ANTHROPOLOGICAL PAPERS OF
THE UNIVERSITY OF ARIZONA
NUMBER 73

T0168829

In the Aftermath of Migration

Renegotiating Ancient Identity in Southeastern Arizona

Anna A. Neuzil

THE UNIVERSITY OF ARIZONA PRESS
TUCSON
2008

About the author

ANNA A. NEUZIL began studies in the American Southwest as a student with the Chevelon Archaeological Research Project and University of Virginia Field School in 1998. She received her B.A. from the University of Virginia in 1999, majoring in Anthropology and Archaeology, and earned her Master's (2001) and doctoral (2005) degrees from the Department of Anthropology, University of Arizona, Tucson. She participated in archaeological field work in many areas of the Southwest, including Chevelon Canyon, Silver Creek, Forestdale Valley, San Pedro Valley, and Tucson Basin, prior to conducting her dissertation research in the Safford and Aravaipa valleys of Arizona as a Preservation Fellow (2003–2005) of the Center for Desert Archaeology, Tucson. Neuzil served as Ceramic Analyst and Project Director in the Archaeology Department of Tierra Right of Way Services in Tucson and was appointed in 2008 as Project Director and Principal Investigator with Ecoplan Associates, Inc., Tucson, Arizona.

Cover: Vessels of Kiet Siel Polychrome (*top*), Maverick Mountain Polychrome (*middle*), and Casa Grande Red-on-buff, Safford Variety (*bottom*) near their places of manufacture in eastern Arizona.

About the cover vessels

Kiet Siel Polychrome canteen (*top*, ASM Gila Pueblo collection GP5500) from the Flagstaff vicinity, Arizona; maximum diameter 17.9 cm; photograph by Jannelle Weakly, Photographer, Arizona State Museum, Tucson.

Maverick Mountain Polychrome jar (*middle*, Mills Collection Catalog 6025D) from the Dinwiddie Site, New Mexico, with permission of Eastern Arizona College, maximum diameter 41.9 cm; photograph by Patrick D. Lyons, Head of Collections and Associate Curator of Anthropology, Arizona State Museum, Tucson.

Casa Grande Red-on-buff, Safford Variety jar (*bottom*, Mills Collection Catalog 7574CS) from Buena Vista Ruin, with permission of Eastern Arizona College, maximum diameter 29.6 cm; photograph by Patrick D. Lyons, Head of Collections and Associate Curator of Anthropology, Arizona State Museum, Tucson.

THE UNIVERSITY OF ARIZONA PRESS
© 2008 The Arizona Board of Regents
All Rights Reserved

www.uapress.arizona.edu

Library of Congress Cataloging-in-Publication Data

Neuzil, Anna A.
  In the aftermath of migration : renegotiating ancient identity in southeastern Arizona / Anna A. Neuzil.
    p. cm — (Anthropological papers of the University of Arizona ; no. 73)
    Includes bibliographic references and index.
    ISBN 978-0-8165-2736-6 (pbk. : alk. paper)
    1. Pueblo Indians —Arizona —Safford Valley —Migrations. 2. Pueblo Indians —Arizona —Aravaipa Canyon —Migrations. 3. Pueblo Indians —Ethnic identity. 4. Pueblo pottery —Themes, motives. 5. Migration, Internal —Arizona —Safford Valley. 6. Migration, Internal —Arizona —Aravaipa Canyon. 7. Safford Valley (Ariz.)—Antiquities. 8. Aravaipa Canyon (Ariz.)—Antiquities. I. Title.
E99.P9N277   2008
304.8089'91411 —dc22   2008022935

Manufactured in the United States of America on acid-free, archival-quality paper containing a minimum of 30% post-consumer waste and processed chlorine free.

13 12 11 10 09 08   6 5 4 3 2 1

Contents

PREFACE   vii
Acknowledgments   viii

1. MIGRATION AND IDENTITY IN
   THE ARCHAEOLOGICAL PAST   1
   Bordieu and *Habitus*   2
   Giddens and the Duality of Structure   2
   Communities of Practice and Practice
       Theory   3
   Technological Style in Migration Research   3
   Migration   5
   Models of Migration in the Past   5
       Why Do People Migrate?   6
       How Do People Migrate?   7
       What Are the Social Consequences
          of Migration?   7
       Why is Migration Important?   8
   Identity, Past and Present   8
       Defining Identity   8
       Why Is Identity Important?   9
   Migration Research in the Safford
       and Aravaipa Valleys   10
   Migrants and Locals in the Safford
       and Aravaipa Valleys   10
   Modeling the Consequences of
       Migration on Identity   14

2. ARCHAEOLOGICAL SETTING OF
   THE SAFFORD AND ARAVAIPA
   VALLEYS   16
   Previous Archaeological Research   16
       The Safford Valley   18
       The Aravaipa Valley   23
   Chronology and Cultural Changes   24

3. IDENTIFYING MIGRANTS IN THE
   ARCHAEOLOGICAL RECORD   28
   Corrugated Ceramics   28
       Corrugated Ceramics at Classic Period
          Safford and Aravaipa Valley Sites   29
   Corrugation Technology   30

Domestic Architecture   32
    Site Layout   33
    Room Area   36
    Construction Techniques   41
        Wall Construction Materials   41
        Header versus Stretcher   42
    Technological Style Variations   45

4. EXAMINING MIGRANT AND
   INDIGENOUS IDENTITY IN THE
   POSTMIGRATION SOCIAL
   ENVIRONMENT   46
   Identity in the Archaeological Record   46
   Decorated Ceramic Assemblages   47
       Richness and Evenness   47
       Cluster Analysis and Measures of
          Diversity Within Sites   54
   Architecture and Space Syntax   56
   Settlement Location on the Landscape   64
   Social Integration   67

5. DIFFERENTIATING MIGRATION AND
   EXCHANGE THROUGH STUDIES OF
   OBSIDIAN AND DECORATED
   CERAMICS   69
   Obsidian   69
   Ceramic Compositional Analyses   73
       Oxidation Analyses   73
       Petrographic Analyses   76
   Local Diversity   85

6. THE SCALE AND EFFECT OF
   MIGRATION IN THE SAFFORD
   AND ARAVAIPA VALLEYS   87
   Social Scale of Migration and
       Migrant Enclaves   87
   Social Scale of Migration and
       Nonenclave Settlements   89
   Extent of Migration During the Thirteenth
       and Fourteenth Centuries A.D.   92

The Effect of Migration on Identity   94
A Model of Migration and Identity Refined   96
Social Consequences of Migration in
    the Safford and Aravaipa Valleys   97
Migration Research in the Greater
    Southwest   98

REFERENCES   101

INDEX   117

ABSTRACT, RESUMEN   123

FIGURES

1.1. Eastern Arizona, showing the Kayenta
      and Tusayan areas and locations of sites   11
1.2. Plan of the Goat Hill Site   13
2.1. Location of the Safford and
      Aravaipa valleys   17
2.2   Chronologies for the Safford and
      Aravaipa valleys   20–21
3.1. Unobliterated corrugated sherd   29
3.2. Obliterated corrugated sherd   29
3.3. Average Room Contiguity Index
      for all sites   35
3.4. Plan of Crescent Ruin   36
3.5. Average Room Contiguity Index
      for select sites   37
3.6. Mean area of all rooms by site   37
3.7. Mean area of habitation rooms
      only, by site   38
3.8. Header and stretcher wall
      construction techniques   43
4.1. Plot of richness and Brillouin statistics
      for ceramic wares through time   51
4.2. Plot of richness and Brillouin statistics
      for ceramic types through time   52
4.3. Plot of richness and Brillouin statistics
      for ceramic wares through time
      at sites with perforated plates   53
4.4. Plot of richness and Brillouin statistics
      for ceramic wares through time
      at sites without perforated plates   53
4.5. The Krider Kiva Site   55
4.6. The Pentagon Site with total site
      area following Potter (1998)   57
4.7. The Pentagon Site with total site

      area following Ferguson (1996)   57
4.8. Locus C of the Eagle Pass Site with
      round structures transformed to
      create convex space   58
4.9. Plot of open space/total site area,
      without walls included in
      architectural space   60
4.10. Plot of integration score, without walls
      included in architectural space   61
4.11. Plot of convex articulation and grid
      convexity, including walls in archi-
      tectural space and total site area   62
4.12. Large versus small Goat Hill and
      Safford phase sites   65
4.13. Large versus small Middle Classic
      and Fort Grant phase sites   66
4.14. Potential migrant enclave sites   67
4.15. Sites with and without perforated
      plates   68
5.1. Locations of obsidian sources in
      southeastern Arizona and
      southwestern New Mexico   70
5.2. Locations of petrofacies in the Safford
      and Aravaipa valleys   78
5.3. Ceramic production and provenience
      matrices by site and ceramic category,
      Safford Valley   80
6.1. Migrant and indigenous features at
      Goat Hill or Middle Classic and
      Safford or Fort Grant phase sites   90
6.2. Sites with components postdating
      A.D. 1275 ranked by the number of
      migrant indicators present   93

TABLES

1.1. Scale of migration   6
1.2. Site designations   12
1.3. Social consequences of migration   14

2.1. Characteristics of Classic period
      phases in the Safford and
      Aravaipa valleys   26

3.1.	Expected results of Kruskal-Wallis tests of metric attributes of corrugated ceramics	31
3.2.	Room Contiguity Index summary	34
3.3.	Area of habitation rooms only, before and after migration	38
3.4.	Area of habitation rooms only, at sites with and without perforated plates	38
3.5.	Kruskal-Wallis test of room area by site	39
3.6.	Kruskal-Wallis test of room area by phase	39
3.7.	Kruskal-Wallis test of room area by occupation before or after migration	39
3.8.	Mann-Whitney U test of room area by presence or absence of perforated plates	40
3.9.	Kruskal-Wallis test of room area by settlements in the same phase	40
3.10.	Kruskal-Wallis test of room area by settlements occupied before and after migration	40
3.11.	Kruskal-Wallis test of room area by settlements with and without perforated plates	40
3.12.	Wall construction techniques by site	42
3.13.	Wall construction techniques at settlements occupied before and after migration	43
3.14.	Wall construction techniques at settlements with and without perforated plates	43
3.15.	Header or stretcher wall construction by settlement	44
3.16.	Header or stretcher wall construction by phase	44
3.17.	Header or stretcher wall construction at settlements occupied before and after migration	44
3.18.	Header or stretcher wall construction at settlements with and without perforated plates	45
4.1.	Dates of ceramics recovered in the Safford and Aravaipa valleys	48–49
4.2.	Richness and Brillouin (evenness) statistics by phase for ceramic wares and types	50
4.3.	Number of spatial clusters defined at each site	55
4.4.	Patterns evident in spatial clusters	56
4.5.	Integration score with wall space included	59
4.6.	Integration score with wall space excluded	59
4.7.	Convex articulation and grid convexity, total site area following Potter (1998)	63
4.8.	Convex articulation and grid convexity, total site area following Ferguson (1996)	63
5.1.	Total obsidian collected and sampled	70
5.2.	Locations of obsidian sources by site	71
5.3.	Locations of obsidian sources by dominant phase	71
5.4.	Locations of obsidian sources before or after migration	72
5.5.	Locations of obsidian sources at sites with and without perforated plates	72
5.6.	Ceramics sampled for oxidation analysis by site	74
5.7.	General color categories with corresponding Munsell designations	74
5.8.	Results of oxidation analyses	75
5.9.	Ceramics sampled for petrographic analysis by site and petrofacies	79
5.10.	Temper source, specific (TSS) summary of analyzed sherds	81
5.11.	Unknown temper source, specific (TSS) summary of analyzed sherds	81
5.12.	Perforated plate petrofacies summary	82
5.13.	Maverick Mountain Series petrofacies summary	82
5.14.	Roosevelt Red Ware petrofacies summary	83
5.15.	Mimbres Black-on-white petrofacies summary	84
5.16.	Middle Gila Buff Ware, Safford Variety petrofacies summary	84
5.17.	San Carlos Red-on-brown petrofacies summary	84
6.1.	Decorated ceramic assemblage from site AZ CC:2:23 (BLM)	88
6.2.	Selected ceramic counts for Fort Grant Pueblo, the Spear Ranch Site, and the Krider Kiva Site	91
6.3.	Decorated ceramic assemblage from site AZ CC:2:33 (BLM)	92
6.4.	Refined scale of migration model	97

Preface

In the late thirteenth and early fourteenth centuries, portions of the northern Southwest experienced widespread depopulation when people who had lived there for many years chose to leave their homelands. Although this abandonment has been referred to as the mysterious disappearance of the "Anasazi" (ancestral Puebloans) in popular literature, archaeologists and Native Peoples know that ancestral Puebloans did not disappear but migrated to other regions, including areas far to the south. Significant speculation and research has gone into determining why these groups chose to move, focusing mainly on environmental factors such as changing climatic conditions affecting rainfall and growing seasons (Ahlstrom and others 1995; Dean 1996; Dean and others 1994; Lipe 1995; Van West and Dean 2000). Although the motivation to migrate may have been largely environmental, this series of migrations impacted both the physical and social world of the migrants and the groups they settled among along their migration route.

The impact of migration on a given landscape or environment can be quantified through a variety of methods, but the social consequences of migration in prehistory are much more difficult to measure. Even so, the study of the social consequences of migration can help archaeologists better understand how migration affected the people involved at all social levels, from the individual to the group. Numerous questions arise from the study of migration. Were migrants anxious about interacting and living with groups with whom they had little previous contact? Were they able to successfully grow crops and gather wild resources independently, or did they have to rely on local groups for guidance on agriculture or resource procurement in their new environment? Did migrants maintain their established rituals and religious practices, or did they adopt those of the local groups in their new home? Although the answers to these questions are not directly reflected in the artifacts and features of the archaeological record, the research presented here examines the evidence that is available to provide some insight into this human side of migration. With this information, a better understanding of the social consequences of this dynamic process can be developed.

Because migration has been studied so intensively in the last 15 years, not only in the Southwest, but in both ethnographic and archaeological contexts around the world, the archaeological understanding of migration has matured considerably. Migration research has covered a broad geographic range, providing an unparalleled knowledge base of past migrations and a diversity of case studies available for comparison. However, many of these studies focus on identifying episodes of migration, and the social consequences of migration on both migrant and indigenous populations are less frequently addressed. Based on studies from throughout the world, it is clear that migration research is at an important turning point, and an understanding of the impacts of migration, which is crucial to comprehending migration as a social process in its entirety, is now possible. The theoretical tools for assessing the results of migration are currently available, and research addressing migration's consequences will provide the next step in enhancing the archaeological and anthropological understanding of this important process.

This study builds on this previous research to examine the scale and impact of Classic period (A.D. 1200–1450) migration in the relatively unexplored Safford and Aravaipa valleys. This region is ideal for refining models of migration because previous research suggests household and suprahousehold migration into and through the area occurred during the Classic period (Brown 1973, 1974; Woodson 1999). Thus, these areas contain a high degree of variation in material culture that can be used to operationalize the archaeological identification of migration. In a two-stage approach, I first look at the extent of migration in these two valleys by determining which Classic period sites were likely inhabited by migrants based on material culture that reflects enculturative processes, such as utilitarian ceramics and domestic architecture (Clark 2001; Neuzil 2005a). Second, I examine the consequences of migration through the expression of identity of both migrant and indigenous populations by looking at patterning in more conspicuous forms of material culture such as decorated ceramic assemblages and settlement architecture (Crown 1994; Ferguson 1996; Mills 2004; Van Keuren 2001). These two research foci feed into a multiscalar model of the social impacts of migration.

Understanding the social impact of migration in the Safford and Aravaipa valleys increases our comprehension of the larger processes of aggregation and reorganization occurring not only in these areas, but also throughout the Greater Southwest during this time period. This research uses a theoretical approach that ties studies of migration to recent anthropological research on social identity, and these topics are bridged through the construction of a model that looks at both the processes of migration as well as its effects on local and migrant populations under different conditions. Additionally, research on late prehispanic migration in the Southwest, including the research presented here, may also help strengthen cultural affiliation studies between past and present native groups.

Many of the sites examined in this study have been heavily damaged by pothunting and systematic looting, and the remainder are under a constant threat of further rapid damage and destruction in the near future. This report not only examines these sites to answer specific questions about migration in the past, but also provides a minimal baseline of data about each. Although significant research has been conducted at a select few of these sites, such as Goat Hill (AZ CC:1:28 ASM); Murphy (AZ CC:1:52 ASM); Crary (AZ CC:1:53 ASM); Dewester (AZ CC:1:56 ASM); Owens-Colvin (AZ CC:1:19 ASM); and Eagle Pass (AZ BB:4:1 ASM), prior to this study the vast majority of sites in the sample analyzed here had only been recorded in a cursory manner, often with no map provided. As a result of this study, a map and systematic ceramic collections are now available for each.

The following chapters provide an in-depth look at migration and its social consequences in the Safford and Aravaipa valleys. Chapter 1 summarizes the theory underlying research on migration and identity in anthropology, as well as some research that is specific to examining migration in the archaeological record. Chapter 2 provides an overview of the previous re-

search conducted in the Safford and Aravaipa valleys, and Chapter 3 assesses the social scale and organization of migration in the archaeological record of Classic period Safford and Aravaipa valley sites. This chapter specifically examines evidence from corrugated ceramics and domestic architecture to determine if migrants arrived and settled as household, suprahousehold, or community level groups. Chapter 4 examines the evidence for spatial and social integration of migrant and indigenous populations in the late thirteenth and fourteenth centuries by looking at spatial patterning, diversity, and richness in ceramic assemblages, as well as at measures of built space that reflect on spatial integration. Results of oxidation and petrographic sourcing analyses of ceramics and X-ray fluorescence sourcing of obsidian, which provide information on the interaction network of Classic period Safford and Aravaipa valley populations, are detailed in Chapter 5. In Chapter 6 I evaluate the evidence and examine the effects of migration on the expression of identities of both migrant and local groups in the Safford and Aravaipa valleys and demonstrate that ancestral Puebloan migrants arrived in groups organized in at least two social scales, as both household and suprahousehold groups. Although migrants initially distanced themselves from the local population, shortly thereafter local and migrant groups lived side-by-side, as reflected in increased social integration and changes in the expression of their social identity.

Acknowledgments

The Center for Desert Archaeology in Tucson, Arizona, supported this project in numerous ways. During the course of this research I enjoyed the many benefits of having a Center Preservation Fellowship, provided by an anonymous donor to whom I express my gratitude. The Safford District Office of the Bureau of Land Management supplied additional funding through a Cooperative Agreement with the Center. Also, funding for this project was furnished by a National Science Foundation Dissertation Improvement Grant (BCS–0354671). The staff at the Center for Desert Archaeology, notably William Doelle, Jeff Clark, Patrick Lyons, Linda Pierce, Char Ackerman, Brett Hill, Doug Gann, Sally Thomas, Chip Colwell-Chanthaphonh, Jacquie Dale, Tobi Taylor, Debra Lee, and Matt Devitt provided me with substantial assistance in things scholarly and logistical that are far too numerous to mention, but made this entire process significantly more intellectually stimulating and enjoyable than it would have been otherwise. And under the auspices of Bill Doelle, the Center graciously provided a subsidy for the publication of this monograph.

Numerous people provided assistance and guidance throughout this project. Barbara Mills, Jeff Clark, Suzy Fish, Nancy Parezo, and Tsianina Lomawaima aided this work significantly with theoretical and practical insights. Many volunteers offered their time to help me in the field and in the lab. Georgie Boyer, Peter Boyle, Elizabeth Burt, Tony Callan, Katherine Cerino, Joan Clark, Bob Conforti, Jackie Cuyler, Rene Donaldson, Ken Fite, Cherie Freeman, Michael Gleeson, Ken and Ethel Haber, Cecelia Hessler, Walt and Carol Hoffman, Albert Lannon, Kyle Molloy, Irma Moreno, Christa Mulloy, Don Reser, Dwight Riggs, Tom Robinson, Mary Star, and Donna Tang, as well as interns Megan Kennedy and Takis Weekes endured tedious artifact washing and labeling and windy field days to help get the fieldwork and artifact analysis completed in a timely manner. Their efforts made the day-to-day field and analysis time substantially more fun and faster than if I had been working alone.

Several landowners and leaseholders allowed me to access sites on their property and generously donated the artifacts I collected to the Arizona State Museum. My thanks go to Ross and Fawn Bryce, Otis and Teddy Carney, Robert and Verna Rae Colvin, Gem Cox, Tom and Betty Clonts, Brooks and Myrna Curtis, the Fort Grant Prison Complex, particularly Deputy Warden Bruce Schiflet, Roy and Bea Hall, Carroll and Barbara Hart, Richard and Karen Holcomb, Robert and Toby Jansen, Don and Kim Lackner, Harold and Caroline Lackner, Julian and Rose Montelongo, the Pacific Western Land Company, particularly Ty Bays, the Phelps Dodge Mining Company, particularly John Korolsky and Jerry Sako, Jim and Rebecca Post, the Safford School District, particularly Superintendent Mark Tregaskes, Angela and Gary Von Bergen, and Leroy and Brenda Zachek.

Several land managing agencies also allowed me access to sites on their land and to their site files, and I thank Anna Rago at the Safford Field Office of the Bureau of Land Management, Mary Farrell and Bill Gillespie at the Coronado National Forest, Gene Sturla and Emily Brown at the Arizona Game and Fish Department, Rick Karl and the Arizona State Museum Site Files Office staff, John Ware at the Amerind Foundation, and David Wilcox at the Museum of Northern Arizona for facilitating this access. Several institutions allowed me to examine existing collections from sites in the Safford and Aravaipa valleys, and I thank Art Vokes at the Arizona State Museum; Mark Bryce, Brent McEuen, and Linda Blan at Eastern Arizona College; Raydene Cluff at the Graham County Historical Society; Bill Gillespie at the Coronado National Forest; and Anna Rago at the Bureau of Land Management for this opportunity to add to my data set. Betty Lee, Rex Owens, and Karl Ronstadt provided me with valuable information about several sites in my study area, and Betty Lee generously gave me copies of her personal notes concerning sites in the Aravaipa Valley. Mike Brack acted as my GPS guru, making me more technologically savvy than I could have been on my own.

Catherine Gilman produced most of the maps in this monograph. Matt Devitt took the photographs of the corrugated sherds in Figures 3.1 and 3.2. Matt Reynolds created Figure 2.1. Julie Wilson provided technical support during the course of the editing process. President Mark Bryce of Eastern Arizona College allowed me to use photographs of whole vessels from the Mills Collection on the front cover. Personnel at the Arizona State Museum, Tucson, assisted with the cover image and I am grateful for the time and efforts of Head of Collections Patrick Lyons, who photographed the lower two vessels, and Senior Curatorial Specialist G. Michael Jacobs and Photographer Jannelle Weakly who provided the top vessel image. At the University of Arizona, Carol Gifford, Department of Anthropology, gets my unending appreciation for shepherding this manuscript into monograph form and lending her expertise to make it a better document than it would have been otherwise. She received computer assistance from Dirk J. Harris, Desktop Services Manager, and David C. Thompsen, Support Systems Analyst, in the College of Social and Behavioral Sciences. María Nieves Zedeño, Bureau of Applied Research in Anthropology, kindly translated the Abstract.

Deep appreciation goes to my family for supporting me in so many ways during the last several years, especially to my husband Jeremy and my sweet daughter Gracie, who make it all worthwhile.

Anna A. Neuzil
March 2008

CHAPTER ONE

Migration and Identity in the Archaeological Past

During the formative years of Southwest archaeology, researchers translated identifiable sets of material culture into archaeological "culture areas" and used them as heuristic tools to better understand changes in culture through time and space (Gladwin 1957; Haury 1985; Kidder 1924; McGregor 1965; Morris 1934). Culture areas proved crucial to developing the general scheme for prehistory in the Greater Southwest. Although more recent research has greatly refined and sometimes contradicted parts of this scheme, this pioneering work provided an important basis on which future research was grounded. Early on, archaeologists recognized that it was important to understand social processes, such as migration, that could obscure or confuse the larger patterns in material culture they sought to define. With this in mind, near the peak of the culture area paradigm, Haury (1958: 1) developed a methodology for detecting migration in the archaeological record based on four criteria:

1. new traits that appear suddenly without local prototypes,
2. products from the immigrant group that reflect borrowed elements from the host group and preserve elements from their own pattern,
3. identification of an area in which the intrusive traits are the normal pattern, and
4. contemporaneity in expressions of the intrusive traits in the new place and the intrusive traits in the homeland where they are the normal pattern.

Archaeologists used these criteria to recognize a constellation of intrusive material traits that they assumed reflected the identity, or at least the presence, of their ancient makers. Researchers interpreted the differences in material trait constellations at a given site or within a given area as representing cultural heterogeneity in the resident population resulting from a recent influx of migrants. At that time, however, there was little explicit consideration of material culture variability and how this variability articulated with identity and other types of human behavior.

Later archaeological research challenged the assumption that the appearance of intrusive or new forms of material culture within a region could be equated with migration, and cultural diversity and other processes such as evolution, exchange, emulation, and environmental change were proposed as possible alternative explanations (Chilton 1998; David and others 1991; Esse 1992). Furthermore, it became clear that archaeological cultures, defined by material culture signatures left in the archaeological record by a variety of groups living in the past, did not necessarily reflect self-defined cultural groups. Therefore, although archaeologically defined culture areas did carry broad similarities in material culture, the people within these areas probably defined themselves at multiple levels based on a variety of factors that may or may not have been clearly reflected in material culture and preserved in the archaeological record.

The problem for archaeologists became how to identify groups at various levels that held meaning not only for archaeologists studying the past, but also were meaningful for the people who were members of those groups in the past as well. In searching for a solution to this problem, archaeologists have borrowed from theoretical developments outside the discipline to develop methods that isolate the material correlates of the identity palimpsest. These methods are largely based on the work of Giddens (1979, 1984) and Bourdieu (1977), who have influenced the development of practice theory in anthropology (Barrett 2001; Ortner 1996, 2001; Pauketat 2001). Such theoretical developments have steered archaeologists toward relating items of material culture, on the basis of technological and design styles, to groups and individuals in the past at both individual and group levels (Cameron 1998; Clark 2001; Gosselain 2002; Stark and others 1998; Van Keuren 1999). In addition, archaeologists have also been able to separate active expressions of identity from more subtle indicators of identity indicative of enculturation and group membership. These developments are key to understanding processes of migration and how they affect the expression of identity.

BOURDIEU AND *HABITUS*

Bourdieu's (1977) concept of *habitus* postulates that people are predisposed to acting in certain ways as a result of their ideational environment. *Habitus* exists in the everyday actions of people, but people can never be fully aware of their own *habitus*. *Habitus* is learned through the experience of socialization, and is often not explicitly taught (Jenkins 1992; Nash 2003). Most importantly for this project, Bourdieu (1977) argues that *habitus* provides the basis for practices by disposing people to do certain things while taking their social environment into account. This formulation of *habitus* has been extended to archaeological discussions of technological style (Dietler and Herbich 1998; Lechtman 1977; Lemonnier 1992; Stark 1998), which propose that people make certain items of material culture in specific ways depending on their learning environment (*habitus*), and that these items of material culture thus reflect enculturation, or basic cultural training. Different techniques and raw materials that are used to manufacture objects with similar functions constitute technological styles that can reflect differences in enculturation (Stark 1998). Techniques and raw materials used to manufacture an object of material culture that are not readily visible in the final product can be used as passive indicators of enculturative background specific to a social group because they are not intended to signal messages to others, including messages pertaining to identity (Gosselain 1998; Stark and others 1998). Thus, differences in manufacturing techniques and raw materials can be used to distinguish between social groups with different backgrounds and settlement histories.

Research has demonstrated this understanding of *habitus* to be a powerful methodological tool in recognizing and identifying migration and migrants in the archaeological record, but such a formulation does not effectively account for other social processes in the

creation of material culture, such as agency, innovation, or exchange. Other independent lines of evidence must be brought to bear in order to evaluate the role of these processes in social change or stability. *Habitus* assumes that under some circumstances people will act strictly within the boundaries set by their social structure and will only change if the circumstances around them change. Individuals cannot introduce change themselves. In conservative interpretations of *habitus*, people become "social automatons" going about their daily routine with little free will or thought (Nash 2003). Numerous scholars acknowledge these interpretations as a weakness of Bourdieu's theoretical framework (Gardner 2002; Nash 2003; Sewell 1992), but Bourdieu himself pointed out that *habitus* was meant to be a concept that bridged the divide between individual decision making and supraindividual structures (Bourdieu 1977; Jenkins 1992: 74). Under this characterization, *habitus* and its extension into technological style still is useful in differentiating between people who undertake activities and create items of material culture in different ways. Its utility is particularly relevant during times of social change, such as migration, when actively expressed identity may be manipulated to achieve social goals, whereas the more subtle *habitus*, as expressed in technological style, is less likely to undergo changes. Other scholars, particularly Giddens (1984), have further operationalized how practice bridges the gap between individual agency and social structures.

GIDDENS AND THE DUALITY OF STRUCTURE

Giddens' (1979, 1984) concept of structuration and the duality of structure is an attempt to integrate the parameters set by structure and the agency of individuals and groups within a single theory. Structuration bridges the gap between conscious and unconscious action, or active and passive expression, and proposes that human agency and structure are in a reciprocal relationship where agency is not predetermined by structure, but reproduces it, sometimes transforming it in the process (Gauntlett 2002). In other words, actions produce structure, which in turn, structures action, and individuals influence the way their society, and by extension material culture, is constituted (Craib 1992). Social practices both constitute social actors and embody structures and are the physical realization of this relationship between structure and action (Craib 1992). Thus, structuration works reciprocally, and Giddens' (1984) concept of agency provides a framework to examine the active dimension of identity in material culture and the manner in which it is impacted through migration.

Giddens (1984), however, does not develop a methodology for operationalizing his theory using empirical data. Sewell (1992) approached this problem by expanding the definition of both structure and agency. Whereas agency is "the actor's capacity to reinterpret and mobilize an array of resources in terms of cultural schemas other than those that initially constituted the array," structure can be viewed as "sets of mutually sustaining schemas and resources that empower and constrain social action and that tend to be reproduced by that social action...but their reproduction is never automatic" (Sewell 1992: 19). Thus, agency mediates between the reproduction and transformation of structure. Often, structure is transformed in social situations that are unprecedented, which result in unintended consequences (McCall 1999).

COMMUNITIES OF PRACTICE
AND PRACTICE THEORY

Recently, archaeologists have started using the concept of "communities of practice" as a way to conceptualize how structure is transformed or reproduced in material culture (Fenn and others 2005; Minar 2001; Minar and Crown 2001; Sassaman and Rudolphi 2001). Communities of practice are learning groups through which cultural knowledge, in this case, that pertaining to the production and use of material culture, is transmitted. Practice, the process of learning and reproducing cultural knowledge, is often passed down in group settings, and every community contains several communities of practice. However, contrary to what is often assumed, communities of practice are dynamic even though they are based on history and tradition (Minar and Crown 2001). This fluidity can lead to changes in the way material culture is made, as reflected in the end product. Understanding the social changes that instigate innovation in material culture in the context of practice theory can elucidate how agency can modify structure and how this is reflected in material culture. Practice theory is where tradition, agency, and structure intersect in the archaeological record.

Practice theory unites Bourdieu's (1977) concept of *habitus* and Giddens' (1979) duality of structure by providing a means to understand how people perceived

themselves through material culture. Under this rubric, material culture itself reflects the interaction of structure and agency as played out in the social practice that creates material culture in everyday life (Pauketat 2001). As Pauketat (2001: 88) states:

> Material culture, as a dimension of practice, is itself causal. Its production— while contingent on histories of actions and representations—is an enactment or an embodiment of people's dispositions—a social negotiation that brings about changes in meanings, dispositions, identities, and traditions.

Thus, material culture can be interpreted as a representation of social practices and can provide information not only on how material culture and the practice that creates it remain the same through time, but also how certain types of material culture can be transformed in social situations that challenge structure, such as those resulting from migration (Minar and Crown 2001).

Furthermore, an analysis of practice embodied in material culture can include both a passive dimension useful in detecting migration and a conscious active dimension useful in assessing the impact of migration on expressions of identity, much as Giddens' (1984) duality of structure brings the interaction of structure and agency to light. In the archaeological record, practice, *habitus*, and the duality of structure are all evident in material culture. *Habitus* embodied in practice is manifest in everyday activities, such as those that engage with items like ceramics and architecture. By examining the style of these items of material culture, it is possible to discern groups with similar practice and *habitus*, as well as discerning when such practice was transformed by changes in social structure. When combined with an examination of other attributes of items that actively express identity, such as decorated ceramics, these analyses provide an understanding of the relationship between structure and action, practice and identity, and how these interact to both reproduce and transform tradition through practice.

TECHNOLOGICAL STYLE IN
MIGRATION RESEARCH

Previous ethnographic research has demonstrated the utility of technological style in identifying discrete groups (Gosselain 1998; Hardin 1977; Lemonnier 1986, 1989, 1992). These ethnographic studies have been particularly useful in providing case studies on which to model research projects that have identified past migrant groups throughout the Southwest who may be outwardly attempting to reconstitute their identity to fit in with existing indigenous groups. In these cases, it may not be possible to see migrant groups in the archaeological record by examining only classes of material culture that actively express identity. Instead, technological styles associated with domestic architecture and utilitarian ceramics reflect differences between groups with different learning frameworks such as migrant and indigenous populations (Clark 2001; Hegmon and others 2000; Meyer 1999; Stark and others 1995; Stark and others 1998). By analyzing these subtle technological styles in everyday domestic material culture that reflects enculturation, migrant groups have been and can be identified in the archaeological record.

In this research, I use the technological styles of corrugated ceramics and domestic architecture to differentiate between distinct social groups in the archaeological record. I measured and recorded several attributes of corrugated ceramics and domestic architecture and used both intersite and intrasite differences in these attributes to evaluate whether the people living at settlements within the Safford and Aravaipa valleys (see Fig. 1.1; Table 1.1) could be considered part of the same social group. I then evaluated decorated ceramics and measures of built space to determine if social groups were socially and spatially integrated. Decorated ceramics, particularly their provenance (Chapter 5), can provide information on the affiliation of the inhabitants of settlements. Space syntax analyses of architecture can provide information on spatial integration. By combining these two lines of evidence, it is possible to delineate how the inhabitants of Classic period (A.D. 1200–1450) Safford and Aravaipa valley sites defined themselves and their identity before and after ancestral Puebloan migrants arrived in the region.

The advantage of using analyses of technological style as well as information from decorated ceramics and measures of built space lies in the subtlety of the information available in the archaeological record. Trait lists rely on robust indicators that leave clear signatures in the archaeological record, only allowing the identification of large, cohesive, and well defined groups. Furthermore, trait lists implicitly assume normative patterns in material culture, where objects equal people or groups, without taking into account other cultural processes, such as exchange and emulation. Moreover,

evidence from other areas of the Southwest has suggested that migration also occurred on the household, and potentially individual, level (Mills 1998; Reid 1997; Slaughter and Roberts 1996). Such small scale migration would be archaeologically invisible with a trait list approach.

A technological style approach to identifying migrants, such as that used here, highlights more subtle indicators of their identity and affiliation. Analyses of technological style identify smaller groups in the archaeological record and provide a more sound theoretical framework for understanding their interaction with other small groups by focusing on indicators of identity that are less likely to change as the social milieu shifts. Because previous research in the Safford and Aravaipa valleys suggests that ancestral Puebloan migrants may have arrived in household level groups, analyses that better characterize these smaller groups are appropriate for understanding the social dynamics of this region during the Classic period. Practice theory provides a framework for understanding how small social groups are structured and differentiated and how social groups can both reproduce and transform social practices simultaneously, as seen through material culture (Pauketat 2001). Because of recent developments in understanding identity in the archaeological record, archaeologists are able to better conceptualize how changes in practice may reflect changes in other aspects of social life that are more difficult to see in the archaeological record, such as identity (Gardner 2002; G. Jones 1999).

The research presented here first identifies cases of migration in the archaeological record through material culture that reflects the enculturative dimension of identity and then seeks to understand the results or consequences of migration by examining the active dimension of identity of both migrant and indigenous populations. Although these two areas of research are often discussed separately in archaeological literature on migration (Herr and Clark 1997), they are both theoretically and methodologically linked. To study migration it is first necessary to identify migrant and nonmigrant groups, which is best accomplished by understanding how the members of each group identified themselves and differentiated themselves. Migration into the Safford and Aravaipa areas in the late thirteenth and early fourteenth centuries provides an ideal case to examine these issues and gain a more complete understanding of the expression of identity in the past and how it can be reconstructed from the archaeological record.

MIGRATION

Since Anthony (1990) inspired a resurgence of migration research in archaeological inquiry, significant advances have been made in identifying occurrences of migration and in understanding why migration occurs, how people migrate, and the social and economic consequences of migration. Underlying this research is an understanding of migration as a patterned and structured process with recognizable and understandable causes and consequences, both in the past and present (Anthony 1990). Migration was an almost taboo topic in American archaeology during the 1960s through 1980s, and very little research on migration was conducted during this time. As a result, more recent archaeological inquiry into migration has been enriched by research on migration conducted in a variety of other disciplines, particularly sociology (Brettell and Hollifield 2000).

In archaeological research, migration has been defined as "a long-term residential relocation beyond community boundaries by one or more discrete social units as the result of a perceived decrease in the benefits of remaining residentially stable or a perceived increase in the benefits of relocating to prospective destinations" (Clark 2001: 2). This fundamental social process affects the dynamics of social and economic relationships, the expression of social identities, and the intensity of interaction between groups and individuals. Situations involving migration have the potential to reveal a great deal about the core social practices of a given group. Because migration often challenges these practices, migrants may reevaluate their own beliefs as well as their relationships to new social groups encountered along migration routes and in destination areas.

Since the 1980s, archaeologists have become increasingly cognizant of the importance of migration in interpreting the past. Recent reinvigoration of migration research has led to increased theoretical and methodological rigor and a broader understanding of the social contexts of migration in past societies (Anthony 1990; Burmeister 2000; Clark 2001; Comas d'Argemir and Pujadas 1999; Marshall and Foster 2002). Advances in migration research have been particularly prevalent in the Greater Southwest (Bernardini 2002; Cameron 1995a; Clark 2001; Duff 2002; Ennes 1999; P. Fish and others 1994; Hegmon and others 2000; Herr 2001; Herr and Clark 1997; Lindsay 1987; Lyons 2003; Spielmann 1998; Woodson 1999) and have demonstrated that migration played an important role in the prehistory of many regions of the Southwest, including the Tonto Basin (Clark 2001; Elson and others 1995), Silver Creek (Herr 2001; Mills 1998; Neuzil 2005a; Newcomb 1999), San Pedro River Valley (Clark and Lyons 2008; Lyons 2003), Grasshopper (Reid 1997), Upper Gila Valley (Lekson 2002; Lekson and others 2002), Tucson Basin (S. Fish and others 1992; Slaughter and Roberts 1996), Mimbres (Hegmon and others 2000), and Point of Pines regions (Haury 1958; Lindsay 1987).

MODELS OF MIGRATION IN THE PAST

Voluntary migration occurs at a variety of scales, each having a different impact depending on the size and composition of migrant groups and the level of interaction between migrant and indigenous groups (Table 1.1). Migrant group sizes range from the individual, to the household, to the suprahousehold group, to the community. Household level migration is generally the smallest level that can be recognized in the archaeological record through material culture that signals shared kinship and settlement history. Many researchers have used evidence from decorated and utilitarian ceramics to examine household level migration in the archaeological record (Bernardini 2002, 2005; Mills 1998; Neuzil 2001; Van Keuren 1999). Suprahousehold level migration (a "site-unit intrusion") consists of the movement of multiple households organized as a larger social unit (Wauchope 1956). It is well represented by the classic example at Point of Pines defined by Haury (1958) and by cases ientified by Di Peso (1958) in the San Pedro Valley (see Fig. 1.1) and can be recognized by the appearance of nonlocal material culture such as ceramics, architecture, and burial practices that contrast markedly with local material culture and practices and can be traced to a known homeland. Communities are the largest migrant groups; they represent the movement of multiple households and suprahousehold groups into an area and are recognized by the appearance of nonlocal material culture combined with a substantial increase in population. All three scales of migration are recognized by the appearance of nonlocal material culture and an increase in population (Table 1.1). Variability in the relative abundance of nonlocal material culture and the magnitude of population increase distinguish among the three levels of migration: intrusive material culture is more apparent and population increases are more pronounced for community level

Table 1.1. Scale of Migration

Scale of Migration	Destination Area	Archaeological Signature	Examples	References
Household	Occupied	New houses or enclave(s) established within an existing settlement Appearance of subtle differences in domestic architecture (construction and room size) and ceramics (design style, technology), sometimes focused within one area of a settlement Rapid construction of domestic architecture	Bailey Ruin Grasshopper Pueblo Gibbon Springs Site	Mills (1998) Reid (1997) Slaughter and Roberts (1996)
	Unoccupied	Single settlement established in a previously unoccupied area Population increase Widespread exchange networks between areas with preexisting social contacts	Silver Creek Great Kiva sites	Herr (2001)
Supra-household "site-unit intrusion"	Occupied	Establishment of new settlement Distinctive and nonlocal material culture associated with new settlement: ceramic design style and technology, ritual and domestic architecture, food remains, lithic technology, burial practices, and architectural features, traceable to a homeland	Point of Pines Goat Hill Reeve Ruin	Haury (1958) Woodson (1999) Di Peso (1958)
	Unoccupied	—	—	—
Community	Occupied	Multiple large settlements established suddenly in a previously occupied area Significant differences in domestic technology from the indigenous population (ceramics, domestic architecture, site layout) traceable to a homeland	Griffin Wash Locus A	Clark (2001)
	Unoccupied	Substantial population influx Multiple socially linked large settlements established around the same time and general location in a previously unoccupied area Distinct material culture traceable to a homeland	Homol'ovi sites	Adams (1998)

migration than for suprahousehold or household migration.

Why Do People Migrate?

As is evident from Clark's definition (2001:2), migration results from changes in the social and economic benefits of remaining in place in contrast to moving to a new location. Migration involves risk, which can be reduced by interaction between populations in the source and destination of migration through kin relations, information flow, and previous migration experiences. The reduction of risk further increases the probability of movement in response to declining living conditions (Anthony 1990).

Motives for migration are usually framed in terms of push factors from the homeland and pull factors into the destination (Anthony 1990; Herr and Clark 1997; Jett 1964; Lipe 1995; Schwartz 1970). Economics are often cited as the main reason for contemporary migrations (Frayne and Pendelton 2001; Heleniak 2004), along with rootedness of a population, political parties in power, and attitudes toward migrants in their destinations (Heleniak 2004). In instances of migration in small-scale society contexts in the ancient past, changes in the environment are most often cited as push and pull factors. This is the case in the Mesa Verde region during the late thirteenth century, where Ahlstrom and others (1995) and Lipe (1995) cite changes in precipitation, agricultural potential, water supply, erosion, and average temperature as the main reasons for the abandonment of the region. Similar environmental triggers are cited for migration from the Kayenta area around the same time (Dean 1996; Dean and others 1994; Van West and Dean 2000), despite the fact that other research has demonstrated that the environment could have supported the existing population (with drastic changes in social organization) at the time people chose to move south (Kohler and others 2005).

Migration is ultimately a social strategy developed within the context of the daily life of a particular group. Social factors, perhaps influenced by the environment, likely play an important role in most migrations (Anthony 1994). Recent research on contemporary and historic migrations supports this assertion (Comas d'Argemir and Pujadas 1999; Herr and Clark 1997; Marshall and Foster 2002), as is the case among contemporary pastoral migrants in northern Sudan where lack of rainfall was the primary reason for migrating from their homeland in the Sahel, but political and social factors also played a role (Haug 2002). Understanding the social motivations behind migrations is crucial, as some researchers have argued that framing the decision to migrate in terms of push and pull factors oversimplifies the process and ignores the agency of the migrating individuals and groups, which is key to understanding the process in its totality (G. Jones 1999; Marshall and Foster 2002).

How Do People Migrate?

As a patterned process, migration has a number of recurrent elements in prehistoric, historic, and contemporary contexts. The process of migration to previously known areas differs dramatically from the colonization of new and completely unknown lands or frontiers that are uninhabited or sparsely inhabited (Rockman and Steele 2003). Migrants to empty landscapes or frontiers must deal with an entirely different suite of challenges than migrants who settle in areas that are known and inhabited, and models dealing with this type of migration are most applicable for understanding the movements of early small-scale forager groups (Herr 2001). Migrants that move into already occupied territory either move into unoccupied niches or settle alongside first-comers and original inhabitants of the area as in a diaspora (Lilley 2004).

Migration into known areas first requires a flow of information between the homeland and the destination, which can be developed by long distance trade, exogamy, or shared resource procurement (Anthony 1990; Cameron 1995b; Marshall and Foster 2002). This flow of information helps migrant groups make informed decisions about the benefits of potential destinations. Although initial information flow to migrant groups is often along kin lines, migrant groups are not always kin-based (Cameron 1995b). However, social networks are crucial to the survival of migrants both during the process of migration and after arrival at the destination (Haug 2002).

Once the destination has been chosen, migration itself can occur in a number of different ways. Anthony (1990: 902–904; 1994) sets out two models of long distance migration seen in the archaeological record. In the first, alternately called the leapfrogging and chain migration model, scouts bypass large areas while collecting information on resource potentials to relay back to the homeland, creating islands of settlement separated by significant expanses of land. The second model, the migration stream model, posits that migrants "proceed along well-defined routes toward specific destinations" (Anthony 1990: 903), resulting in recognizable artifact distributions following a specific route. This model has been updated recently to recognize the multidirectionality of migration, as well as its time depth (Bernardini 2005). Current research on migration in the Southwest suggests that prehispanic migrations are best characterized by a combination of these two models, where migrants had specific destinations, and left routes traceable through artifacts, but also bypassed large areas and created islands of settlement (Haury 1958; Lyons 2003; Mills 1998).

What Are the Social Consequences of Migration?

Inevitably, migration results in changes in both migrant and indigenous populations as new social situations arise between culturally and structurally distinct groups. The scope of these changes is dependent on the relative size and organization of the indigenous and migrant populations, the scale and organization of migration, previous relations between migrant and indigenous groups, and the level of integration between migrant and indigenous groups following migration. Substantial economic and social power inequalities may develop between migrant and indigenous groups following migration (Burmeister 2000), and this imbalance will necessitate new social institutions to integrate these disparate groups thereby increasing social complexity, or lead to instability, conflict, and possibly further migration (Bernardini 1998; Herr and Clark 1997; Lekson and Cameron 1995).

A feeling of belonging or a sense of place can help to mitigate the desire to move again or to return to the homeland, although such a sense takes time to develop (Frayne and Pendelton 2001; Haug 2002; Heleniak 2004; G. Jones 1999). The platform mounds of the Classic Period Tonto Basin and the ritual architecture of the Silver Creek area during the Pueblo III to Pueblo IV period transition are evidence of the integration of migrant and indigenous populations into a new social structure (Clark 2001; Mills 1998).

A part of the integration process may be a renegotiation of identity and sense of place, and consequently *habitus*, for both groups (Marshall and Foster 2002; Schnapper 1994; Torres-Saillant 1997). Broadly, the identity of both migrant and indigenous groups may be renegotiated, persist, or be subsumed within others (Anthony 1997). Migrants are not likely to retain a distinct identity for an extended interval (Lucassen and Lucassen 1997b), but may retain conservative elements of their premigration cultural background, while renegotiating their identity to fit in to their new social space (Levy and Holl 2002; Mills 2004).

Change in identity can be seen in contemporary migrant populations, as at San Cristobal de las Casas, Mexico, where migrant women created a new social space and identity for themselves through a women's collective (Enciso and Guerrero 1995). Such renegotiations of identity can lead to a feeling of belonging in two places, the homeland and the destination of migration, and can lead to multiple definitions of migrant identity, common among modern transnational migrants (Vertovec 2001). Additionally, the consequences of migration on identity may be different for people at different stages of life. In a study of modern migrants on Cape Cod, Cuba and Hummon (1993) found that older migrants constructed a sense of home and identified themselves as being from Cape Cod based on their domestic dwellings, whereas younger migrants based their sense of home and identity on their social ties to the area.

Why Is Migration Important?

Understanding migration as a process with predictable motives, patterned movement, and potential for dramatic social and economic impacts underscores its importance in archaeology and anthropology evidenced by its reemergence in the literature. Different motives, for example, can affect interaction at the receiving end, as migrants who are escaping social persecution or unfavorable environmental conditions may be more willing to acculturate with the indigenous population, accept unfavorable economic conditions, and reformulate aspects of their identity than are migrants who are exploring new areas or who have an intention of eventually returning to their homelands. Furthermore, migration creates the opportunity for the emergence of social complexity resulting from unprecedented social interaction, which can lead to integration, differentiation, and potentially, conflict. Research in a number of different areas has demonstrated that migration was an important social phenomenon in the past (Bugocki 1987; Burmeister 2000; Levy and Holl 2002; Lucassen and Lucassen 1997a), and thus modeling its consequences will enhance the understanding of migration, not only in the ancient Greater Southwest, but also at a global scale. Increasing our understanding of ancient migrations will also help us predict and better plan for contemporary migrations at all scales. Additional research into other cases of migration will help establish robust cross-cultural patterns, differentiate it from other social processes, such as exchange, which may have similar signatures in the archaeological record, and expand archaeological understanding of the implications of migration.

IDENTITY, PAST AND PRESENT

Characterizing identity and its negotiation is an essential part of understanding the consequences of the process of migration. The manner in which identity is expressed provides an indication of the type and level of integration between migrant and indigenous populations, especially because identity is situational and is challenged in unique social situations that confront the structure of the expression of identity (Jenkins 1996). Therefore, reconstructing the scale and impact of migration will lead to a greater understanding of its effect on the expression of identity of both migrant and indigenous populations.

Defining Identity

Despite, or perhaps as a result of its importance, identity has become a somewhat problematic concept in anthropological and archaeological literature. Researchers variably use the terms identity, social identity, ethnic identity, and ethnicity to refer to broadly similar concepts, often assuming that they can be used interchangeably (with some notable exceptions, see Jenkins 1996). Identity is both social, being shared between individuals, and specific to certain individuals (Jenkins 1996; Meskell 2001; Wiessner 1983). For the purposes of this project, identity is defined following Jenkins (1996: 4) as "the ways in which individuals and collectivities are distinguished in their social relations with other individuals and collectivities." These "ways of distinguishing" are operationalized and embedded in the social practices that constitute daily life (Jenkins 1996).

The concept of identity connotes both similarity and difference, often operationalized as an internal/external dichotomy: individual identity emphasizes differences between each individual, and social identity emphasizes similarities among individuals within a group and differences between groups (Jenkins 1996; G. Jones 1999). Similarly, identity can be characterized as the interaction between self and the other (Gardner 2002). Despite this dichotomy, ultimately all identities are social, in that they require another individual or group to exist and are constructed at social boundaries (Barth 1969; Jenkins 1996). Furthermore, differences in social boundaries result in the situational construction and expression of identity. Interpretations of expressions of identity are similarly fluid among groups (Meskell 2002).

Identity is generally expressed on a number of overlapping levels, depending on the situation and the audience. Individuals can express their identity based on their gender, family group, household membership, ethnic background, country or place of origin, occupation, beliefs, and a number of other levels. Some of these expressions of identity are more mutable than others. Jenkins (1996: 21), for example, states that some of the ways that identity is expressed, such as gender, are primary identities that are less likely to change. The propensity to not change the expression of identity is directly related to how that particular expression is embodied. Those identities that are more embodied are less prone to be altered than others (Jenkins 1996). These distinct ways of expressing identity are not mutually exclusive, as an individual may present herself simultaneously as an American (country of origin) female (gender) student (occupation). This was also true in the past, where a comparable identity may have been expressed as a female potter from the Water clan.

Why Is Identity Important?

Identity is necessary for individuals to understand who they are in relation to those who interact with them (Jenkins 1996), particularly in social situations where notions of identity are challenged, such as periods following migration (Jenkins 1996; Meskell 2002). In these situations, social identity is essential to understanding the meaning of practice, as identity is both reproduced and transformed through practice, which can be recognized through its material expression in the archaeological record (Gardner 2002). Thus, reconstructing identity and its material expression can lead to greater understanding of the effects of new social situations that lead to unintended consequences, such as migration. Identity, through which the outcomes of actions can be manifested, provides a key to understanding the duality of structure.

Archaeological studies of identity are also important for connecting the past to the present and thus have particular importance for contemporary society. Identity research has implications for nation building, understanding questions of origins, the legitimacy of cultural claims, and as a means of addressing cultural affiliation for legislation such as NAGPRA (the Native American Graves Protection and Repatriation Act; see also Meskell 2002). Research that moves beyond the boundaries of traditional archaeological culture areas, such as that described herein, posits a different conception of social groups in the past. Such a conception is more consistent with how groups define themselves now and probably defined themselves in the past. This research has substantial use for NAGPRA cultural affiliation studies, as it uses a more nuanced approach to understanding identity with an emic, rather than etic, focus (Ferguson 2004). Although research on past identity is often politically charged and embedded in contemporary notions of identity, ultimately understanding identity is essential to better understanding ourselves and others in a world that is becoming increasingly interconnected through time.

The concept of identity has many advantages over similar concepts often used interchangeably with identity, such as ethnicity. Most research on identity explicitly recognizes that identity shifts with changing social situations, whereas ethnicity is often characterized as static, and ethnic identity is often assumed to have a one-to-one correlation with a well-defined social group that can be set apart from others on the basis of the cultural characteristics it exhibits (S. Jones 1997: 56–64). Furthermore, ethnicity is often characterized on a larger social group level, whereas identity acts at many levels, ranging from the individual, to the household, to other larger social entities such as clans and moieties. Thus, while the concept of ethnicity has its place in anthropological and archaeological research, identity is a much more flexible, and therefore useful, concept in characterizing how people and groups in the past distinguished themselves in relation to others.

MIGRATION RESEARCH IN THE SAFFORD AND ARAVAIPA VALLEYS

Although several researchers had previously speculated that migrants from the Kayenta and Tusayan areas of northeastern Arizona settled in the Safford Valley and Aravaipa Creek areas (Brown 1973; Lindsay 1987; Wasley 1962; Welch 1995), excavations at the Goat Hill Site (Figs. 1.1, 1.2; site designations are listed in Table 1.2) in the early 1990s were the first to definitively demonstrate that ancestral Puebloan migrants settled in this region during the late thirteenth century (Woodson 1994, 1995, 1999).

Before and after Woodson's (1995, 1999) research, several other studies undertaken by Brown (1973); Clark, Neuzil, and Lyons (2004); the Millses (J. Mills and Mills 1978); and others (Jernigan 1993; Lee 1996; Rinker 1998) have provided further evidence of the presence of migrants in the region. Additional information from landowners with small artifact collections has supplied tantalizing clues about the presence of migrants in these valleys. Extremely little research has been conducted in the Aravaipa Valley, let alone research specifically focused on migration, although anecdotal information concerning indicators of Kayenta and Tusayan migration was available for a select few sites (Betty Lee, personal communication 2003). None of this research has systematically evaluated how many migrants traveled to the Safford and Aravaipa valleys, where these migrants settled, how they interacted with the existing local population, and how their presence affected both migrant and indigenous groups.

As a result, the Safford and Aravaipa valleys have proved to be somewhat of an enigma in migration research because of the lack of data available from many of the sites in these areas. However, numerous archaeologists have conducted research in the surrounding regions (Clark and Lyons 2008; Di Peso 1958; Gerald 1975; Haury 1958; Lindsay 1987), demonstrating that the Safford and Aravaipa valleys were bordered by areas in which it is known that Kayenta and Tusayan migrants settled. Haury's (1958) research at Point of Pines (AZ W:10:50 ASM; see also Lindsay 1987), located north of the Safford Valley, demonstrated that Kayenta and Tusayan migrants settled and lived alongside local groups at this location during the late thirteenth century.

Recent research along the San Pedro (Clark and Lyons 2008), just southwest of the Aravaipa Valley, has demonstrated that Kayenta and Tusayan migrants settled at several locations in this valley in the thirteenth and fourteenth centuries. In addition, sparse research and anecdotal evidence from the Clifton/Morenci and Duncan areas to the east suggest Kayenta and Tusayan migrants may have settled in this area for a time during the thirteenth and fourteenth centuries as well. Along with the Safford and Aravaipa valleys, these areas appear to be on a pathway of migration from the north through southeastern Arizona used by Kayenta and Tusayan migrants during the thirteenth and fourteenth centuries. This route may have been established by earlier migrants to the Safford and Aravaipa valleys, who originated in east-central Arizona and west-central New Mexico (Clark and Lengyel 2002). Understanding the scale and effect of migrant populations in the Safford and Aravaipa valleys helps to clarify the role of migration in these surrounding regions, as well as the larger demographic processes that shaped the last centuries before the arrival of Europeans in the Southwest.

MIGRANTS AND LOCALS IN THE SAFFORD AND ARAVAIPA VALLEYS

The Goat Hill Site (Fig. 1.2), which provided the first conclusive evidence of Kayenta and Tusayan migrants in the Safford Valley, was excavated during the summer of 1994 by a field school from the University of Texas at Austin, led by M. Kyle Woodson. The site is located atop a steep butte in Lefthand Canyon, about 10 km (6.2 miles) southwest of the town of Pima in the foothills of the Pinaleño Mountains. The pueblo consisted of 35 rooms constructed of coursed masonry separated into two room blocks, with entries at the north and south sides of the butte. A D-shaped kiva was located in the center of the pueblo, surrounded on all sides by the two room blocks.

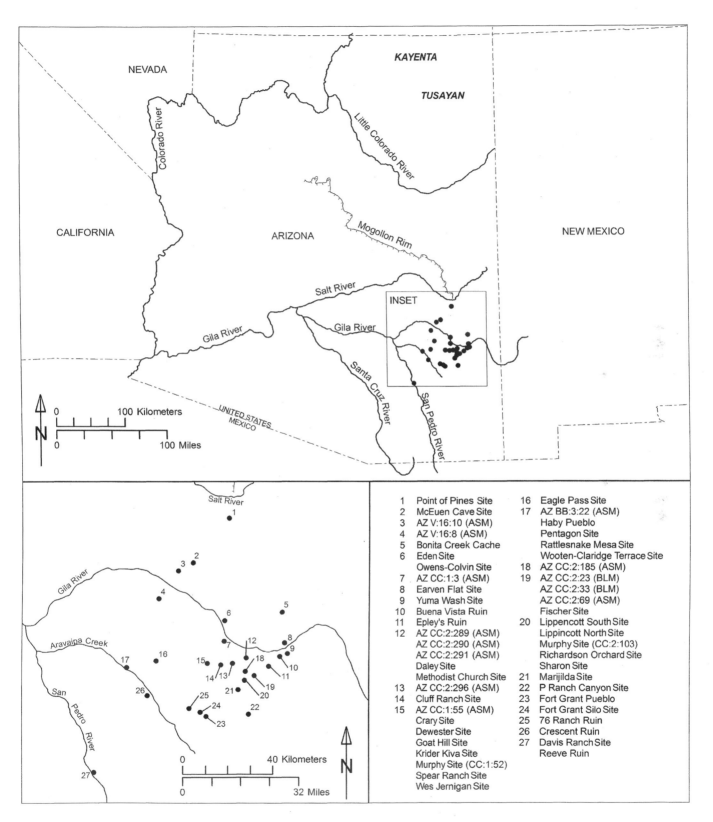

Figure 1.1. Eastern Arizona, showing the Kayenta and Tusayan areas and locations of sites mentioned in the text (see Table 1.2). The Hooker Ranch Site, Layton Site, Mesa Site, Sunset School Site, Two Dog Site, and Whitmer Site were not used in the analyses and are not displayed on this map.

Table 1.2. Site Designations

Name	Site Survey System Number	Secondary Name	Name	Site Survey System Number	Secondary Name
Arizona State Museum System (ASM)	**AZ**		**Arizona State Museum System (ASM)**	**AZ**	
Bonita Creek Cache	W:14:1		Spear Ranch Site	CC:1:11	
Buena Vista Ruin	CC:2:3	Solomonsville Site, Curtis Site	Sunset School Site	No number	
			Two Dog Site	W:13:14	
Cluff Ranch Site	CC:1:1		Wes Jernigan Site	CC:1:38	
Crary Site	CC:1:53		Whitmer Site	No number	
Crescent Ruin	BB:8:6		Wooten-Claridge		
Daley Site	CC:2:235		Terrace Site	BB:3:19	Wootton Ranch
Davis Ranch Site	BB:11:36		Yuma Wash Site	CC:2:16	
Dewester Site	CC:1:56		*No name*		
Eagle Pass Site	BB:4:1			BB:3:22	
Earven Flat Site	CC:2:5			CC:1:3	
Eden Site	CC:1:4			CC:1:55	
Epley's Ruin	CC:2:64			CC:2:69	
Fischer Site	CC:2:100			CC:2:185	
Fort Grant Pueblo	CC:5:8	Fort Grant		CC:2:289	
Goat Hill Site	CC:1:28			CC:2:290	
Haby Pueblo	BB:3:16	Haby Ranch		CC:2:291	
Hooker Ranch Site	No number			CC:2:296	
Krider Kiva Site	CC:1:43			V:16:8	
Layton Site	No number			V:16:10	
Lippencott South Site	CC:2:102				
Lippincott North Site	CC:2:104				
Marijilda Site	CC:5:6		**Amerind Foundation System (AF)**	**ARIZONA**	
Methodist Church Site	CC:2:15		Fort Grant Silo Site	CC:5:3	
McEuen Cave Site	W:13:6		Rattlesnake Mesa Site	BB:3:5	
Mesa Site	CC:2:177				
Murphy Site	CC:1:52				
Murphy Site	CC:2:103		**Bureau of Land Management System (BLM)**	**AZ**	
Owens-Colvin Site	CC:1:19		P Ranch Canyon Site	CC:6:89	
Pentagon Site	BB:3:18	Wootton-Haby Terrace	Richardson Orchard Site	CC:6:33	
			No name		
Point of Pines Site	W:10:50			CC:2:23	
Reeve Ruin	BB:11:26			CC:2:33	
76 Ranch Ruin	BB:8:1				
Sharon Site	CC:2:101				

Woodson and his team excavated all or part of 11 rooms, the kiva, the north entrance, and two geomorphological trenches, and found several lines of evidence pointing toward a Kayenta and Tusayan migrant occupation. First, the Goat Hill site was constructed entirely of coursed masonry (with the exception of the kiva), a construction technique most often associated with Puebloan regions of the northern Southwest and practiced widely at only one other settlement in the valley, the Marijilda Site. Second, the pueblo was laid out in room blocks, a plan that differed radically from other contemporaneous and previously occupied settlements in the area, which were almost exclusively arranged into compounds. Third, the D-shaped kiva, a

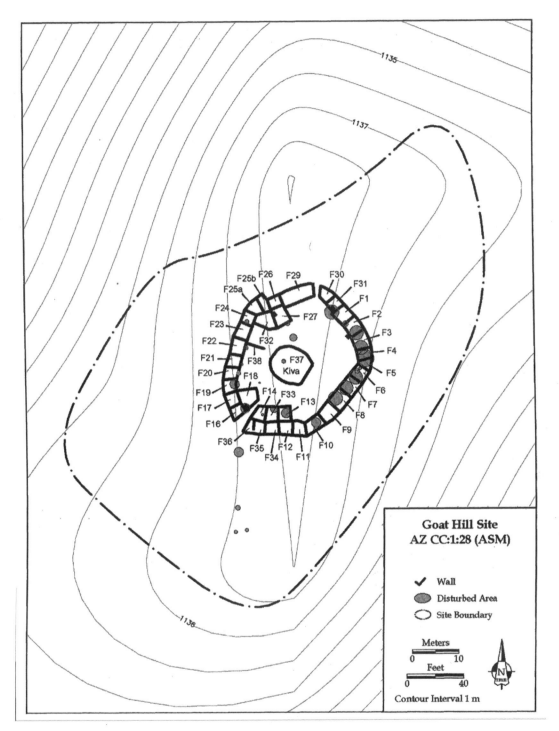

Figure 1.2. Plan of the Goat Hill Site

puebloan form of ritual architecture, is one of only two found south of the Mogollon Rim; the other is at Point of Pines associated with the migrant room block found there. Fourth, Woodson (1995, 1999) found entrybox complexes, a unique northern puebloan architectural form, only in rooms inhabited by Kayenta migrants in the western room block. Fifth, the pueblo was in a defensible location compared with nearby contemporaneous local settlements. And finally, the ceramic assemblage at Goat Hill was dominated by Maverick Moun-

Table 1.3. Social Consequences of Migration

Scale	Size of Indigenous Population	Distance Traveled by Migrants	Consequences for Identity
Household	Smaller	—	—
	Larger	Long Short	Migrants adopt indigenous identity OR identities are renegotiated
Suprahousehold	Smaller	Long Short	Indigenous population adopts migrant identity Identities are maintained
	Larger	Long Short	Migrants adopt indigenous identity OR identities are renegotiated
Community	Smaller	Long Short	Indigenous population adopts migrant identity Identities are maintained
	Larger	Long Short	Migrants adopt indigenous identity OR identities are renegotiated

tain Series ceramics, which are locally manufactured versions of Tsegi Orange Ware that is found primarily in northeastern Arizona (Lindsay 1987). Fragments of several perforated plates, which have been clearly associated with the presence of Kayenta and Tusayan migrant populations in southeastern Arizona (Lyons and Lindsay 2006), were also present. From this evidence, Woodson (1999, 1995) concluded that Goat Hill was a Kayenta and Tusayan site-unit intrusion, or migrant enclave, occupied from about A.D. 1290 to 1315.

In contrast, the local pattern in the Safford Valley was characterized by cobble reinforced adobe architecture arranged into compounds, no obvious ritual or communal architecture with the exception of a handful of ballcourts (Fewkes 1904; Wilcox and Sternberg 1983: 104–106), settlement locations in the middle of the broad and flat Gila River floodplain, and a ceramic assemblage with both "local" types such as San Carlos Red-on-brown, and nonlocal types likely brought in by both exchange and previous migrations, including Safford Variety Middle Gila Buff Ware, White Mountain Red Ware, Cibola White Ware, and corrugated ware.

In combination with these listed trait markers, I use several other lines of evidence to look for migrant populations at Safford and Aravaipa valley settlements and evaluate the effect of migration on identity. Differences in the technology and manufacture of corrugated ceramics and domestic architecture aid in discerning distinct and discrete social groups. Decorated ceramics help to determine who these groups were and if they

identified themselves as "local," "nonlocal," or some combination thereof. Provenance analyses of these ceramics and obsidian more definitively establish that "nonlocal" decorated ceramics were the result of distinct groups living at settlements and not exchange relationships. And finally, measures of space syntax of architecture and built space determine the degree to which distinct groups were integrated.

MODELING THE CONSEQUENCES OF MIGRATION ON IDENTITY

Just as the archaeological signatures of different scales of migration vary, so do their impacts, depending on the relative size of migrant and indigenous populations and the social means available for integration. Table 1.3 presents a model of the impacts of long distance migrations to an occupied area on the expression of identity. Although changes in the expression of identity are most likely to have been the result of a disparity in size between migrants and indigenous groups, other factors may also have played a role, such as the availability of social methods to integrate outsiders, the historical tolerance for outsiders due to earlier migrations, and the social and physical distance between groups. Migrants are usually at a disadvantage as a result of their newcomer status (Clark 2001).

Migration can have a variety of impacts on the identities of migrant and indigenous populations. Identities can be maintained as distinct from one another, renegotiated into a new identity, or be subsumed into one another such that one population takes on the identity of the other. When indigenous populations outnumber migrants of relatively equal technological and organizational complexity, identities of these groups may be renegotiated, or migrants may be assimilated into the indigenous population. In cases where migrants are more numerous than the indigenous population and migration occurred across only a short distance, identities may be maintained, as there is a greater possibility that migrants may return to their homeland if that option is available. Alternatively, in cases of long distance migration, the indigenous group may transform their identity to fit in with that of the migrants, particularly if the latter outnumber the former.

The research presented here examines a case of migration into the Safford and Aravaipa valleys in the late thirteenth and fourteenth centuries to understand both the scale of these migrations and their effect on the expression of identity of both the migrant and indigenous populations. Evidence shows both suprahousehold and household level groups migrated into the Safford and Aravaipa areas during this time. Initially, migrant groups segregated themselves from the local population, but shortly after their arrival they moved in with these local groups and both migrants and the indigenous populations renegotiated their identity, taking on aspects of both the migrant and local identities to form a new, cohesive, and distinctive group.

This study is important because most research on migration that has been undertaken in anthropology, and archaeology specifically, has focused on identifying cases of migration in the archaeological record. The research presented here goes a step further, not only identifying cases of migration, but also assessing the consequences of migration on the identity of those involved. The model and approach used here can be applied to other cases of migration, taking migration research in archaeology beyond its culture history roots and allowing archaeologists to understand migration as a process, rather than an isolated event.

CHAPTER TWO

Archaeological Setting of the Safford and Aravaipa Valleys

The Safford and Aravaipa valleys are located in southeastern Arizona (Fig. 2.1). The Safford Valley extends from the modern town of San Carlos on the west to the Gila Box area on the east, just west of the Greenlee-Graham County line. It is bounded by the Gila Mountains on the north and by the Pinaleño Mountains on the south. Based on previous research, archaeologists split the Safford Valley into two distinct districts, the San Carlos district to the west and the Pueblo Viejo district to the east, divided approximately at the modern town of Bylas. The research that has been conducted in these two districts has demonstrated that there are definite distinctions between the two. The San Carlos district appears to have been more influenced by the Hohokam inhabitants of the Phoenix Basin to the west, and the Pueblo Viejo district was more influenced by highland Mogollon populations (Black and Green 1995; Clark, Nials, and Vint 2004; Crary 1997; Johnson and Wasley 1966). Here I focus on the eastern Pueblo Viejo district, hereafter termed the Safford Valley. The Aravaipa Valley is bounded on the east by the town of Bonita and the Fort Grant Prison complex, and on the west by the confluence of the Aravaipa Creek and Turkey Creek in the Galiuro Mountains. North of this area are the Pinaleño and Santa Teresa Mountains; to the south are the Galiuro and Winchester Mountains.

The Safford and Aravaipa valleys are located in the Arizona Upland subdivision of the Sonoran Desertscrub Biome, which is within the Basin and Range Physiographic Zone of central Arizona (Turner and Brown 1994). The town of Safford averages 21.5 cm of rain annually (Turner and Brown 1994: 202), which probably typifies annual rainfall for this region except for the upper elevations of the surrounding mountain ranges that receive more precipitation. Elevations in the study area range from a low of about 850 m (2,800 feet) along the Gila River, to more than 3050 m (10,000 feet)

atop Mount Graham in the Pinaleño Mountains. Most major habitation sites in the area are situated between 850 m and 1500 m in elevation. Neither the Aravaipa Creek nor the Gila River currently flow year round due to groundwater pumping for agricultural pursuits, although in the past the Gila River is known to have flowed and the Aravaipa Creek likely ran year round (Waters and Ravesloot 2001). Aravaipa Creek is mainly fed from rainwater runoff and flows during the summer monsoon season after rainstorms. The Gila River is fed by both precipitation and groundwater and flows most frequently and with the most volume in the eastern end of the valley. The Safford Valley had one of the largest arable floodplains in the past, second only to the Phoenix Basin (Neely 2004).

PREVIOUS ARCHAEOLOGICAL RESEARCH

Research concerning the ancient past in the Safford and Aravaipa valleys has been relatively sparse in comparison to much of the rest of the Greater Southwest. Early in the history of the discipline, much of the archaeological research was conducted by large universities and their distance from these valleys and hot summer temperatures made these areas less than ideal for summer field schools. The Safford and Aravaipa valleys were not suited to answering many of the important research questions of the early twentieth century, when archaeologists were focused on working out regional chronologies and large-scale culture areas (Clark, Neuzil, and Lyons 2004). Many of the sites in the area also experienced extensive damage from agriculture and looting, making them less attractive for study. Later in the twentieth century, population growth and development in these two areas was slow, and cultural resource management (CRM) work here has

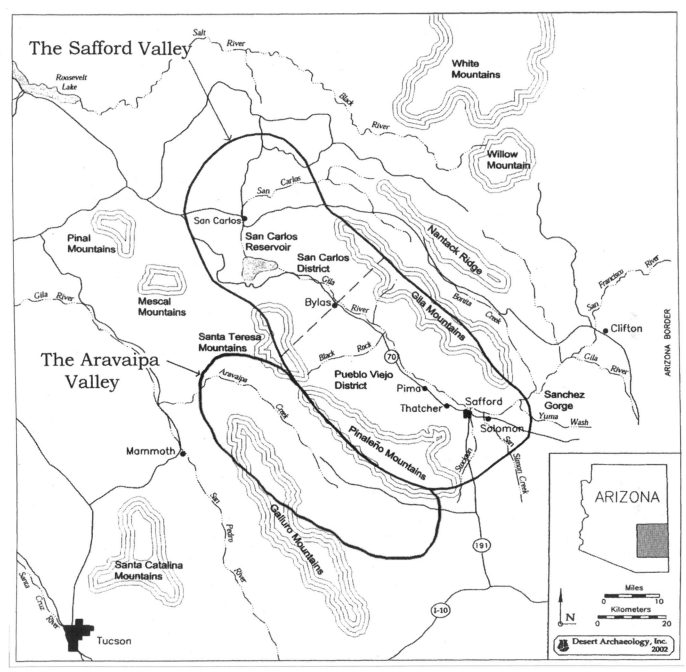

Figure 2.1. Location of the Safford and Aravaipa valleys. (Map reprinted with permission of Desert Archaeology, Inc., Tucson, Arizona.)

been limited. The number of CRM projects completed in the Safford area has increased during the last decade, however, and archaeological research in advance of development projects in the area is becoming more commonplace (Clark 2004; Lascaux and Montgomery 2008; Purcell 2004; Seymour and others 1997). Local land managing agencies, particularly the Bureau of Land Management and the Coronado National Forest, have also recently conducted a number of CRM projects on lands that they administer (Bronitsky and Merritt 1986; Farrell and others 2002; Gillespie and Schrager 2002; Hadley and others 1993; LeBlanc and others 2003; Taylor and others 2002), increasing the overall amount of research in these areas. Nonetheless, the general understanding of basic culture history and chronology of the Safford and Aravaipa valleys lags well behind much of the Southwest.

The Safford Valley

The Safford Valley has been the subject of far more archaeological research than the Aravaipa Valley. Its archaeological resources were well known to early American explorers who visited the area in the nineteenth century and were first mentioned in the report submitted by Lieutenant Colonel Emory and the journal of his associate Captain Johnston who traveled to the area on an exploratory mission for the U.S. military (Emory 1848; Johnston 1848). Archaeological sites in the Safford area were also discussed in publications shortly after the initial arrival of Anglo settlers in the area in the 1870s (Hamilton 1884; Hodge 1875). Bandelier (1890) visited shortly thereafter, but confined much of his visit to the western half of the Gila Valley around the area of Fort Thomas. He did, however, describe canals that carried rainwater runoff from the Pinaleño Mountains north to the Gila River Valley. Hough (1907) and Fewkes (1898, 1904) visited around the turn of the century and made a much more thorough investigation of local sites. They visited sites in the eastern part of the valley, including Buena Vista Ruin (see Table 1.2 for Arizona Site Survey designations) and Epley's Ruin, conducting test excavations and collecting artifacts to send back to the Smithsonian Institution for museums in Washington, D.C. Fewkes (1898) was the first to note the presence of rock-bordered grids and ballcourts in the valley, although he mistakenly identified the ballcourts as large reservoirs. Undoubtedly, archaeological sites were more visible along the Gila River at that time, as they had experienced little disturbance since their inhabitants left several centuries prior. Fewkes (1898) did note, however, that disturbance of these sites through farming activities had already begun. Although only some of these early descriptions can be matched to known sites today, they give an important glimpse of the density of sites present in the Safford Valley before the sites were impacted by modern agriculture and development.

Oscar Tatman was the first to conduct research in the Safford Valley under the auspices of a large academic institution, the University of Colorado, in the early 1930s. Tatman spent one field season at Buena Vista Ruin, excavating numerous structures in a variety of locations throughout the site (Tatman 1931). In his Master's thesis for the University of Colorado at Boulder, Tyberg (2000) reexamined the collections made by Tatman at the Buena Vista Ruin. Tyberg's work demonstrated that Tatman had excavated late components of the site that were likely occupied after the arrival of Kayenta and Tusayan migrants in the valley. Tyberg's (2000) research provided valuable insights into Tatman's collection and reaffirmed the importance of this site in the Safford phase (A.D. 1325–1450; Fig. 2.2).

Along with Tatman's research, early CRM projects were some of the first to lay out the basic cultural framework of the ancient past in the Safford Valley. Tuohy (1960) conducted one of the first systematic surveys in the area in advance of realignments of the Gila River channel, recording 48 new sites and locating the second known ballcourt in the valley (at the Eden Site). He also undertook a series of test excavations at the six sites most affected by the proposed realignment of the river channel and proposed additional excavations be undertaken at three of these sites. Following Tuohy's (1960) survey, Johnson and Wasley (1966) conducted excavations at two of the affected sites, AZ V:16:8 (ASM) and AZ V:16:10 (ASM). Johnson and Wasley's work remains important today, because they provided the first chronological framework for the Safford Valley, and designated AZ V:16:8 (ASM) and AZ V:16:10 (ASM) as the type sites for the Bylas phase, which they placed in the twelfth century (A.D. 1100–1200). Although later research cast doubt on their chronological placement of the Bylas phase (Neily and others 1993), these sites remain two of only a handful that have been professionally excavated in the area.

Shortly thereafter, Jeffrey Brown (1973, 1974) conducted research in the Safford Valley in the late 1960s for his dissertation at the University of Arizona. Brown looked at ten sites in the area, including Earven Flat, Yuma Wash, Rincon Canyon (no known site number, but may be AZ CC:2:103 ASM, also known as the Murphy Site), Methodist Church, Bonita Creek Cache, Marijilda, Whitmer, Spear Ranch, and Goat Hill, as well as Buena Vista Ruin. He mapped, carried out test excavations, and analyzed existing collections from each site.

Brown (1973) tested several hypotheses in an attempt to account for the appearance of so-called "Saladoan" traits in the Pueblo Viejo area beginning in the fourteenth century, focusing both on migration and in situ development. Based on his ceramic data, Brown suggested that most sites in his sample were culturally affiliated with the Point of Pines-Reserve area to the north and that three sites (Methodist Church, Spear Ranch, and Goat Hill) were specifically affiliated with the Maverick Mountain phase inhabitants of the Point of Pines area. As a result, Brown suggested some inhabitants of these sites may have migrated from Point of Pines to the Safford Valley in the late thirteenth century. Brown also recognized the similarities in material culture between the Reeve Ruin on the San Pedro River and Safford Valley sites, as well as similarities between design layouts on decorated ceramics from the Kayenta area and those found in the Safford Valley, particularly Roosevelt Red Ware vessels. Although Brown did not explicitly recognize the presence of Kayenta and Tusayan migrants in the Safford Valley, he did acknowledge their influence in the development of fourteenth century settlements in the area.

During the course of the next decade, a few projects were undertaken by amateur archaeologists and CRM companies. Jack and Vera Mills (1978) conducted the largest amateur project in the valley in the 1970s, excavating approximately 80 rooms and 90 cremations over the course of several years at the Buena Vista Ruin. The Millses self-published report describes the excavations as well as many of the artifacts they found, which are curated at Eastern Arizona College. Their excavations demonstrated that this settlement was occupied for at least 400 years, perhaps longer, and was likely one of the most persistent and largest settlements in the Safford Valley. At about the same time, Fitting (1977) conducted a CRM survey of approximately four square miles south of the town of Solomon, centered on Foote Wash and No Name Wash. This survey recorded limited habitation in this area just west of the San Simon River. Fitting (1977) found only artifact scatters and small, round cobble features. Based on the sparseness of the artifacts, both on the surface and in test excavation units, Fitting concluded that all the sites he recorded had been used for a only a short period of time, perhaps seasonally, for resource procurement activities.

Amateur archaeologists continued to advance what was known of Safford Valley prehistory in the 1980s and 1990s. The Eastern Arizona College Minutemen, a group of local amateurs, conducted excavations at the Daley Site in advance of ground leveling work for agricultural purposes in the early 1980s (Lee 1981). Lee and her crew excavated portions of several cobble-reinforced adobe rooms as well as several test pits.

Ceramics at the site suggested an occupation during the Bylas phase (A.D. 1200–1275/1300). Shortly thereafter, Rex Owens, a long time resident of the area, conducted excavations in one structure at the Owens-Colvin Site, uncovering what may have been a ceremonial structure with an unusual artifact assemblage (Owens 1990). Much of the site was excavated later by Eastern Arizona College (Rule 1993) and another group of amateur archaeologists led by professionals (Neily and others 1993), but the structure excavated by Owens provided a glimpse into the ritual and ceremony of this time period, which had never been adequately characterized. Owens also wrote limited circulation reports of excavations of five structures and a trash mound conducted by other avocational archaeologists at Two Dog Site, the type site of the Two Dog phase (A.D. 1000–1100; Owens 1993). Although the chronological assignment of this site is somewhat questionable, Owens' report remains one of the few excavation reports of any structures predating the Classic period. Owens also wrote a short report detailing the Eastern Arizona College excavations at the Fischer Site, led by Thomas Scott (Owens 1992). Excavations at this site sampled three separate cobble-reinforced adobe room blocks and a cremation area. Ceramics recovered suggest a late thirteenth- and early fourteenth-century occupation.

Eastern Arizona College (EAC), located in Thatcher, Arizona, continued the trend of academic research in the Safford Valley through the 1970s, 1980s, and 1990s (Crary 1995; Lee 1996; Rule 1993). Professors at EAC conducted excavations at several sites, including Owens-Colvin, Eagle Pass, Fischer, Layton, Mesa, Spear Ranch, and Krider Kiva. Other sites may have been excavated also but remain undocumented. Betty Graham Lee (1996) excavated at the Eagle Pass Site for an independent study project through the University of Arizona to investigate whether it could have been the fabled ruins of Chichilticale described by Coronado's chronicler Castañeda in 1540. This work was later published (Lee 1996) as a monograph from Eastern Arizona College. In the two excavated rooms Lee (1996) found a typical Safford or Fort Grant phase (A.D. 1325–1450) assemblage, dominated by plain and corrugated vessels, along with several Gila Polychrome jars. The location of this late site is unique, situated in Eagle Pass between the Santa Teresa and Pinaleño mountains and well away from major rivers and flood plain agricultural areas. Pamela Rule's (1993) excavations at Owens-Colvin Site revealed a typical Bylas

Time	Gregory (1995) Safford Valley		Crary (1997) Pueblo Viejo District Safford Valley	Aravaipa Valley	Clark, Neuzil, and Lyons (2004) Pueblo Viejo District Safford Valley	
A.D. 1500	Late Ceramic Period A.D. 1150/1200-1500	Late Ceramic Period II A.D. 1300-1450/1500	Classic Period A.D. 1100/1150-1450		Classic Period A.D. 1200-1450	
A.D. 1450			Safford phase A.D. 1300-1400/1450	Fort Grant phase A.D. 1300-1400/1450		Safford phase A.D. 1300-1450
A.D. 1400						
A.D. 1350						
A.D. 1300		Late Ceramic Period I/Bylas A.D. 1150/1200-1300	Bylas phase A.D. 1175-1300	Haby Ranch phase A.D. 1050/1100-1300		Bylas phase A.D. 1200-1300
A.D. 1250						
A.D. 1200	Middle Ceramic Period A.D. 600/700-1150/1200		Late Formative Period A.D. 800-1100/1150		Late Formative (pre-Classic) Period A.D. 800-1200	Eden phase A.D. 1100-1200
A.D. 1150		Middle Ceramic Period II A.D. 900/1000-1150/1200	Eden phase A.D. 1100-1175			
A.D. 1100			Two Dog phase A.D. 950/1000-1100			Two Dog phase A.D. 1000-1100
A.D. 1050				Early Encinas A.D. 950-1050/1100		
A.D. 1000						Talkali phase A.D. 800-1000
A.D. 950			Talkali phase A.D. 800-950/1000	Galiuro phase A.D. 800-950		
A.D. 900						
A.D. 850		Middle Ceramic Period I A.D. 600/700-900/1000				
A.D. 800			Pinaleño phase A.D. 700-800			Pinaleño phase A.D. 700-800
A.D. 750						
A.D. 700			Dos Cabezas phase A.D. 600-700			Dos Cabezas phase A.D. 600-700
A.D. 650						
A.D. 600			Early Formative Period 150 B.C. – A.D. 800		Early Formative (pre-Classic) Period 150 B.C. – A.D. 800	
A.D. 550						
A.D. 500						
A.D. 450			Peñasco phase A.D. 150/200-600			Peñasco phase A.D. 150-600
A.D. 400	Early Ceramic Period A.D. 100-600/700	No phases defined				
A.D. 350						
A.D. 300						
A.D. 250						
A.D. 200						
A.D. 150						
A.D. 100						Whitlock phase 150 B.C. – A.D. 150
A.D. 50			Whitlock phase 150 B.C. – A.D. 150/200			
50 B.C.	Archaic Period 8000 B.C. – A.D. 100					
100 B.C.						
150 B.C.			No periods defined		Archaic Period 8500 – 150 B.C.	
8000 B.C.	Paleoindian Period ? – 8000 B.C.				Paleoindian Period ? – 8500 B.C.	

Figure 2.2a. Chronologies for the Safford and Aravaipa valleys.

Time	Neely (2004) Safford Valley		Neuzil (2005b) Pueblo Viejo District Safford Valley	Aravaipa Valley
A.D. 1500				
A.D. 1450	Classic Period A.D. 1150-1450	Late Classic Period A.D. 1300-1450	Classic Period A.D. 1200-1450	Safford phase A.D. 1325-1450	Fort Grant phase A.D. 1325-1450
A.D. 1400				
A.D. 1350				Goat Hill phase A.D. 1275/1300-1325	Middle Classic phase (prov.) A.D. 1275/1300-1325
A.D. 1300		Early Classic Period A.D. 1150-1300		Bylas phase A.D. 1200-1275/1300	Early Classic phase (prov.) A.D. 1200-1275/1300
A.D. 1250				
A.D. 1200	Late Formative Period A.D. 800-1150	Phases undefined	Late Formative Period A.D. 800-1200	Eden phase A.D. 1100-1200	Phases undefined
A.D. 1150				
A.D. 1100				Two Dog phase A.D. 1000-1100	
A.D. 1050				
A.D. 1000				Talkali phase A.D. 800-1000	
A.D. 950				
A.D. 900				
A.D. 850				
A.D. 800	Early Formative Period 150 B.C. – A.D. 800	Phases undefined	Early Formative Period 150 B.C. – A.D. 800	Pinaleño phase A.D. 700-800	Phases undefined
A.D. 750				
A.D. 700				Dos Cabezas phase A.D. 600-700	
A.D. 650				
A.D. 600				Peñasco phase A.D. 150-600	
A.D. 550				
A.D. 500				
A.D. 450				
A.D. 400				
A.D. 350				
A.D. 300				
A.D. 250				
A.D. 200				
A.D. 150				Whitlock phase 150 B.C. – A.D. 150	
A.D. 100				
A.D. 50				
50 B.C.				
100 B.C.				
150 B.C.	Paleoindian and Archaic Periods ~8000-150 B.C.		Archaic Period 8000-150 B.C.	
8000 B.C.			Paleoindian Period ? – 8000 B.C.	

Figure 2.2b. Chronologies for the Safford and Aravaipa valleys (*continued*).

phase (A.D. 1200–1275/1300) assemblage, with some ceramics representative of an earlier Eden phase (A.D. 1100–1200) component. Later excavations (Neily and others 1993) demonstrated that several pit houses and compounds were located east of the area Rule excavated and were probably the source of the Eden phase ceramics. Although Rule (1993) thought this site may have been occupied seasonally, comparison with other excavated sites and the sheer volume of habitation debris point to year-round occupation. Jernigan's (1993) work at the Krider Kiva Site uncovered one of the two definitive kivas in the Safford Valley (the other is at the Goat Hill Site). Cumulatively, these excavations helped better define the Classic period in the Safford Valley. Although the excavations carried out at the rest of the sites studied by EAC have never been formally published, this research was done in advance of later significant disturbance and remains a major contribution to the archaeological understanding of the Safford area.

As the largest government land managing agency in the Safford area, the Bureau of Land Management has conducted and overseen a number of CRM projects in the region. Most important are an overview of the archaeology of southeastern Arizona, including the Safford and Aravaipa areas, an ethnoecological study of Aravaipa Creek, and an ethnoecological study of the Bonita Creek watershed (Bronitsky and Merrit 1986; Hadley and others 1991; Hadley and others 1993). Although these reports do not focus specifically on the Safford area, they do provide important regional contexts.

The United States Forest Service (USFS) also manages a significant portion of land in the Safford area, mostly in the Pinaleño and Santa Teresa mountains to the southwest and northwest of Safford, respectively. Over the years, the USFS has conducted a number of surveys in these areas in advance of prescribed burns, road improvements, and other projects (Farrell and others 2002; Gillespie and Schrager 2002; LeBlanc and others 2003; Taylor and others 2002). Although many of these surveys are relatively small, they provide one of the few sources of information on sites outside the floodplain and lower bajada areas of the Safford Valley.

One of the most interesting projects sponsored by the USFS in the Safford Valley was the recovery of several ceramic vessels, baskets, and raw cotton from a cave on the north side of the Pinaleño Mountains (Haury and Huckell 1993). Discovered by local residents, the artifacts were carefully removed from the cave under the supervision of Forest Service archaeologists and airlifted to Safford. Subsequent analyses of the vessels, cotton, and baskets revealed that they were probably deposited in the cave over several episodes ranging from the tenth or eleventh to the thirteenth centuries (Haury and Huckell 1993). This cache provided important evidence for the prehistoric cultivation of cotton in the Safford Valley.

Several surveys conducted by SWCA Environmental Consultants in the 1990s found that upland areas on the north side of the Gila River were likely used seasonally for resource procurement (Doak and Ahlstrom 1995; Lyon and others 1999; Seymour 1992; Seymour and others 1997). Both survey and excavations revealed relatively little material culture in this upland zone, and Ahlstrom and others (1997) suggest that the area was exclusively used for short term seasonal resource procurement activities; there is no evidence that long term occupation ever took place there. This pattern stands in contrast to the floodplain zone and adjacent terraces along the Gila River, which were extensively used for long term habitation throughout the ancient past. Survey in the early 1990s by Archaeological Consulting Services, Inc. (Black and Green 1995) demonstrated that this habitation pattern of heavy floodplain use continued west into the San Carlos district of the Safford Valley as well.

More recently, several projects undertaken by students and professors from the University of Texas at Austin, the University of California at Berkeley, and the University of New Mexico have made significant strides in improving our understanding of the Classic period, the Archaic period, the role of migration in the Safford area, and the role and extent of water control features in agriculture throughout the valley (Doolittle and Neely 2004; Rinker 1998; Shackley 2005a; Woodson 1995, 1999). In their research on fields with rock-bordered grids north of Pima, Doolittle and Neely (2004) determined that these fields represented an important advance in the utilization of upland areas for agave production, much like rockpiles in the Tucson Basin (S. Fish and others, 1992). Similarly, canals fed by runoff in the Pinaleño Mountains supported increased upland farming on the south side of the Gila River (Neely 1997, 2001; Neely and Crary 1998; Rinker 1998).

Woodson's (1995, 1999) work at the Goat Hill Site for his Master's thesis at the University of Texas at Austin conclusively demonstrated that the Safford Valley was a destination for migrants from the Four

Corners area in the late thirteenth century. Work conducted by Rinker (1998) at the Murphy (AZ CC:1:52 ASM), Crary, and Dewester sites significantly advanced our understanding of site structure and morphology through time and showed evidence for the transition from pit houses, to compounds, and ultimately to room blocks during the Late Formative and Classic periods.

Recent excavations at the McEuen Cave site in the Gila Mountains north of the Safford Valley, undertaken to provide new light on older excavations at the site, have provided valuable insight into the Archaic period occupations of the Safford Valley. This research has demonstrated that late Archaic period inhabitants of the Safford Valley practiced mixed farming and foraging, in which they utilized resources from many ecological zones, in addition to farming maize and squash (Schmidt 2005; Shackley 2005a). The shift to dependence on agriculture over wild resources was gradual and is reflected in several material culture classes (Schmidt 2005).

CRM research by contract companies has also been on the rise in the Safford valley in recent years. In the late 1990s, Desert Archaeology conducted excavations at the Daley Site, as well as at AZ CC:2:289 (ASM), AZ CC:2:290 (ASM), and AZ CC:2:291 (ASM). The results of these investigations made several important contributions to the understanding of the ancient past in the Safford Basin. First, two canal segments (AZ CC:2:296 ASM) were excavated and dated to 100 B.C. to A.D. 300 (Nials and others 2004), providing conclusive evidence that canal irrigation has a long history in this region, much like in the Tucson Basin (Mabry 2003). Second, excavations at the Daley Site revealed several ephemeral pit structures that were heavily associated with Maverick Mountain Series ceramics, indicating the structures may have been occupied by migrants from the Kayenta and Tusayan areas (Hall and Clark 2004). Because many sites that are located in the Gila River floodplain are in areas currently under cultivation, like the Daley Site, this work provides not only an important record of the Daley Site but also an insight into how it fits into the settlement pattern of the rest of the valley.

Other recent CRM projects in the area include excavations at the Methodist Church Site conducted by Aztlan Archaeology (Laurie Slawson, personal communication 2003), excavation of sites along US 191 by Archaeological Research Services (Purcell 2004; Purcell 2006), excavation of Eplcy's Ruin by Tierra Right of Way Services (Lascaux and Montgomery 2008), survey and excavation in upland areas north of the Gila River by SWCA (Joe Ezzo, personal communication 2006) and survey in the eastern part of the valley around the Yuma Wash Site and Buena Vista Ruin (Dale 2005). The recent research on Late Formative period settlements south of Safford by Archaeological Research Services has contributed significantly to our understanding of this time and demonstrated that the inhabitants of these sites appear to be "multicultural," exhibiting material culture traits of both the Mogollon and Hohokam culture areas (Purcell and Coriell 2004). Numerous other small projects, both survey and test excavation, have been conducted in other areas in the Safford Valley as well (Bierer 1995; Bierer and Motsinger 1994; Dart 1999; Gilman and Sherman 1975; Jernigan 1990; J. Jones 2000; Phillips 1984; Roth 1993; Stull 1998). In total, these projects have contributed substantially to the growing body of knowledge about this region.

The Aravaipa Valley

Archaeological research along Aravaipa Creek has largely been in the form of informal small-scale surveys conducted by professional archaeologists (Crary 1997, Hartmann and Lee 2003, Sauer and Brand 1930) and small CRM projects (Gilman and Richards 1975; Gutierrez and Tucker 2003; J. Jones 1996; Kaldahl and Dart 2002). Sauer and Brand (1930) were the first to describe any of the sites in the area, and they focused on six in the Aravaipa and upper Sulphur Springs valleys, including Haby Pueblo (called Haby Ranch, Sauer and Brand number 31), the Wooten-Claridge Terrace Site (called Wootton Ranch, Sauer and Brand number 32), the Pentagon Site (called Wootton-Haby Terrace, Sauer and Brand number 33), Fort Grant Pueblo (called Fort Grant, Sauer and Brand number 28), and two sites with unknown site numbers called Hooker Ranch (Sauer and Brand number 29) and Sunset School (Sauer and Brand number 30). The description they provide of Haby Pueblo as a defensible pueblo with thick walls and at least two distinct room blocks is particularly useful, because this site has since been destroyed.

Shortly after Sauer and Brand's initial work, Duffen undertook excavations at the 76 Ranch Ruin (also known as Webb Ruin), excavating nine rooms over the course of a summer (Duffen 1937; Duffen and Hartmann 1997). These excavations clearly demonstrated that the site was arranged into multiple adobe room blocks surrounding a plaza or plazas. Duffen believed one of the rooms he excavated, which was about twice the size of the other rooms, was a kiva. Other northern influences were visible in architectural attributes such as wall niches and mealing bins and in the presence of artifacts such as full grooved axes. Unfortunately, no maps of the excavations or the site were made, and artifacts from the excavations were subsequently distributed as souvenirs to ranch guests. However, Duffen's work represents the only formal excavations of any site in this area.

William Hartmann later collaborated with Betty Graham Lee (Hartmann and Lee 2003) to summarize her work at sites along the Aravaipa. Lee had informally surveyed many of the sites in the area over the course of many years in an effort to locate the ruin of Chichilticale. Hartmann and Lee (2003) describe several sites and provide rough ceramic counts for each. This work represents a lasting contribution to the understanding of the archaeology of the Aravaipa Valley.

Several small CRM projects have recorded other sites in the Aravaipa area. Gilman and Richards (1975) surveyed a portion of the Aravaipa Canyon Primitive Area, managed by the BLM, recording or revisiting eleven sites and three isolated activity areas. More recently, J. Jones (1996) and Kaldahl and Dart (2002) recorded two sites on the grounds of the Fort Grant Prison complex in advance of improvements to prison infrastructure. Gutierrez and Tucker (2003) surveyed a portion of Arizona State Trust land that included the 76 Ranch Ruin to evaluate the impacts of a proposed road improvement project. Because our basic understanding of culture history in the Aravaipa area is minimal, the archaeologists who conducted these projects had difficulty tying their research into an overarching cultural scheme. However, small projects like these have made a significant contribution to our understanding of parts of the Aravaipa area, and those parts can now be unified by regional research such as that presented here.

Some of the research conducted in the Safford and Aravaipa valleys has been published, but a large portion of the data collected from sites in these areas has not been analyzed to its full potential. Much of the research that has been published has experienced only limited distribution, so that many Southwest archaeologists are unaware of the archaeological importance of the Safford and Aravaipa areas. Recent efforts to conduct fieldwork in these areas have been hampered by the poor preservation of many sites, which have been heavily disturbed by pothunting and other activities. These disturbances only emphasize the importance of making full use of existing collections and information from previously conducted fieldwork, because they more often provide more representative assemblages than can be obtained by current research.

CHRONOLOGY AND CULTURAL CHANGES

Current understanding of the chronological sequence of human settlement in the Safford and Aravaipa valleys is poor, and the chronological divisions archaeologists currently use are provisional and subject to change with future research. Most scholars have discussed chronology in the Safford and Aravaipa valleys either as an outgrowth of chronologies in surrounding areas (Gregory 1995; Neely 2004), or in general terms, such as Sauer and Brand's (1930) Middle Gila Polychrome period. Several authors have attempted to refine time and space systematics in both valleys, but consensus has only been reached on the definition of periods and phases of the Classic period in the Safford Basin (Clark, Nials, and Vint 2004; Crary 1997; Gregory 1995; Neely 2004).

Johnson and Wasley (1966) were the first to attempt phase definitions in the Safford Basin. Based on their excavations of 73 rooms at AZ V:16:10 (ASM) and 15 rooms from AZ V:16:8 (ASM) near the modern town of Bylas on the San Carlos Indian Reservation, they defined the Bylas phase, which extended from A.D. 1100 to 1200. However, a review of the ceramic types that Johnson and Wasley (1966: 250) included in their definition of the Bylas phase reveals that these ceramics actually were prevalent during a much longer period of time, from as early as A.D. 1050 to as late as 1300 (Lyons 2004; Mills and Herr 1999: 280). Additionally, some of these ceramic types were later demonstrated to postdate (wholly or almost completely) the Bylas phase range proposed by Johnson and Wasley (1966), including Tularosa Black-on-white, Snowflake Black-on-white, and San Carlos Red-on-brown (Lyons 2004; Mills and Herr 1999: 280). Neily and others (1993) and Gregory (1995) recently suggested that the original definition of the Bylas phase might have conflated two phases that have distinct material culture, the twelfth century Eden phase, and the revised Bylas phase, which makes up much of the thirteenth century. The totality of evidence from AZ V:16:8 (ASM) and AZ V:16:10

(ASM), in both the ceramic assemblage as well as the architecture, suggests that occupation of these settlements spanned much of the twelfth and thirteenth centuries, and the Bylas phase should be restricted to the thirteenth century.

Brown (1973) also attempted to place the sites he worked on in the Safford Valley into a temporal context based on nonlocal decorated wares, particularly White Mountain Red Ware and Cibola White Ware, that had been reliably dated at other sites with tree-ring dates. However, Brown (1973) did not assign any phase or period names to the time periods he defined. In his work in the San Carlos district of the Safford Basin, Gregory (1995: 124) defined five provisional periods: Paleoindian, Archaic, Early Ceramic, Middle Ceramic, and Late Ceramic (Fig. 2.2). Differences among these periods were based on changes in architecture and sedentism, and in the later ceramic periods, on changes in the ceramic assemblages. Gregory (1995) further divided the Late Ceramic period into the Late Ceramic I or Bylas phase (A.D. 1150/1200–1300) and the Late Ceramic II phase (A.D. 1300–1450), based mainly on changes in ceramic assemblages.

Crary (1997) was the first to define phases for both the Safford and the Aravaipa areas, but due to the limited amount of research completed in both areas, his chronology should still be considered provisional, particularly at sites dating to the Formative period. Crary (1997) defined three periods (Early Formative, Late Formative, and Classic), presumably preceded by Paleoindian and Archaic periods. He divided these periods into multiple phases (Fig. 2.2) and through the development of these phases noted a transition from cultural homogeneity throughout southeastern Arizona to cultural heterogeneity within smaller valleys and other topographically subscribed regions. Notably, the boundaries of the periods defined by Crary (1997) are roughly the same as those defined by Gregory (1995).

Clark, Nials, and Vint (2004: 14) mainly base their phase sequence on Crary's (1997) research, although they collapse the Talkali and Galiuro phases together. Periods in their sequence are divided at roughly the same intervals as periods defined by Crary (1997) and by Gregory (1995). Neely's (2004) chronology also defines periods at roughly the same intervals, although he refrains from dividing periods into phases.

I propose two changes to the chronologies for the Classic period that were presented in this previous research. First, in the Pueblo Viejo district of the Safford Basin I name a new Goat Hill phase in the Classic period intermediate between the Bylas phase and Safford phases. This new phase reflects changes in ceramic assemblages and architectural layout commensurate with the arrival of immigrants from the Kayenta and Tusayan areas in the late thirteenth century. These changes in material culture reflect the emergence of a new region-wide identity incorporating elements from both migrants and indigenous populations. Second, the phases of the Classic period for the Aravaipa area proposed by Crary (1997) are refined, and I define two new provisional phases, Early Classic and Middle Classic. Because there has been so little research at sites in this area, these phases will remain provisional until more data can be collected to confirm that their definition is warranted. Notably, the use of phase names in this research is not intended to suggest that each was homogenous and that no cultural changes were occurring during the length of the phases, whereas abrupt changes took place between phases. Instead, because chronology in these areas is not refined, phase names are intended to highlight general cultural trends for which the exact chronology may be further refined with future research. Table 2.1 summarizes the trends in architecture, ceramics, and social organization of each phase of settlement in the Safford and Aravaipa valley Classic period.

Although previous research in the Safford and Aravaipa valleys is more sparse than in other areas of the Southwest, several general trends and patterns are apparent, particularly during the Classic period. Overall, it appears that the Safford area had a significant and cosmopolitan local population that interacted regularly with groups in surrounding areas. Thereafter these local groups experienced an influx of migrant populations from the Kayenta and Tusayan areas of northeastern Arizona in the late thirteenth century. Along the Aravaipa, settlement appears to have been sparse until the late thirteenth century, when Kayenta and Tusayan migrants, perhaps accompanied by groups indigenous to the Safford Valley, moved into the valley. It is unclear what the extent of the local population of the Aravaipa Valley was previous to the arrival of the migrants.

In sum, Classic period inhabitants of the Safford and Aravaipa valleys were relatively diverse, as reflected in their material culture. As research in these areas has progressed, our understanding of each area's chronological sequences has improved significantly, highlighting how quickly some of these changes took place. Evidence from ceramics and other sources visibly portray

Table 2.1. Characteristics of Classic Period Phases in the Safford and Aravaipa Valleys

Phase	Architecture	Ceramics	Social Organization
SAFFORD VALLEY			
Bylas (A.D. 1200–1275/1300)	Early transition from subsurface pit structures to above ground cobble and adobe compounds Stepped entries Circular clay-lined hearths	Dominated by utilitarian wares, both plain and corrugated San Carlos Red-on-brown Middle Gila Buff Ware, Safford Variety Cibola White Ware White Mountain Red Ware	Waning Hohokam and Mimbres influences Dominated by household level social organization
Goat Hill (A.D. 1275/1300–1325)	"Clustered room blocks," multiple room blocks clustered around an open space Most constructed of cobble reinforced adobe, though some masonry architecture occurs Late pit houses underlying some room blocks	Dominated by utilitarian wares, both plain and corrugated Cibola White Ware White Mountain Red Ware San Carlos Red-on-brown Middle Gila Buff Ware, Safford Variety Ancestral Zuni Glaze-decorated Ware Maverick Mountain Series Early Roosevelt Red Ware	Ancestral Puebloan migrants played a large role Increased aggregation
Safford (A.D. 1325–1450)	Large, contiguous room blocks surrounding plazas Most constructed of cobble reinforced adobe, though some masonry architecture occurs	Dominated by utilitarian wares, corrugated becomes less common Roosevelt Red Ware Cibola White Ware Ancestral Zuni Glaze-decorated Ware White Mountain Red Ware San Carlos Red-on-brown Maverick Mountain Series	Increasing aggregation at increasingly larger sites Ancestral Puebloan migrants played a large role
ARAVAIPA VALLEY			
Early Classic, provisional (A.D. 1200–1275/1300)	Sparse evidence, probably very little occupation in the Aravaipa Valley during this time		
Middle Classic, provisional (A.D. 1275/1300–1325)	"Clustered room blocks," multiple room blocks clustered around an open space Late pit houses underlying some room blocks	Dominated by utilitarian wares, particularly plain Maverick Mountain Series Early Roosevelt Red Ware Cibola White Ware Middle Gila Buff Ware, Safford Variety White Mountain Red Ware Ancestral Zuni Glaze-decorated Ware	Settled by new groups, probably combinations of migrants and indigenous populations from the Safford Valley
Fort Grant (A.D. 1325–1450)	Large, contiguous room blocks surrounding plazas Exclusively cobble reinforced adobe	Dominated by utilitarian wares, particularly plain Roosevelt Red Ware Maverick Mountain Series Middle Gila Buff Ware, Safford Variety San Carlos Red-on-brown	Continued settlement by new groups, probably combinations of migrants and indigenous populations from the Safford Valley

ancestral Pueblo migrants from the Kayenta and Tusayan areas of northeastern Arizona entering the Safford Valley during the late thirteenth and fourteenth centuries. Evidence from the Aravaipa Valley is less abundant, but provides hints of a similar pattern. Understanding this wave of migration not only has implications for reconstructing the cultural past in the Safford and Aravaipa valleys, but also sheds light on larger cultural processes occurring throughout much of the Greater Southwest during this time.

CHAPTER THREE

Identifying Migrants in the Archaeological Record

In this chapter I use analyses of the technological styles of corrugated ceramics and domestic architecture to determine the social scale at which ancestral Puebloan migrants arrived and where they settled in the Safford and Aravaipa valleys. The scale of migration must be determined before inferences about its effects on the expression of identity can be made. I analyzed four attributes of corrugated ceramics to determine if any differences were apparent that could be tied to discrete households. I also analyzed domestic architecture with the same goal in mind. Understanding where migrants settled in the Safford and Aravaipa valleys makes it possible to examine how migrants and local groups may have changed the expression of their identity as a result of increased interaction with new and different people in the time following migration (Chapter 4).

CORRUGATED CERAMICS

Corrugated ceramics have posed an interesting problem for Southwest archaeologists throughout the history of the discipline. Whereas most ceramics found at prehistoric sites from the Greater Southwest can be and have been classified according to Colton's (1953) divisions of class, ware, and type, corrugated ceramics have never fit easily into these categories. With a few select exceptions (Gifford 1980; Kidder 1924; Martin and others 1952; Mauer 1970; Olson 1959), attempts to categorize corrugated ceramics beyond the ware level have not been successful (Gifford and Smith 1978). Corrugation technology is a continuum in its exuberance, execution, and overall appearance, all qualities used to define types. Although all ceramic wares and types could be conceived of as part of a technological and stylistic continuum, distinctions among corrugated ceramics are particularly difficult, and there is considerable overlap in the characteristics normally used to define types. Thus, corrugated types do not have the same weight in helping to explain behavioral and cultural differences as do types associated with most other defined wares in the Southwest.

There are exceptions to this observation. Types like McDonald Corrugated (Gifford 1980; Olson 1959) and Cibicue Painted Corrugated (Hagenbuckle 2000; Mauer 1970) can be easily recognized on the basis of distinctive painted and textured designs and vessel forms. Other types, such as Tularosa Fillet Rim, also have distinctive corrugation technology as well as other attributes, such as high polishing, a smudged interior, and a semiflared incurved vessel form, which make this type easily distinguishable from most other corrugated vessels (Kidder 1924; Martin and others 1952). Furthermore, general distinctions in the surface treatment of corrugated vessels, such as indented, obliterated, and clapboard, have some utility in describing the outward appearance of vessels and have temporal variability that can be used to seriate and compare sites across broad regions throughout much of the Southwest (Pierce 1999).

Corrugation technology, when viewed from a technological style perspective, can be used to identify differences among social groups from the regional to the household level (Clark 2001; Ennes 1999; Hegmon and others 2000; Neuzil 2001; Stark and others 1998). There is general consensus that corrugated ceramic vessels served a utilitarian function, likely for cooking, storage, and other daily household activities (Pierce 1999; Rohn 1971: 144). In addition, it is usually assumed that corrugated ceramics were produced and used locally and at a household level (Reid and Montgomery 1998; Zedeño 1994), although there are some exceptions where the exchange of corrugated vessels has been demonstrated (see Anna Shepard's work in Judd 1954). Because many corrugated vessels served a household utilitarian function, they probably were not intended to signal messages to others concerning the identity of their producers or users, although the way they were produced reflected the identity of their producers in a subtle way (Clark 2001). Moreover, the techniques used to create corrugated ceramics were likely passed down within family groups or communities of practice (Arnold 1989; Duwe 2005; Fenn and others 2005) with the same learning frameworks and enculturative practices. With this in mind, I collected corrugated ceramics from all sites examined except the Marijilda Site (where no ceramics were collected) to determine if differences in technological style reflecting discrete social groups could be detected, and if so, whether these differences in technological style could be attributed to differences in household level production resulting from the arrival of migrant groups in the Safford and Aravaipa areas. (Full site designations are in Table 1.2.)

Corrugated Ceramics at Classic Period Safford and Aravaipa Valley Sites

In addition to the attributes recorded for all ceramics, such as type, ware, weight, thickness, vessel form, vessel shape, and others, I recorded several other attributes of corrugated ceramics to address questions of technological style. These additional attributes were coil width, indentation width, indentation depth, and percent of obliteration. Coil width was defined as the distance between coil junctures. Although this measurement is not the true width of the original ceramic coil used to construct the vessel, which is obscured during the vessel's manufacture, it does serve to quantify the coil width as part of the outward appearance of the vessel. Indentation width was defined as the widest part of each indentation created during the process of building up a vessel and was usually at a coil juncture. Indentation depth was defined as the deepest part of an indentation, also usually at a coil juncture. Percent of obliteration was defined as the ratio of the number of obliterated coil junctures to the total number of coil junctures, ranging from a low of 0.01 (no obliteration), to a high of 1.00 (fully obliterated; Figs. 3.1, 3.2). These metric measurements quantify the differences among corrugated ceramics without resorting to typologies that can conflate and confuse variability. Some of the variation in these attributes is undoubtedly temporal, as in the case of obliteration (Mills 1999: 264), but comparing sherds from individual sites or sites that date to the same phase helps to separate temporal variability from variability

Figure 3.1. Unobliterated corrugated sherd (measure of obliteration = 0.01).

Figure 3.2. Obliterated corrugated sherd (measure of obliteration = 1.00).

that is the result of other factors, such as technological style.

For these analyses, "textured" corrugated included all unslipped, undecorated, and unpolished corrugated sherds, often otherwise classified as obliterated, indented, clapboard, or with other qualitative descriptors. The rest of the corrugated sherds analyzed were placed into a "painted and other textured" corrugated category, including sherds that showed signs of decoration, such as Cibicue Painted Corrugated and McDonald Corrugated and those that were slipped, polished, or had fillets, such as Tularosa Fillet Rim, Salado Red, unidentified painted corrugated (probably Mogollon), and unidentified obliterated red slipped, which sometimes had signs of white paint on the exterior as well. Hagenbuckle (2000) and Stone (1987) demonstrated that these vessels may have been produced and consumed for different purposes and in different social situations than the so-called textured corrugated ceramics. Thus analyses aimed at understanding differences in technological style that reflect different social groups would be clarified by the separation of these groups of types. The so-called textured and painted and other textured corrugated ceramics were also grouped together to compare with the results of the analyses of the separate groups described above.

Corrugated ceramics were collected in bulk in collection areas, as well as individually point provenienced, with the goal of collecting at least 100 corrugated sherds from each site. Collection areas were placed within or adjacent to discrete areas of architecture, such as a room block, compound, or single room structure. However, if only one such discrete area of architecture was present at a given site, a second collection area was placed in a dense artifact scatter to ensure that a sufficient sample was gained from each site. The number collected at each site ranged from a low of 5 corrugated sherds at the P Ranch Canyon Site and Haby Pueblo to a high of 653 sherds at Fort Grant Pueblo. The sample for each attribute varies from the total number of corrugated ceramics in each group at each site because every attribute could not be measured on every sherd. Not all sites contained painted and other textured corrugated pottery. No ceramics were collected at the Marijilda Site because the surface assemblage was too sparse, and no corrugated ceramics were collected from the Goat Hill Site because surface collections had already been made by Woodson (1995).

Corrugation Technology

Because utilitarian corrugated ceramics were likely produced within the settlements in which they were used, the technological styles associated with their production were probably shared and passed down among producers at a settlement and perhaps even at a household level. Therefore, it should be possible to see differences in corrugated ceramic technology at settlements that were occupied by multiple households in the past (Neuzil 2005a). Differences in corrugation technology may be most visible among general areas at sites, rather than between specific rooms. With this in mind, corrugated ceramics from spatially segregated areas of sites were compared to see if differences in the technological style of their corrugation technology could be detected. I conducted nonparametric tests of difference to compare metric attributes measured on sherds among collection areas to ascertain if such differences existed and whether they could be meaningfully tied to discrete areas of architecture or social groups.

The results of tests of difference performed on assemblages from 14 sites that had large enough samples of corrugated ceramics from each collection area to yield meaningful results are listed in Table 3.1. I ran tests at various levels, comparing (1) textured, (2) painted and other textured, and (3) all corrugated ceramics, and in some cases, comparing assemblages representing (a) discrete habitation areas only, (b) habitation areas and judgmentally dense artifact scatters, and (c) collection area assemblages with a sample size greater than five. Differences were mainly expected at large sites likely inhabited by several household groups, such as Fort Grant Pueblo, Buena Vista Ruin, and AZ CC:2:69 (ASM).

As expected, differences occurred in collection area assemblages in all four metric attributes measured at Fort Grant Pueblo when comparing only textured corrugated sherds, as well as when comparing all corrugated sherds (not enough decorated corrugated sherds were available for comparison). This settlement, which is estimated to have had more than 100 rooms, clearly housed multiple household groups, which are reflected in the differences seen in corrugated ceramics.

Differences were expected at Buena Vista Ruin and were detected in three out of four attributes when comparing textured and all corrugated sherds. This settlement was the largest and longest occupied in the Safford Valley (Mills and Mills 1978; Tyberg 2000) and was undoubtedly occupied by numerous household groups. Similarly, differences in corrugated ceramic technology were expected at AZ CC:2:69 (ASM), as it likely was one of the larger and later occupied settlements in the Safford Valley, along with Buena Vista

Table 3.1. Expected Results of Kruskal-Wallis Tests of Metric Attributes of Corrugated Ceramics

Site	Differences expected in K-W test	Differences seen in K-W test	Attribute differences seen in:
Buena Vista Ruin (AZ CC:2:3 ASM)	Yes	Yes	Coil width Indentation width Obliteration
Fort Grant Pueblo (AZ CC:5:8 ASM)	Yes	Yes	Coil width Indentation width Indentation depth Obliteration
AZ CC:2:69 (ASM)	Yes	No	
Crescent Ruin (AZ BB:8:6 ASM)	Maybe	Yes	Indentation depth Obliteration
Owens-Colvin Site (AZ CC:1:19 ASM)	Maybe	Yes	Obliteration
Wes Jernigan Site (AZ CC:1:38 ASM)	Maybe	Yes	Coil width Indentation depth Obliteration
Fischer Site (AZ CC:2:100 ASM)	Maybe	Yes	Coil width Indentation width Indentation depth Obliteration
Sharon Site (AZ CC:2:101 ASM)	Maybe	Yes	Coil width Indentation depth
AZ CC:2:185 (ASM)	Maybe	Yes	Obliteration
Yuma Wash Site (AZ CC:2:16 ASM)	Maybe	No	
Rattlesnake Mesa Site (ARIZONA:BB:3:5 AF)	Maybe	No	
Murphy Site (AZ CC:2:103 ASM)	No	Yes	Indentation width Indentation depth
Cluff Ranch Site (AZ CC:1:1 ASM)	No	No	
Lippencott South Site (AZ CC:2:102 ASM)	No	No	

Ruin. However, no significant differences were detected in the metric attributes of corrugated sherds gathered in collection areas at this site. Disturbance at CC:2:69 has made the original site layout impossible to determine, and the number of rooms may be smaller than the density of the surface scatter at first suggests, and it may not have been occupied by multiple households. Alternatively, the two collection areas at the site may not have provided an adequate sample to capture the variability that was present there.

Somewhat surprisingly, significant differences also occurred in all four metric attributes of corrugated ceramics from collection areas at the Fischer Site. This settlement was not particularly large, but has been disturbed to the point that discerning the original ar-

rangement of rooms is now impossible without extensive excavation. Previous excavations at the Fischer Site (Owens 1992) did not clarify the overall site layout or room count. It is therefore possible that this settlement contained enough rooms to accommodate several household groups, accounting for the differences in metric attributes that reflect corrugation technology.

Based on the estimated number of rooms, intrasite differences in corrugation technology might also be present at several other sites, such as Rattlesnake Mesa, Crescent Ruin, Owens-Colvin, Wes Jernigan, Yuma Wash, Sharon, and AZ CC:2:185 (ASM). These sites contained at least 15 rooms each, which may have been enough to accommodate several households (Hill and others 2004; Lowell 1991). The patterns for these sites were mixed, however. Differences in one to three metric attributes of corrugated ceramics were present at Crescent Ruin, the Owens-Colvin Site, the Wes Jernigan Site, the Sharon Site, and AZ CC:2:185 (ASM). I detected no differences in corrugation technology in sherds from the Rattlesnake Mesa Site or the Yuma Wash Site.

Moreover, differences in corrugation technology were not expected at the Cluff Ranch, Lippencott South, or Murphy (AZ CC:2:103 ASM) sites based on the small number of rooms present at each (fewer than 10). Differences were not detected at the Cluff Ranch Site or the Lippencott South Site but were detected at the Murphy Site (CC:2:103) where there may have been more rooms than currently estimated. The surface of the Murphy Site (CC:2:103) has been disturbed to the extent that room outlines and walls are no longer visible.

In these tests, I found significant differences in corrugation technology at two of the three sites where they were expected, such as Buena Vista Ruin, and did not find any differences at two of the three sites where they were not expected, such as the Cluff Ranch Site. These results suggest that the patterning and implications behind differences in the attributes of corrugated ceramic technology may be more complex than originally thought. At AZ CC:2:69 (ASM) the lack of difference may be due to its late occupation, which may have extended into the mid-fifteenth century, so that households had time to integrate and thus produce similar corrugated pottery. The only other settlement that was occupied this late was Buena Vista Ruin, but the differences observed in the assemblage from this site may be in part temporal. The Buena Vista Ruin assemblage conflates approximately 400 to 600 years of occupation, which may be the source of differences in corrugation technology. Unexpected differences, as found at the Murphy Site (CC:2:103), may be explained by the large social distance among residents of settlements occupied immediately following migration. In this case, differences in corrugation technology may have been the result of disparate household groups living side-by-side immediately following settlement, but before social mixing due to intermarriage and other social mechanisms would have taken place.

At the Rattlesnake Mesa Site and the Yuma Wash Site it was unclear whether differences could be expected and none were found (Table 3.1). These sites date to the Goat Hill or Middle Classic (A.D. 1275/1300–1325) and Safford or Fort Grant phases (A.D. 1325–1450), so the lack of differentiation was probably not a temporal phenomenon but instead the result of social closeness on the part of the groups living there, or perhaps only one household produced corrugated ceramics for use by the rest of the inhabitants. Regardless, this lack of differentiation in corrugated ceramics suggests a small or limited social distance among the inhabitants of these settlements.

These data demonstrate that distinct, discrete household level groups were present at many Safford and Aravaipa valley settlements. Differences in corrugation technology and technological style provide supporting evidence for the presence of distinct households at settlements dating to the Goat Hill or Middle Classic phase and after. The presence of perforated plates, a ceramic vessel form closely associated with Kayenta and Tusayan migrant populations (Lyons and Lindsay 2006), as well as kivas and masonry room blocks at several Safford and Aravaipa area sites suggest some of these households were composed of Kayenta and Tusayan migrants. Based on the size of settlements where differences were detected, these differences suggest migrants arrived in household or suprahousehold level groups. Next, attributes of the technological style of domestic architecture are examined to see if the patterns observed in corrugated ceramics are repeated.

DOMESTIC ARCHITECTURE

Domestic architecture has long been an avenue of research for reconstructing identity and its expression (Aldenderfer and Stanish 1993; Ferguson 1996; Hegmon 1989; Hillier and Hanson 1984; Meyer 1999; Munson and others 2005; Shapiro 1999), but there have been numerous recent advances in understanding the role architecture plays in shaping social interaction (Cameron 1998; Clark 2001; Hegmon 1989; Liebmann and others 2005; Riggs 2001). Architecture and domestic spatial organization have always been presupposed to be reflections of identity and ethnicity (Bagwell 2004; Barth 1994, 2000; Bentley 1987; Meskell 2001; Stone 2003; Yelvington 1991), but early research into architecture often simply assumed that the style of construction and settlement layout were expressions of the identity of the settlement's inhabitants (Baldwin 1987; Conrad 1993). This conceptualization of architectural style glossed over significant variation in its function, visibility, and the background of its builders and users, all of which affect aspects of construction, organization, and use. Recent research on architecture has taken a more nuanced approach, looking at technological style and focusing especially on construction techniques and settlement layout in identifying different social groups and interaction between them (Cameron 1998; Clark 2001; Dawson 2002; Meyer 1999; Potter 1998). This discussion of architecture focuses on construction techniques and site layout; spatial organization is addressed in the next chapter.

Technological style analyses of architecture have focused on the less visible aspects of construction and raw materials used in order to understand how differences in these fundamental decisions in construction may reflect important information about the people who built it. Differences that are not readily visible in the final product, such as the banded masonry at Chaco Canyon that was covered by a veneer of small stones (Meyer 1999), can be particularly telling. As in the manufacture of corrugated ceramics, it is these differences that hold information about enculturative backgrounds and learning frameworks that are specific to families and household groups. Thus, differences in the technological style of architecture, particularly domestic architecture, can differentiate between diverse social groups at a variety of scales, from the settlement to the region (Clark 2001; Riggs 2001). I examine several elements of the construction techniques employed in the domestic architecture at sites in the Safford and Aravaipa regions, including site layout, room area, raw materials, and construction methods to determine if differences existed and whether those differences can be tied to discrete social groups.

Site Layout

The arrangement of space at sites in the Safford and Aravaipa valleys underwent two dramatic shifts during the Classic period. From the beginning of the Classic period until about A.D. 1275 or 1300, above ground architecture was arranged in open compounds with rooms and open space enclosed by the surrounding walls. Based on well excavated transitional sites in the Hohokam and surrounding regions of the Southwest, this arrangement likely reflects the courtyard

group spatial organization of some earlier pit house settlements translated into above ground architecture with the addition of a compound wall (Clark 2001). Current data do not make it clear whether rooms were constructed first and walls attached, or if walls were constructed and then rooms were built in the resulting enclosure. This settlement layout briefly overlapped with and was followed by small room blocks clustered around a central open space beginning at A.D. 1275–1300, the beginning of the Goat Hill phase. Room blocks were a dramatic departure from earlier compound architecture. This trend of building room blocks continued in the Safford phase (A.D. 1325–1450), when room blocks became more contiguous and compact and central spaces became more formally defined as communal plazas. Clearly, site layout and the arrangement of space at Safford and Aravaipa area sites underwent drastic changes during the Classic period. Furthermore, research suggests that site layout and changes in it such as those that occurred in the Safford and Aravaipa valleys can provide important clues concerning how the inhabitants of the site identified themselves (Aldenderfer and Stanish 1993).

Changes in settlement layout in the Safford and Aravaipa areas can be quantified using the Room Contiguity Index (RCI; Clark 2001: 46–56). This index was created to differentiate between settlements laid out into open compounds with dispersed room arrangements and those laid out in contiguous room blocks. The index is a ratio of the total number of walls to the total number of rooms at a settlement and ranges from 2.0 (a square room block of infinite size) to 4.0 (a site with no contiguous rooms). Sites dominated by noncontiguous rooms have higher RCIs, and sites dominated by rooms that share walls have lower RCIs. In Clark's (2001) study of domestic architecture in the eastern Tonto Basin, he found that compound sites had RCIs between 3.5 to 4.0, linear room block sites had RCIs between 3.1 and 3.4, and compact contiguous room blocks had RCIs under 3.0. A region-wide assessment of sites all across the Southwest corroborated these RCI ranges and lent support to a separate ancestral Puebloan tradition of room block construction in the northern Southwest and a Hohokam tradition of compound construction in southern Arizona during the thirteenth century A.D. Most of the sites in Clark's sample had been excavated, which dramatically improved the resolution at which RCIs could be calculated.

Table 3.2. Room Contiguity Index (RCI) Summary

Phase	Site Name	RCI absolute	RCI provisional	RCI from other source (with citation)
Eden	Pentagon Site	3.80		
	P Ranch Canyon Site			
	Murphy Site (AZ CC:1:52)		4.00	4.00 (Rinker 1998)
	AZ CC:1:55 (ASM)	3.33		
Eden/Bylas	Earven Flat Site			2.60 (Brown 1973)
	Lippencott South Site	4.00		
Bylas	Owens-Colvin Site		3.33	3.21 (Rule 1993)
	Cluff Ranch Site	3.75		
	Richardson Orchard Site		3.50	
	Murphy Site (AZ CC:2:103)			
	Crary Site	4.00		4.00 (Rinker 1998)
Bylas/Goat Hill	Sharon Site		3.36	
Goat Hill or Middle Classic	Fort Grant Silo Site		3.66	
	Yuma Wash Site		3.29	Low (Brown 1973)
	AZ CC:2:23 (BLM)		3.00	
	AZ CC:2:33 (BLM)		2.66	
	Goat Hill Site		3.27	2.80 (Woodson 1995)
	Wes Jernigan Site		3.33 (Locus A)	
	Rattlesnake Mesa Site		3.45	
	AZ CC:2:185 (ASM)	3.47		
Safford or Fort Grant	Crescent Ruin		Low (Locus A) 3.83 (Loci B–D)	
	Fort Grant Pueblo		2.95	
	Spear Ranch Site		3.25	Low (Brown 1973)
	Fischer Site		3.66	Low (Owens 1992)
	AZ CC:1:3 (ASM)			
	Dewester Site	3.50		3.50 (Rinker 1998)
	Eagle Pass Site	4.00 (Locus A) 3.38 (Locus B) 4.00 (Locus C)		3.56 (Lee 1996)
	Haby Pueblo			Low (Gerald 1957)
	Wooten-Claridge Terrace Site		3.33 to 3.25	
	AZ BB:3:22 (ASM)			
	Krider Kiva Site	3.44		
	Lippincott North Site	4.00		
	Marijilda Site	2.83		2.48 (Brown 1973)
	AZ CC:2:69 (ASM)			
	Buena Vista Ruin		3.00	2.98 (Tatman 1931) 2.75 (Mills and Mills 1978)

I calculated RCIs for 30 of the 35 sites in the sample discussed here, which does not include sites for which the arrangement of architecture could not be discerned from the surface as a result of disturbance or other processes. Three different RCI values were calculated or estimated for 30 of the 35 sites (Table 3.2). An absolute RCI value was calculated for sites that had been excavated and mapped, or for which I felt confident that I could see the full layout of the site from the surface. Provisional RCI values were calculated for sites that had some disturbance that obscured or destroyed part of the site layout, or for sites that I did not otherwise feel confident that the full extent of the architecture could be viewed on the surface. RCIs were also calculated based on published maps for several sites. However, many of these maps contained information on only a portion of the entire site. Because these RCI values were not calculated based on

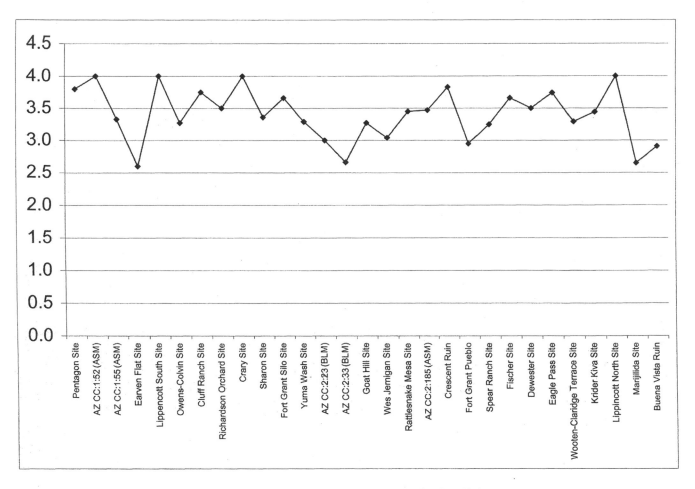

Figure 3.3. Average Room Contiguity Index for all sites.

fully excavated sites, they should be viewed with caution. Despite this fact, some interesting trends emerge.

Figure 3.3 plots the average RCI for each site, with earlier sites at the left end of the graph and later sites at the right. Although there are definite variations, there are more sites that have RCIs above 3.5 on the earlier end of the graph than on the later end. Unusually high or low values may be explained by incomplete data. The low value for the Earven Flat Site was based on a sketch map by Brown (1973) where he depicted the site as a contiguous room block even though he admits he could see very few walls and that he based his size estimate on the extent of wall rubble rather than on actual foundations. On the other end, the high RCI value for the Crescent Ruin is based almost entirely on several single room structures visible in the three southeastern loci of the site (Fig. 3.4). The northern locus, which also happens to be the largest, more than likely contained a large contiguous room

block, but disturbances to the surface have precluded a definite assessment of the architecture. The Lippincott North Site also has an extraordinarily high RCI value. However, it is relatively small, and it appears that smaller Safford or Fort Grant phase sites follow a different pattern than their larger counterparts. This problem cannot be conclusively addressed without further investigation of small Classic period sites.

To get a better idea of trends in RCI values through time, several of the more problematic sites with provisional RCI values were eliminated (Fig. 3.5). This more reliable graph suggests a strong temporal trend in RCI values. Clearly, early Classic period sites had much higher RCI values than later sites. Interestingly, sites that date to the Goat Hill or Middle Classic phase (A.D. 1275/1300–1325), such as the Yuma Wash Site, the Goat Hill Site, and AZ CC:2:185 (ASM) appear to have generally lower RCI values than the Eagle Pass Site and the Krider Kiva Site, their

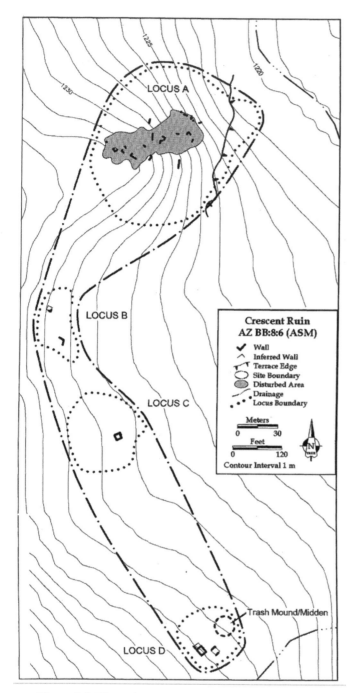

Figure 3.4. Plan of Crescent Ruin (AZ BB:8:6 ASM).

Safford or Fort Grant phase (A.D. 1325–1450) counterparts. However, if RCI values for other Safford or Fort Grant phase sites such as the Spear Ranch Site and Buena Vista Ruin were represented on this graph, their RCI values would undoubtedly be lower than those for earlier Goat Hill or Middle Classic sites.

RCI values for Safford and Aravaipa Classic period sites quantify changes in settlement layout through

time. Earlier Eden and Bylas phase sites have high RCI values, reflecting the tendency toward noncontiguous room layouts at that time. Later Goat Hill or Middle Classic, and Safford or Fort Grant phase sites have substantially lower RCI values, reflecting the trend toward increasingly nucleated settlements and contiguous layouts. These changes in layout likely reflect the influence of Kayenta and Tusayan migrant populations, for whom room block layouts were common. This trend toward room blocks is similar to the trend occurring in the Tonto Basin, where ancestral Puebloan migrants introduced room blocks in the late thirteenth and early fourteenth centuries. As in the Safford and Aravaipa areas, room blocks were without precedent in the Tonto Basin before the arrival of migrant populations (Clark 2001). The influx of migrants appears to be the primary force behind this shift in the Safford and Aravaipa valleys as well.

Room Area

Differences in technological style are also visible in several other architectural attributes that may help distinguish among social groups living at the same settlement or several different settlements within a region. Size of living space is a variable that can reflect cultural background (Baldwin 1987; Conrad 1993; Ferguson 1996; Hillier and Hanson 1984). It may also be an indicator of roof beam raw material availability and other functional constraints, but at sites with equal access to similar roofing materials, room size is unlikely to actively convey social messages. Thus, room size may reflect differences in the technological style of architecture that can be tied to passive differences in social groups, just as the technological style of corrugated ceramics can be tied to passive identity.

I calculated room area on the basis of length and width dimensions of each room at each site for which there was reasonable certainty that most of the walls were visible and the dimensions could be determined. Figure 3.6 summarizes room area for rooms inferred to have been used for habitation at all settlements. These data do not clearly identify any specific trends in room area, as room area varies widely. However, summaries of room area by phase reveal that mean room area decreases steadily through the Goat Hill or Middle Classic phase (if sites that are transitional between the Eden and Bylas phases and the Bylas and Goat Hill phases are eliminated), and then increases

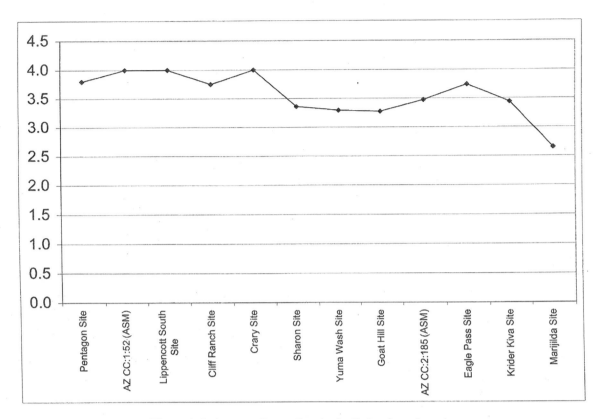

Figure 3.5. Average Room Contiguity Index for select sites.

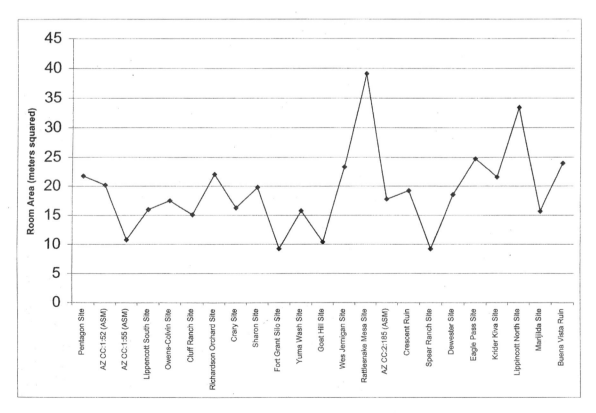

Figure 3.6. Mean area of all rooms by site.

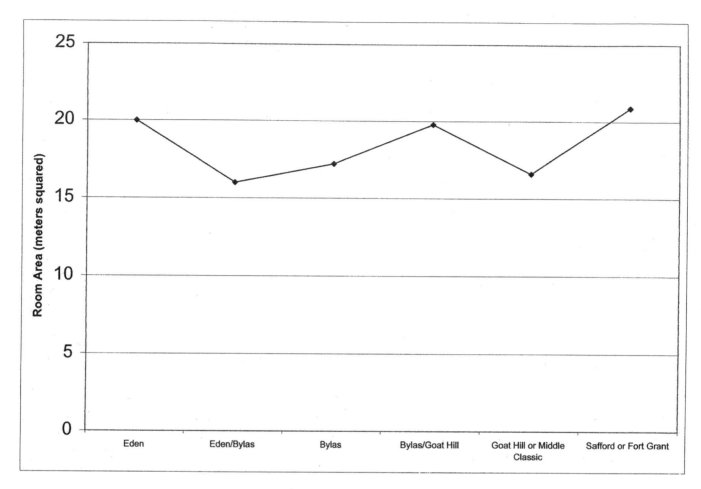

Figure 3.7. Mean area of habitation rooms only, by site.

Table 3.3. Area of Habitation Rooms Only, Before and After Migration

Before or After Migration	No. Rooms	Minimum (sq. m)	Maximum (sq. m)	Median (sq. m)	Mean (sq. m)	St. Dev.	CV
Before (8 sites)	24	7.600	28.050	18.955	18.146	5.972	0.329
Transitional (1 site)	7	9.920	24.440	20.580	19.787	4.669	0.236
After (16 sites)	100	5.200	56.400	17.380	19.374	9.503	0.491
After, including excavated and unexcavated habitation rooms from the Marijilda Site (16 sites)	134	4.160	56.400	16.225	18.315	8.994	0.491

Table 3.4. Area of Habitation Rooms Only, at Sites With and Without Perforated Plates

With or Without Perforated Plates	No. Rooms	Minimum (sq. m)	Maximum (sq. m)	Median (sq. m)	Mean (sq. m)	St. Dev.	CV
With (8 sites)	28	5.640	42.240	15.090	16.206	7.503	0.463
Without (17 sites)	103	5.200	56.400	19.356	19.977	8.906	0.466
Without including all excavated and unexcavated rooms from the Marijilda Site (17 sites)	137	4.160	56.400	17.500	18.792	8.596	0.457

Table 3.5. Kruskal-Wallis Test of Room Area by Site

Variables Tested	K-W test statistic	p	df	Result
Habitation rooms	76.547	0.000	23	Significant difference *
habitation rooms, extra rooms from Marijilda Site added	80.832	0.000	23	Significant difference *

*Results are suspect due to small sample size

Table 3.6. Kruskal-Wallis Test of Room Area by Phase

Variables Tested	K-W test statistic	p	df	Result
Habitation rooms	12.600	0.027	5	Significant difference*
Habitation rooms, extra rooms from Marijilda Site added	7.669	0.751	5	No significant difference*

*Results are suspect due to small sample size

Table 3.7. Kruskal-Wallis Test of Room Area by Occupation Before or After Migration

Variables Tested	K-W test statistic	p	df	Result
Habitation rooms	0.420	0.811	2	No significant difference
Habitation rooms, extra rooms from Marijilda Site added	1.172	0.557	2	No significant difference

again in the Safford or Fort Grant phase (Fig. 3.7). Because assignments of room function were based largely on surface assessments, they may not all be accurate. Therefore, rooms classified as habitation rooms may also include storage rooms and other nonhabitation areas and rooms that may have been built alongside habitation rooms in room blocks or compounds. Because the goal was to tease out general trends in domestic architecture, not just habitation rooms specifically, the possible inclusion of non-habitation rooms seems justified.

Coefficients of variation parallel mean room area and are higher with larger mean room areas. Restricting the data further to sites that date before and after migration also reveals a clear pattern (Table 3.3). In this case, when looking at habitation rooms, mean room area remains stable at about 18 square meters and the periods before and after migration show only about one square meter difference. However, there is a fairly substantial difference in room area of sites with and without perforated plates present in the assemblage (Table 3.4). In general, sites with perforated plates have smaller rooms when looking at mean area of habitation rooms. This implies that migrants, who used perforated plates, may have built smaller rooms

than did the existing indigenous population in the Safford and Aravaipa areas.

I ran Kruskal-Wallis nonparametric tests of difference to determine whether the differences observed in the summary statistics were significant. These tests revealed that there were significant differences in room area among sites when testing habitation structures (Table 3.5). Differences in room area also occurred between phases, except when the extra structures from the Marijilda Site were added (Table 3.6). Tests comparing sites occupied before and after migration resulted in no significant differences in room size (Table 3.7). However, there were significant differences between sites containing perforated plates and those without, except when the extra structures from the Marijilda Site were added (Table 3.8).

To further explore these differences, I performed tests comparing all sites dating to the same phase to each other (Table 3.9). Interestingly, there was no significant difference in room area of sites dating to the Eden and Bylas phases, but significant differences appeared during the Goat Hill or Middle Classic phases and at Safford or Fort Grant phase sites. The implication from these tests is that room area became increasingly heterogeneous through time, perhaps due

Table 3.8. Mann-Whitney U Test of Room Area by Presence or Absence of Perforated Plates

Variables Tested	Mann-Whitney U test statistic	p	df	Result
Habitation rooms	1842.500	0.025	1	Significant difference
Habitation rooms, extra rooms from the Marijilda Site added	2276.000	0.120	1	No significant difference

Table 3.9. Kruskal-Wallis Test of Room Area by Settlements in the Same Phase

Variables Tested	K-W test statistic	p	df	Result
Eden phase sites, habitation rooms	2.044	0.360	2	No significant difference *
Eden-Bylas phase sites, habitation rooms	—	—	—	—
Bylas phase sites, habitation rooms	1.481	0.687	3	No significant difference *
Bylas-Goat Hill phase sites, habitation rooms	—	—	—	—
Goat Hill or Middle Classic phase sites, habitation rooms	28.578	0.000	5	Significant difference *
Safford or Fort Grant phase sites, habitation rooms	30.918	0.000	8	Significant difference *
Safford or Fort Grant phase sites, habitation rooms, extra rooms from Marijilda Site added	40.089	0.000	8	Significant difference *

*Results are suspect due to small sample size.

Table 3.10. Kruskal-Wallis Test of Room Area by Settlements Occupied Before and After Migration

Variables Tested	K-W test statistic	p	df	Result
Habitation rooms occupied before migration	5.055	0.653	7	No significant difference *
Habitation rooms in transitional settlements	—	—	—	—
Habitation rooms occupied after migration	68.616	0.000	14	Significant difference *
Habitation rooms occupied after migration, extra rooms from Marijilda Site added	72.708	0.000	14	Significant difference *

*Results are suspect due to small sample size

Table 3.11. Kruskal-Wallis Test of Room Area by Settlements With and Without Perforated Plates

Variables Tested	K-W test statistic	p	df	Result
Habitation rooms at settlements with perforated plates	11.514	0.042	5	No significant difference*
Habitation rooms at settlements without perforated plate	60.179	0.000	17	Significant difference *
Habitation rooms at settlements without perforated plates extra rooms from Marijilda Site added	66.547	0.000	17	Significant difference *

*Results are suspect due to small sample size

to increased population diversity after Kayenta and Tusayan migrants moved to the area. This assertion is supported by tests comparing sites occupied before and after migrants moved into the area with each other (Table 3.10). Settlements occupied before the arrival of Kayenta and Tusayan migrants contained no significant differences in their room area, whereas those occupied after the arrival of migrants had significantly different room areas.

The most intriguing results came from the test comparing sites with and without perforated plates

(Table 3.11). Sites with perforated plates did not have significantly different room areas in comparison to each other, but sites without perforated plates did have significantly different room areas in comparison to each other. This observation suggests that those sites with perforated plates that are most likely to have been occupied by migrant populations were built by people with similar ideas and enculturative backgrounds concerning the correct size to build a room, which differed from that of the local population. This interpretation does not imply that no migrants lived at sites without perforated plates, but it does imply that if migrants did live at sites without perforated plates, they likely mixed with the local population at such a level that average room area differed from those sites occupied almost exclusively by migrants. It also suggests some level of diversity in the local population, as these groups had somewhat disparate ideas about what size rooms should be.

Construction Techniques

Construction techniques are another good marker of technological style that may be used to differentiate between social groups with different learning frameworks and enculturative backgrounds. The Goat Hill Site, which exhibits horizontally coursed masonry, had substantially different construction techniques than all but one other site in the Safford and Aravaipa areas (the Marijilda Site). Horizontally coursed masonry therefore appears to be one indicator of Kayenta and Tusayan migrant populations in the Safford and Aravaipa areas. I recorded construction techniques for every visible wall to determine if differences in construction technique could be tied to differences in technological style stemming from the disparate social backgrounds of groups living together.

Wall Construction Materials

As Table 3.12 clearly demonstrates, cobble-reinforced adobe was the most common construction technique used in the Safford and Aravaipa areas. Only a small number of sites contained walls with different construction techniques, and some of those techniques occurred at only one site in the area. Although the results are to be viewed with caution due to the high number of cells that have frequencies of fewer than five, a Chi-square test clearly illustrates that there are significant differences in the distribution of construction techniques at Safford and Aravaipa area sites. These differences are still apparent when the data are divided by phase. However, Table 3.12 highlights the fact that horizontally coursed masonry did not appear in the Safford and Aravaipa areas until after the arrival of Kayenta and Tusayan migrants, during the Goat Hill or Middle Classic phase (A.D. 1275/1300–1325).

When the data are further separated into those sites dating before and after the arrival of migrants, the patterns become more apparent (Table 3.13). Although

cobble-reinforced adobe is dominant before migrants arrived in the area, it comprised only 54 percent of the walls after migrants arrived, and horizontally coursed masonry increased from zero to 27 percent of the total after migration.

A comparison of sites with and without perforated plates shows a similar pattern (Table 3.14). Cobble-reinforced adobe was more common at sites without perforated plates than at those with perforated plates. The pattern for coursed masonry is somewhat misleading, however. To date, no perforated plates have been found at the Marijilda Site, but it is likely that excavations there would reveal perforated plates and other signs of a migrant occupation such as a kiva or entrybox complexes. If this were the case, coursed masonry architecture would be entirely associated with sites with perforated plates and migrant populations. Until the relationship between perforated plates and coursed masonry architecture can be demonstrated unequivocally, the decrease in cobble-reinforced adobe through time and its lack of association with sites with perforated plates is both clear and convincing.

What is perhaps most compelling about the architectural data is the trend in layout toward room blocks, combined with the overwhelming dominance of cobble-reinforced adobe construction. Room blocks were generally more common in areas to the north, where they were regularly constructed of horizontally coursed masonry. Their appearance in the Safford and Aravaipa areas after about A.D. 1275 signals a profound shift in the grammar of site layout and arrangement of space that was likely associated with the arrival of migrant populations from the Kayenta and Tusayan areas. A similar trend was evident in the Tonto Basin (Clark 2001). However, the Safford and Aravaipa architectural pattern differed from the Tonto Basin pattern, as in the Safford and Aravaipa valleys room blocks were constructed almost entirely with techniques associated with the local area, most commonly cobble-reinforced adobe. Combined with other data, these patterns suggest that both migrants and indigenous populations influenced settlement architecture, with migrants controlling the room block layout and indigenous groups guiding the choice of raw materials and construction methods used. Such a coalescence of techniques indicates that these populations coresided in the same settlements shortly after the arrival of migrants in the area.

Table 3.12. Wall Construction Techniques by Site

Site	No. upright cobble footer and adobe walls	%	No. coursed cobble and adobe walls	%	No. cobble reinforced adobe walls	%	No. coursed adobe walls	%	No. coursed masonry walls	%	No. other walls	%	Total
Pentagon Site					27	100.00							27
Murphy Site (AZ CC:1:52 ASM)					12	66.67	6	27.78			1	5.56	19
AZ CC:1:55 (ASM)					20	100.00							20
Earven Flat Site	5	62.50			3	37.50							8
Lippencott South Site					13	100.00							13
Owens-Colvin Site					58	100.00							58
Cluff Ranch Site					20	100.00							20
Richardson Orchard Site					8	100.00							8
Murphy Site (AZ CC:2:103 ASM)					15	100.00							15
Crary Site					11	100.00							11
Sharon Site					38	100.00							38
Fort Grant Silo Site					20	95.24	1	4.76					21
Yuma Wash Site			11	26.19	31	73.81							42
AZ CC:2:23 (BLM)					3	100.00							3
AZ CC:2:33 (BLM)			7	100.00									7
Goat Hill Site									86	100.00			86
Wes Jernigan Site					14	100.00							14
Rattlesnake Mesa Site					38	100.00							38
AZ CC:2:185 (ASM)					65	100.00							65
Crescent Ruin					38	82.61	8	17.39					46
Fort Grant Pueblo	65	70.65			27	29.35							92
Spear Ranch Site			1	1.75	44	77.19	12	21.05					57
Fischer Site					9	100.00							9
Dewester Site					8	100.00							8
Eagle Pass Site					3	3.49			83	96.51			86
Haby Pueblo					1	100.00							1
Wooten-Claridge Terrace Site					2	66.67			1	33.33			3
AZ BB:3:22 (ASM)					10	100.00							10
Krider Kiva Site					30	76.92	8	20.51	1	2.56			39
Lippincott North Site					8	100.00							8
Marijilda Site									22	100.00			22
AZ CC:2:69 (ASM)					1	100.00							1
Buena Vista Ruin			8	21.62	28	75.68	1	2.70					37
Total	65	6.98	32	3.44	605	64.98	36	3.76	193	20.73	1	0.11	932

NOTE: Pearson Chi-square = 2126.063; p = 0.000; df = 160.000.
   When "Upright cobble footer and adobe" and "Other" are eliminated from the analysis, the results are:
      Pearson Chi-square = 1345.490; p = 0.000; df = 96.000.
   Results are suspect, more than one-fifth of fitted cells are sparse (frequency < 5).

Header versus Stretcher

Cobbles in cobble-reinforced adobe walls are generally placed between courses of adobe in order to anchor the courses together. They can either be vertically coursed so they are taller than they are wide, or horizontally coursed so they are wider than they are tall. When placed in the adobe matrix of the wall, they can be oriented so that their width is either parallel (header) or perpendicular (stretcher) to the length of

Table 3.13. Wall Construction Techniques at Settlements Occupied Before and After Migration

Before or after migration	No. upright cobble footer and adobe walls	%	No. coursed cobble and adobe walls	%	No. cobble reinforced adobe walls	%	No. coursed adobe walls	%	No. coursed masonry walls	%	No. other walls	%	Total
Before (10 sites)			5	2.51	187	93.97	6	3.02			1	0.50	199
Transitional (1 site)					38	100.00							38
After (22 sites)	65	9.35	27	3.89	380	54.68	30	4.32	193	27.77			695
Total (33 sites)	65	6.97	32	3.43	605	64.91	36	3.86	193	20.71	1	0.11	932

NOTE: Pearson Chi-square = 140.389; p = 0.000; df = 10.000
   When upright cobble footer and adobe and other are eliminated from the analysis, the results are:
      Pearson Chi-square = 108.052; p = 0.000; df = 6.000.
   Results are suspect, more than one-fifth of fitted cells are sparse (frequency < 5).

Table 3.14. Wall Construction Techniques at Settlements With and Without Perforated Plates

With or without perforated plates	No. upright cobble footer and adobe walls	%	No. coursed cobble and adobe walls	%	No. cobble reinforced adobe walls	%	No. coursed adobe walls	%	No. coursed masonry walls	%	No. other walls	%	Total
Without (25 sites)			23	4.06	429	75.80	7	1.24	106	18.73	1	0.18	566
With (8 sites)	65	17.76	9	2.46	176	48.09	29	7.92	87	23.77			366
Total (33 sites)	65	6.97	32	3.43	605	64.91	36	3.86	193	20.71	1	0.11	932

NOTE: Pearson Chi-square = 157.578; p = 0.000; df = 5.000.
   When upright cobble footer and adobe and other are eliminated from the analysis, the results are:
      Pearson Chi-square = 51.550; p = 0.000; df = 3.000

the wall (Fig. 3.8). However, once the wall is fully constructed, the cobbles are no longer visible. In this way, cobbles act as a marker of a technological style that is not visible in the final product. With this in mind, I compared the orientation of wall cobbles to see if differences could be detected.

A cross-tabulation of header and stretcher cobble orientation by site is shown in Table 3.15. No patterns are immediately apparent, except that builders at individual sites favored one orientation over another. For example, at the Yuma Wash Site all visible walls contained cobbles that were oriented in the stretcher position, or perpendicular to the length of the wall. Conversely, all the walls at AZ BB:3:22 (ASM) had cobbles oriented in a header position, or parallel to the length of the wall. A Chi-square test of this table revealed that these differences were significant, but the results are suspect due to the high number of cells in the table that had a frequency of fewer than five.

When sites dating to the same phase were combined, significant differences also appeared in a Chi-square test (Table 3.16). The greatest differences ap-

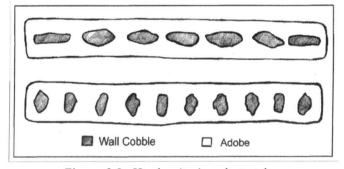

Figure 3.8. Header (top) and stretcher (bottom) wall construction techniques.

pear in the Bylas, transitional Bylas to Goat Hill, and Goat Hill or Middle Classic phases. During the Bylas phase (A.D. 1200–1275/1300), 72 percent of the walls contained cobbles in a header orientation. This percentage went up to 100 percent during the transitional Bylas to Goat Hill phase, but because this interval is only represented by one site, the results are suspect. During the following Goat Hill or Middle Classic phase (A.D. 1275/1300–1325), the majority of walls

Table 3.15. Header or Stretcher Wall Construction by Settlement

Settlement	No. header walls	%	No. stretcher walls	%	Total
Pentagon Site	27	100.00			27
Murphy Site (CC:1:52)	4	36.36	7	63.64	11
AZ CC:1:55 (ASM)			18	100.00	18
Earven Flat Site	8	100.00			8
Lippencott South Site	2	15.38	11	84.62	13
Owens-Colvin Site	59	100.00			59
Cluff Ranch Site	20	100.00			20
Richardson Orchard Site			8	100.00	8
Murphy Site (CC:2:103)	1	6.67	14	93.33	15
Crary Site			9	100.00	9
Sharon Site	23	100.00			23
Fort Grant Silo Site	19	90.48	2	9.52	21
Yuma Wash Site			41	100.00	41
AZ CC:2:23 (BLM)	2	100.00			2
AZ CC:2:33 (BLM)	5	71.43	2	28.57	7
Goat Hill Site	3	100.00			3
Wes Jernigan Site	8	57.14	6	42.86	14
Rattlesnake Mesa Site	27	71.05	11	28.95	38
AZ CC:2:185 (ASM)	5	7.69	60	92.31	65
Crescent Ruin	20	58.82	14	41.18	34
Fort Grant Pueblo	36	49.32	37	50.68	73
Spear Ranch Site	13	40.63	19	59.38	32
Fischer Site	8	88.89	1	11.11	9
Eagle Pass Site	17	89.47	2	10.53	19
Haby Pueblo	1	100.00			1
Wooten-Claridge Terrace Site	3	100.00			3
AZ BB:3:22 (ASM)	10	100.00			10
Krider Kiva Site	10	38.46	16	61.54	26
Lippincott North Site			8	100.00	8
AZ CC:2:69 (ASM)			1	100.00	1
Buena Vista Site	2	5.71	33	94.29	35
Total	333	51.00	320	49.00	653

NOTE: Pearson Chi-square = 376.140; p = 0.000; df = 30.000.
  Results are suspect, more than one-fifth of fitted cells are sparse (frequency < 5).

Table 3.16. Header or Stretcher Wall Construction by Phase

Dominant phase	No. header walls	%	No. stretcher walls	%	Total
Eden (3 sites)	31	55.36	25	44.64	56
Eden/Bylas (2 sites)	10	47.62	11	52.38	21
Bylas (5 sites)	80	72.07	31	27.93	111
Bylas/Goat Hill (1 site)	23	100.00			23
Goat Hill or Middle Classic (8 sites)	69	36.13	122	63.87	191
Safford or Fort Grant (12 sites)	120	47.81	131	52.19	251
Total (31 sites)	333	51.00	320	49.00	653

NOTE: Pearson Chi-square = 60.275; p = 0.000; df = 5.000

Table 3.17. Header or Stretcher Wall Construction at Settlements Occupied Before and After Migration

Before or After Migration	No. header walls	%	No. stretcher walls	%	Total
Before (10 sites)	121	64.36	67	35.64	188
Transitional (1 site)	23	100.00			23
After (20 sites)	189	42.76	253	57.24	442
Total (31 sites)	333	51.00	320	49.00	653

NOTE: Pearson Chi-square = 47.538; p = 0.000; df = 2.000

contained cobbles arranged in a stretcher orientation, representing a shift from the previous phase. It is notable that this shift occurred between the Bylas and Goat Hill phases, because the transition between these two phases also signaled the beginning of a sizeable presence of Kayenta and Tusayan migrants in the Safford and Aravaipa areas. Interestingly, this trend declined in the following Safford or Fort Grant phase, when the distribution of header and stretcher oriented cobbles was more even. It is unclear exactly what this shift signals, as both header and stretcher oriented cobbles were common before migrants arrived during the Eden and the transitional Eden to Bylas phases.

Table 3.17 clarifies this pattern somewhat. Although both cobble orientations were present before and after migration, header oriented cobbles became less common through time, whereas stretcher oriented cobbles became more common. These differences are significant in a Chi-square test. It is clear that stretcher oriented cobbles were significantly more common at sites with perforated plates than at those without perforated plates (Table 3.18). The differences shown in these two tables are mutually supportive, in that stretcher oriented cobbles became more common through time and were also more common at settlements that were more likely occupied by migrants. Although the differences in Table 3.18 are not completely clear cut, the overwhelming patterns seem to suggest that migrants used stretcher oriented cobbles

Table 3.18. Header or Stretcher Wall Construction at Settlements With and Without Perforated Plates

With or Without Perforated Plates	No. header walls	%	No. stretcher walls	%	Total
Without (24 sites)	248	55.23	201	44.77	449
With (7 sites)	85	41.67	119	58.33	204
Total (31 sites)	333	51.00	320	49.00	653

NOTE: Pearson Chi-square = 10.332; p = 0.001; df = 1.000

more frequently than did local indigenous groups. Furthermore, the relatively equal representation of these two orientations in the Safford or Fort Grant phase (A.D. 1325–1450) may be indicative of migrant and indigenous populations constructing and living at the same settlements by this time.

TECHNOLOGICAL STYLE VARIATIONS

The data presented in this chapter provide compelling evidence of the presence of various social groups living in the Safford and Aravaipa areas, particularly after about A.D. 1275. Technological attributes of corrugated ceramics showed a varied pattern, but overall indicated that there were distinct and discrete household level groups making corrugated ceramics with different technological styles at several settlements in the area. Some of these households were undoubtedly composed of Kayenta and Tusayan migrants, who arrived in the area in the last quarter of the thirteenth century.

This pattern is mirrored in the technological style of domestic architecture of Safford and Aravaipa valley sites. Settlement layout changes around A.D. 1275–1300, as reflected in higher Room Continguity Index values at and after this time. Room area reflects similar changes through time, and Kruskal-Wallis nonparametric tests of difference demonstrated that settlements with perforated plates in their ceramic assemblages had significantly smaller rooms than those without. Similar temporal trends appeared in construction technique, where coursed masonry occurred and cobble reinforced adobe became more prevalent after A.D. 1275/1300, when Kayenta and Tusayan migrants arrived. The orientation of cobbles shifted from header dominated before A.D. 1275/1300 to stretcher dominated afterward. Clearly the interval around A.D. 1275/1300 signaled a shift in many attributes of technological style of everyday material culture in the Safford and Aravaipa areas, undoubtedly due to the arrival of Kayenta and Tusayan migrants in the area. Together these data highlight the movement of household level migrant groups who had a substantial influence on the material culture into the Safford and Aravaipa valleys during this time. We can now investigate how migrant and indigenous populations interacted after the arrival of migrants in the area, and how the expression of identity of both groups and the total social landscape changed in the Safford and Aravaipa region during the late Classic period.

CHAPTER FOUR

Examining Migrant and Indigenous Identity in the Postmigration Social Environment

Evidence from utilitarian ceramics and domestic architecture has demonstrated that migrants from the Kayenta and Tusayan areas of northeast Arizona began arriving in the Safford and Aravaipa valleys in the late thirteenth century. Other distinctive material culture, including masonry room blocks, kivas, and perforated plates provided further evidence of their presence. The Kayenta and Tusayan migrants who arrived at this time established settlements spatially segregated from the local population, as at the Goat Hill Site, and also lived alongside the local population at other settlements. Decorated ceramics, measures of built architectural space, and regional settlement patterns help us determine if the demonstrated spatial integration led, in turn, to social integration and changed the expression of identity of both migrant and indigenous groups during the Classic period in the Safford and Aravaipa valleys.

Decorated ceramics provide clues to understanding the cultural affiliation of the inhabitants of settlements and groups with whom they traded. Decorated ceramics do not positively demonstrate the presence of manufacturing groups at a given settlement because of the possibility that ceramics were obtained through exchange, but they can shed light on group and individual identity and social networks once various migrant and local groups have been differentiated by other means (Chapter 3). Similarly, significant research has been conducted on the relationship of the construction of space to social groups and their identity at various levels (Baldwin 1987; Dawson 2002; Ferguson 1996; Hillier and Hanson 1984; Hillier and Penn 1992; Liebmann and others 2005; Oetelaar 2000; Potter 1998; Schriwer 2002; Shapiro 1999; Van Dyke 1999). Much of this research has suggested that groups with the same identity (realizing that this term is problematic and identities can be both multifaceted and mutable) will arrange space in

similar ways in order to structure social interactions and conduct domestic and ritual activities. Innovations, external influences, and exposure to different groups can certainly lead to changes in spatial organization and must be taken into account when inferring the meaning of spatial organization from architecture. The location of settlements on the archaeological landscape can provide clues to the relationships between migrant and indigenous groups based on access to water and prime agricultural land and the location of settlements in relation to one another (Clark 2001). Now that migrants have been located in the Safford and Aravaipa areas with the data presented in Chapter 3, the relationships between various migrant and indigenous populations and the manner in which these relationships impacted the expression of identity of both migrant and indigenous groups can be more closely examined. Data from analyses of corrugated ceramics, site layout, and construction techniques detailed in the previous chapter suggest diverse populations were living in and interacting regularly in the Safford and Aravaipa valleys after A.D. 1275, and it is likely that their identities underwent some changes to accommodate their new social environment, which are explored here.

IDENTITY IN THE ARCHAEOLOGICAL RECORD

Migration can play an important role in social change and identity formation and maintenance from the perspective of both migrant and indigenous groups. In the often fluid and stressful social setting that follows migration, the duality of structure and agency comes into play (Sahlins 1981). Existing social structures of both groups may not be able to accommodate new social interactions and may become susceptible to change by human agency during this time. Preexisting group and individual identities based in established social structures may also be challenged by new realities in the postmigration environment. Although some facets of identity of both migrant and indigenous groups may have remained the same after an episode of migration, the integration of new people may have required changes to the structure of interaction, ritual, and many other aspects of daily life. In theory, changes in identity and structure may differ greatly between migrant and local groups as integration is seldom complete or on equal terms and is dependent on power relations that develop between these groups. These changes are reflected in the practices used to create certain items of material culture, as reflected in the end products found in the archaeological record (Jenkins 1996; Sahlins 1981). The production of material culture as "an enactment…of people's dispositions" (Pauketat 2001: 88) represents the material manifestation of social changes, including changes in identity. Because identity is bounded by both structure and agency, it is one of the most sensitive indicators of change in each of these realms (Gardner 2002; G. Jones 1999).

The model of the social consequences of migration presented in Table 1.3 helps to predict how migration may affect identity and its expression. The outcomes proposed in this model are, in part, based on the scale of migrant and indigenous groups in occupied areas.

DECORATED CERAMIC ASSEMBLAGES

Decorated ceramics in the Greater Southwest have long been associated with traditionally defined archaeological culture areas, despite the fact that many types and wares crosscut these divisions. Nonetheless, decorated ceramics are not equally distributed through time or space, and patterns in their distribution, particularly those outside their expected range, denote a variety of activities including exchange, ideology, political alliances, and when other lines of evidence are considered, migration and identity. Decorated ceramics cannot be universally attributed to a specific group or groups, however, and their presence at a site does not necessarily imply that groups typically associated with their manufacture and decorative style were present at a given settlement. Unlike most utilitarian ceramics, decorated ceramics likely moved through space through a variety of mechanisms that did not necessitate the movement of

the people with whom they are associated (Shepard 1956: 339; Zedeño 1994: 19). With this in mind, it is important to understand whether decorated ceramics at a given site represent the people who lived at the settlement itself or whether they merely indicate the influence of their trading partners or groups they emulated. The wares and types that make up the decorated ceramic assemblages from settlements occupied before and after migration are examined here to determine if they changed after the arrival of migrants in the Safford and Aravaipa areas and whether observed changes can be linked to changes in the expression of identity.

Richness and Evenness

To better understand how the composition of decorated ceramic assemblages changed through time in the Safford and Aravaipa areas, I conducted several statistical tests to examine diversity in the complete assemblages collected for this research. The ceramic types and wares found in the Safford and Aravaipa areas, their date ranges, and references for more information about each are provided in Table 4.1. The tests conducted looked at the number of types and wares represented and the number of sherds that represent each ware or type. Although numerous factors must be taken into account when interpreting the diversity, or lack thereof, in a given ceramic assemblage, generally a more diverse assemblage reflects a greater diversity in the cultural backgrounds or exchange contacts of a settlement's inhabitants (Herr 2001). Therefore, the diversity of decorated ceramic assemblages is expected to go up in the period following the arrival of migrants in the area. However, before ceramic diversity can be considered a reliable measure of social diversity, other lines of evidence must be brought to bear. Furthermore, the implications of such social diversity must be examined on a case-by-case basis.

Before statistics measuring diversity in the decorated ceramics were completed, I ran a series of regressions for the total ceramic assemblage in order to understand how much influence sample size had on diversity in the assemblages analyzed here (Kintigh 1989). In general, regression analyses revealed that very little of the variation within the assemblages from each site can be explained by sample size. Values of squared multiple r ranged from a low of 0.089 to a high of 0.331, demonstrating that only about 9 to 33 percent of the variation in the samples analyzed can be accounted for by their

Table 4.1. Dates of Ceramics Recovered in the Safford and Aravaipa Valleys

Ceramics	Type	Date A.D.	Reference
Chihuahuan Polychromes	Ramos Polychrome	1200–1450	Hendrickson 2003: 5, 86
Cibola White Ware	La Plata Black-on-white	550–750	Mills and Herr 1999: 280
	Puerco Black-on-white	1030–1200	Mills and Herr 1999: 280
	Escavada Black-on-white	1000–1100	Mills and Herr 1999: 280
	Reserve Black-on-white	1100–1200	Mills and Herr 1999: 280
	Tularosa Black-on-white	1180–1300	Mills and Herr 1999: 280
	Snowflake Black-on-white	1100–1275	Mills and Herr 1999: 280
	Pinedale Black-on-white	1270–1320	Mills and Herr 1999: 280
	Reserve/Tularosa Black-on-white	1100–1300	Mills and Herr 1999: 280
	Tularosa/Pinedale Black-on-white	1180–1320	Mills and Herr 1999: 280
	Kiatuthlanna/Red Mesa Black-on-white	850–1040	Mills and Herr 1999: 280
	Roosevelt Black-on-white (Kayenta and Little Colorado White Ware designs)	1150–1300	Vint 2000: 25
Maverick Mountain Series	Maverick Mountain Black-on-red	1275–1325	No source available
	Maverick Mountain Polychrome	1275–1325	No source available
	Tucson Black-on-red	1275–1450	No source available
	Tucson Polychrome	1275–1450	Lindsay 1992: 237
	Nantack Polychrome	Unknown	No source available
	Prieto Polychrome	1275–1400	No source available
Middle Gila Buff Ware	Gila Butte Red-on-buff	725–875	Wallace 2001: 226, 229; Craig 2001: xiv
	Sacaton Red-on-buff	950–1150	Wallace 2001: 234, 236, 239, 241, 244; Craig 2001: xiv
Middle Gila Buff Ware, Safford Variety	Estrella Red-on-buff	625–775	Wallace 2001: 224; Craig 2001: xiv
	Santa Cruz–Rillito Red-on-buff	825–1000	Wallace 2001: 232; Craig 2001: xiv
	Santa Cruz–Rillito/Sacaton–Rincon Red-on-buff	825–1150	Wallace 2001: 232, 234, 236, 239, 241, 244; Craig 2001: xiv
	Sacaton–Rincon Red-on-buff	950–1150	Wallace 2001: 234, 236, 239, 241, 244; Craig 2001: xiv
	Casa Grande–Tanque Verde–San Carlos Red-on-buff	1150–1300	Wallace 2001: 246; Craig 2001: xiv
	Indeterminate Preclassic	825–1150	See above
Mimbres pottery	Three Circle Red-on-white	850–950	Haury 1936: 42
	Mimbres Black-on-white Style I	900–1000	Haury 1936: 42
	Mimbres Black-on-white Style II	950–1050	Haury 1936: 42, Anyon and LeBlanc 1984: 158
	Mimbres Black-on-white Style III	1000–1150	Nelson 1999: 52
	Mimbres Black-on-white Style I/II	900–1050	See above
	Mimbres Black-on-white Style II/III	950–1150	See above

sample size. These tests revealed that the diversity present in the ceramic assemblages from the sites sampled cannot be entirely attributed to sample size, although sample size does influence measures of diversity to a small degree in some cases.

To examine the diversity present in the ceramic assemblages sampled, I calculated richness and Brillouin statistics on the number of types and wares present at each of the sites in the sample. Richness, a mea-

sure of diversity, describes the number of classes present in a sample, in this case, the number of types or the number of wares (Kintigh 1989). Evenness can be calculated with two measures, the Brillouin and the Shannon statistics, which describe how evenly the classes present in the sample are represented. The Shannon statistic differs from the Brillouin statistic in that Shannon is not influenced by abundance and is intended for use with large populations, whereas Bril-

Table 4.1. Dates of Ceramics in the Safford and Aravaipa Valleys (*Continued*)

Ceramics	Type	Date A.D.	Reference
Mogollon Brown Ware	McDonald Painted Corrugated	1150–1280	Mills and Herr 1999: 280
	Point of Pines Punctate	1100–1250	Olson 1959: 101
	Tularosa Fillet Rim	1100–1300	Breternitz 1966: 99
	Tularosa White-on-red	1100–1300	Breternitz 1966: 99
	Plain (throughout ceramic sequence)		No source available
	Cibicue Painted Corrugated	1300–1350	Mills and Herr 1999: 280
	Corrugated	600–1450	Pierce 1999: 73-74
Roosevelt Red Ware	Pinto Polychrome	1280–1330	Lyons 2004: 366
	Gila Polychrome	1300–1450	Lyons 2004: 366
	Cliff Polychrome	1350–1450	Lyons 2004: 388
	Tonto Polychrome	1340/1350–1400	Lyons 2004: 366
	Subtypes (Ninemile, Phoenix, and Dinwiddie polychromes)	1350/1375–1450/1475	No source available
San Simon Series	Dos Cabezas Red-on-brown	650–800	Heckman 2000a: 66
	Galiuro Red-on-brown	700–900	Heckman 2000a: 66
	Encinas Red-on-brown	950–1200	Heckman 2000a: 66
	Cerros Red-on-white	800–1000	Heckman 2000a: 66
	Galiuro/Encinas Red-on-brown	700–1200	Heckman 2000a: 66
Trincheras Series	Nogales Polychrome	700–1150	Heckman 2000b: 75
White Mountain Red Ware	Puerco Black-on-red	1000–1180	Mills and Herr 1999: 280
	Wingate Black-on-red	1050–1200	Mills and Herr 1999: 280
	Wingate Polychrome	1100–1200	Mills and Herr 1999: 280
	St. Johns Black-on-red	1200–1300	Mills and Herr 1999: 280
	St. Johns Polychrome	1200–1300	Mills and Herr 1999: 280
	Springerville Polychrome	1250–1300	Carlson 1970: 45
	Pinedale Black-on-red	1280–1330	Mills and Herr 1999: 280
	Pinedale Polychrome	1290–1330	Mills and Herr 1999: 280
	Wingate/St. Johns Polychrome	1100–1300	Mills and Herr 1999: 280
	Pinedale Black-on-red/Polychrome	1280–1330	Mills and Herr 1999: 280
	Pinedale/Cedar Creek Polychrome	1290–1350	Mills and Herr 1999: 280
	Cedar Creek/Fourmile Polychrome	1300–1390	Mills and Herr 1999: 280
Ancestral Zuni Glaze-decorated Ware	Heshotauthla Polychrome	1270–1380	Mills and Herr 1999: 280
	Kwakina Polychrome	1280–1380	Mills and Herr 1999: 280
Various	Perforated plates	700–1450	Lyons and Lindsay 2006
	Cordmarked vessels	Unknown	No source available
	Playas Red Incised	(approx.) 1250–1450	Sayles 1936: 61
	Rough red slipped corrugated, possibly Thatcher White-on-red	Unknown	No source available
	San Francisco Red Ware?	600–1050	Anyon and LeBlanc 1984: 158, 161
	San Carlos Red-on-brown	1250/1275–1450	Lyons 2004: 107
	San Carlos Red	1200–1400	Foster 1994, Table 4.6
	Salado Red Corrugated	1150–1450	Vint 2000: 80

louin is intended for smaller populations for which all of the members are known (Kintigh 2002). The Brillouin statistic is more appropriate here, as the sample population is not infinitely large. These statistics range between 0.0 and 1.0, with 1.0 representing maximum evenness in the Brillouin statistic and maximum diversity for the scaled richness statistic.

Table 4.2 shows the scaled results of richness and Brillouin statistics for the wares present at each site sampled and the values generally range between 0.4 and 0.6 although higher and lower values occur. In particular, the Lippencott South, Cluff Ranch, Richardson Orchard, and Yuma Wash sites, as well as AZ CC:2:185 (ASM), Fort Grant Pueblo, Buena Vista

Table 4.2. Richness and Brillouin (Evenness) Statistics
by Phase for Ceramic Wares and Types

Dominant Phase	Site Number	Ceramic Wares		Ceramic Types	
		Richness	Brillouin	Richness	Brillouin
Eden	Pentagon Site	0.3846	0.4846	0.1920	0.5111
	P Ranch Canyon Site	0.1840	0.4988	0.4231	0.5421
	Murphy Site (CC:1:52 ASM)	0.5000	0.5761	0.2160	0.5689
	AZ CC:1:55 (ASM)	0.4231	0.5241	0.1600	0.5506
Eden/Bylas	Earven Flat Site	0.4615	0.5286	0.3680	0.5951
	Lippencott South Site	0.6538	0.5052	0.2160	0.4671
Bylas	Owens-Colvin Site	0.5000	0.5405	0.2960	0.5489
	Cluff Ranch Site	0.6154	0.5981	0.2800	0.5778
	Richardson Orchard Site	0.6538	0.5679	0.2960	0.4950
	Murphy Site (CC:2:103 ASM)	0.5769	0.5769	0.2560	0.3864
	Crary Site	0.3462	0.4984	0.1600	0.5393
Bylas/Goat Hill	Sharon Site	0.4231	0.4321	0.2320	0.4116
Goat Hill or Middle Classic	Fort Grant Silo Site	0.5000	0.5616	0.2080	0.5301
	Yuma Wash Site	0.6154	0.4974	0.2880	0.4661
	AZ CC:2:23 (BLM)	0.3077	0.2581	0.1360	0.2188
	AZ CC:2:33 (BLM)	0.5000	0.4692	0.2000	0.4595
	Wes Jernigan Site	0.5769	0.5295	0.2400	0.5213
	Rattlesnake Mesa Site	0.5000	0.4690	0.2320	0.4434
	AZ CC:2:185 (ASM)	0.6154	0.4165	0.2400	0.3737
Safford or Fort Grant	Crescent Ruin	0.4615	0.2555	0.2000	0.3252
	Fort Grant Pueblo	0.6154	0.4595	0.2960	0.4794
	Spear Ranch Site	0.5385	0.3645	0.2480	0.3561
	Fischer Site	0.5385	0.5070	0.2560	0.4806
	AZ CC:1:3 (ASM)	0.6538	0.6594	0.3120	0.6507
	Dewester Site	0.5385	0.5554	0.2400	0.5227
	Eagle Pass Site	0.2308	0.2747	0.1040	0.2479
	Haby Pueblo	0.4231	0.3053	0.1760	0.4002
	Wooten-Claridge Terrace Site	0.3846	0.5419	0.1600	0.5259
	AZ BB:3:22 (ASM)	0.4231	0.3250	0.1760	0.4172
	Krider Kiva Site	0.4615	0.4836	0.2000	0.5085
	Lippincott North Site	0.2692	0.3866	0.1280	0.3802
	AZ CC:2:69 (ASM)	0.4615	0.4610	0.2000	0.4914
	Buena Vista Ruin	0.6923	0.6467	0.4160	0.6308

Ruin and AZ CC:1:3 (ASM) all have scaled richness values over 0.6, indicating that these sites had a higher number of ceramic wares present than other sites in the sample. These high measures of diversity do not appear to correlate with site size, and the sites with the highest diversity in ceramic wares (listed above) are of various sizes.

Evenness values (Table 4.2) for wares at the sites listed in the previous paragraph are also generally high, particularly at the Buena Vista Ruin, but some sites with lower richness values had high values for evenness statistics, such as the Earven Flat Site. Sev-

eral sites also had particularly low richness values, including the Crary site, AZ CC:2:23 (BLM), the Eagle Pass Site, the Wooten-Claridge Terrace Site, and the Lippincott North Site. Although some of these sites also had low evenness values (like Lippincott North, Eagle Pass, and AZ CC:2:23 BLM), others did not. Therefore, the number of distinct wares present at a given site does not dictate how well each ware is represented.

Table 4.2 also shows the scaled results of richness and Brillouin statistics for the ceramic types present at each site sampled. These scaled values are much more

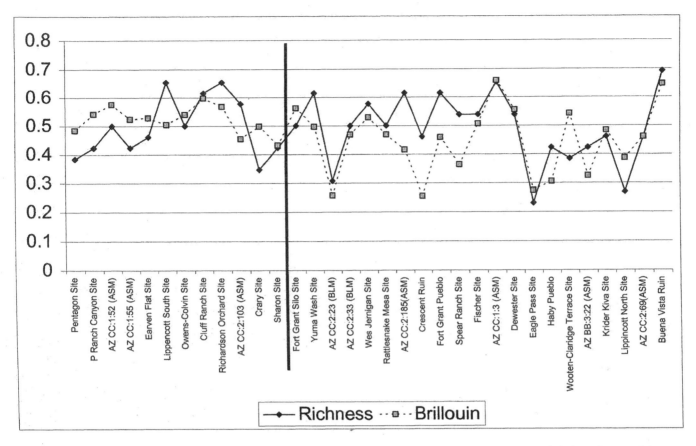

Figure 4.1. Plot of richness and Brillouin statistics for ceramic wares through time (early sites, *left*; late sites, *right*).

variable than those for wares. Values of richness for types are much lower in general than those for wares because fewer types in the total universe of possible types are represented at a site at any given time due to the relatively restricted temporal range of most ceramic types. Values of richness for types range from a low of 0.1040 at the Eagle Pass Site to a high of 0.4160 at the Buena Vista Ruin. These results are not surprising because Buena Vista Ruin was occupied for several centuries and had an example of almost every ware and type found in the Safford Valley in its assemblage, whereas the assemblage from Eagle Pass, a single component Safford or Fort Grant phase site (A.D. 1325–1450), was almost exclusively dominated by a limited number of types of Roosevelt Red Ware and Mogollon Brown Ware. Brillouin statistics for types generally range between 0.3 and 0.6, though there are some sites with higher (AZ CC:1:3 ASM and the Buena Vista Ruin) and lower (AZ CC:2:23 BLM and the Eagle Pass Site) values. Again, these trends do not appear to correlate with site size.

Plots of richness and Brillouin statistics reaffirm these trends. Figure 4.1 plots both statistics through time for ceramic wares, with earlier sites on the left side of the graph and later sites on the right side. Although no temporal trends are immediately apparent, beginning in the Goat Hill or Middle Classic phase (A.D. 1275/1300–1325), which includes all sites to the right of the Sharon Site, both measures become much more variable, particularly the Brillouin statistic. This trend is also apparent in Figure 4.2, which plots both statistics through time for ceramic types, although the differences in the variation of these statistics for types is more subtle than for wares. Nonetheless, these graphs indicate that variation in richness and evenness is greater during and after the Goat Hill phase, from A.D. 1275/1300 to 1450, than for the earlier Eden and Bylas phases (A.D. 1100–1275/1300).

Comparing richness and Brillouin statistics of ceramic wares for sites with and without perforated plates reveals no overall differences (Table 4.2 and Figures 4.3 and 4.4). Richness statistics vary from a

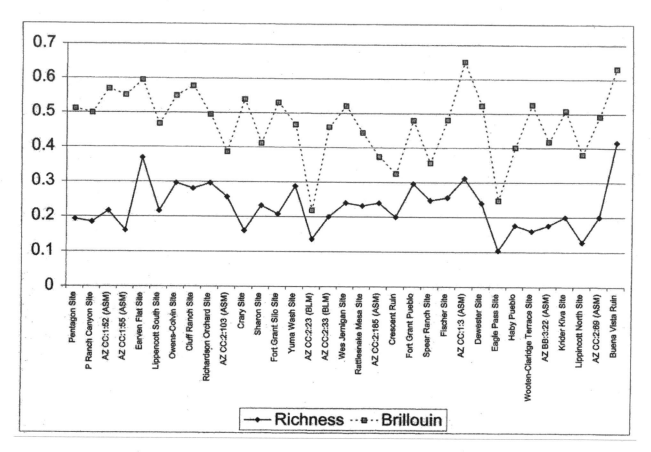

Figure 4.2. Plot of richness and Brillouin statistics for ceramic types through time (early sites, *left*; late sites, *right*).

low of about 0.45 to a high of about 0.7 at sites with perforated plates. Richness statistics for sites without perforated plates are more variable, ranging from about 0.25 to 0.65, but this range encompasses that of richness statistics for sites with perforated plates as well. The Brillouin statistic for ceramic wares has a similar range of variation for sites with and without perforated plates. Comparing both statistics for types at sites with and without perforated plates demonstrates that there are virtually no differences in the distribution of these statistics.

Measures of diversity in ceramics suggest that settlements occupied after A.D. 1275/1300 had greater diversity in the number of types and wares present. Regressions run on the samples demonstrated that little of this variability can be accounted for by differences in sample size, and the variability observed must result from other factors. Considering that the variability in assemblages from Safford and Aravaipa valley sites is most prominent at sites dating after A.D. 1275/1300, it is likely that the variability in these sam-

ples reflects variability in the people living at these settlements and in their exchange partners. Such variability would arise if Kayenta and Tusayan migrants moved into the area at the end of the thirteenth century. Sites that exhibit low richness in their assemblages, such as AZ CC:2:23 (BLM), the Eagle Pass Site, and the Lippincott North Site were probably occupied by people with a similar social background or, alternatively, people who obtained ceramics from a single social group. The opposite was likely true for settlements exhibiting high values of richness for their ceramic assemblage, at which multiple social groups were making or exchanging a wide variety of ceramics. It is at these sites, such as Buena Vista Ruin, AZ CC:1:3 (ASM), and the Yuma Wash Site that Kayenta and Tusayan migrant groups likely settled alongside indigenous populations upon their arrival in the Safford area, resulting in the observed diversity in ceramic assemblages.

A disparity in values of richness between valleys indicates further differentiation in social group com-

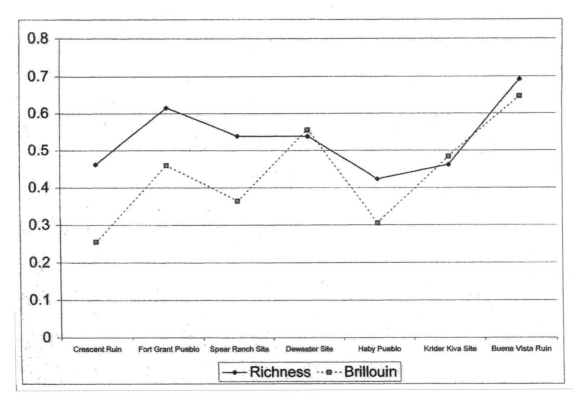

Figure 4.3. Plot of richness and Brillouin statistics for ceramic wares through time at sites with perforated plates (early sites, *left*; late sites, *right*).

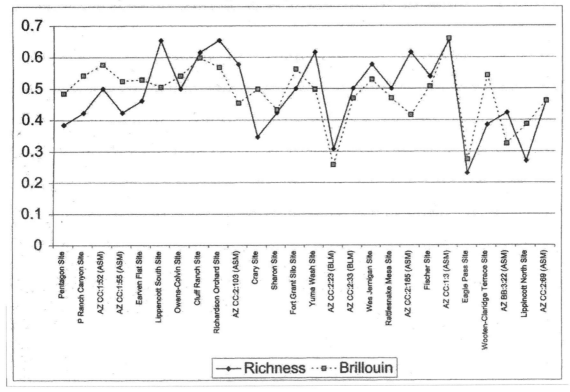

Figure 4.4. Plot of richness and Brillouin statistics for ceramic wares through time at sites without perforated plates (early sites, *left*; late sites, *right*).

position. Low richness values at several Fort Grant phase (A.D. 1325–1450) Aravaipa sites suggest less social diversity among the inhabitants or the exchange partners of these settlements. Perhaps some Aravaipa area sites were settled by groups originating in the Safford Valley that were composed of both Kayenta and Tusayan migrants and indigenous locals who had lived together for a relatively short period of time, but long enough that they had begun to transform their identities. Many of these settlements had decorated assemblages composed primarily of Roosevelt Red Ware, which dominated the decorated assemblages at Safford and Aravaipa sites after A.D. 1325 and may have been part of an economic and social strategy among migrants to both fit in with local groups and continue to thrive. Interestingly, Aravaipa settlements occupied earlier, such as the Rattlesnake Mesa Site and Crescent Ruin have higher richness values than later Aravaipa sites, suggesting the inhabitants of these earlier settlements, composed of a combination of Kayenta and Tusayan migrants and groups indigenous to the Safford Valley, were more cosmopolitan in their composition and social contacts, having lived together for a much shorter period of time.

Variability in values of evenness at sites from both valleys is also very telling. Sites with low values favored one or several ceramic wares or types over others in their assemblage, which likely also reflects low diversity in the inhabitants or their exchange partners. Values of the Brillouin statistic presented in Figures 4.1 and 4.2 vary widely through time and across space. Sites with low values (AZ CC:2:23 BLM, Crescent Ruin, Eagle Pass, and Haby Pueblo) all had assemblages dominated by a select group of wares and types, namely Maverick Mountain Series at AZ CC:2:23 (BLM) and Roosevelt Red Ware at the remaining three sites. At CC:2:23 this dominance of Maverick Mountain Series implies a strong presence of the producers of Maverick Mountain Series pottery, Kayenta and Tusayan migrants. At the other three sites, the dominance of Roosevelt Red Ware suggests strong influences by Kayenta and Tusayan migrants, especially at Crescent Ruin and Haby Pueblo where perforated plates are also in the ceramic assemblage. Although some high values of richness and evenness of ceramic assemblages are the result of the long temporal span these settlements were occupied, in general high values of richness statistics and high values of the Brillouin statistic are found at settlements that

were occupied by and exchanged with a diverse population. For sites dating to the Goat Hill or Middle Classic phase and after (post A.D. 1275/1300), the diversity present among inhabitants undoubtedly resulted from the coresidence of Kayenta and Tusayan migrants with local populations shortly after the migrants' arrival.

Cluster Analysis and Measures of Diversity Within Sites

To understand whether any decorated ceramic wares or types were spatially patterned at sites in this sample, I defined spatial clusters of all ceramics collected based on the Universal Transverse Mercator coordinates (UTMs) of collection areas and point provenienced sherds at each site. Although ceramics on the surface of sites have been subjected to a number of environmental and cultural processes that move them from their original provenience (Schiffer 1987), surface assemblages still hold important information about the distribution of artifacts at a given site (Bayman and Sanchez 1998; Downum and Brown 1998; Sullivan and Tolonen 1998). Clusters of similar wares and types may help delineate whether distinct social groups lived at a settlement and if these groups were segregated or intermingled throughout the settlement.

I ran K-means cluster analyses on the UTMs for each collection area and point provenience using several cluster solutions for each site until the cluster solution that maximized between-group differences and minimized within-group differences had been achieved. Cluster solutions varied among sites and ranged from a low of one cluster at the Murphy Site (AZ CC:2:103 ASM) and AZ CC:2:33 (BLM) to a high of eight clusters at the Pentagon site. Despite the fact that all sherds from each collection area were assigned the same UTMs, these sherds from collection areas do not appear to have overly influenced the cluster solutions by weighing the spatial clusters around these collection areas. Table 4.3 summarizes the number of clusters in the best cluster solution at each site in the sample. Figure 4.5 provides an example of a cluster solution from the Krider Kiva Site.

Measures of diversity were calculated for the clusters defined at each site in the sample with the exception of the Murphy Site (AZ CC:2:103 ASM)

Table 4.3. Number of Spatial Clusters Defined at Each Site

Site	Number of Clusters
Haby Pueblo	3
Pentagon Site	8
Wooten-Claridge Terrace Site	2
AZ BB:3:22 (ASM)	5
Rattlesnake Mesa Site	3
Eagle Pass Site	7
Crescent Ruin	2
Cluff Ranch Site	3
Spear Ranch Site	4
Owens-Colvin Site	4
AZ CC:1:3 (ASM)	3
Wes Jernigan Site	4
Krider Kiva Site	3
Murphy Site (CC:1:52 ASM)	4
Crary Site	2
AZ CC:1:55 (ASM)	7
Dewester Site	4
Fischer Site	3
Sharon Site	2
Lippencott South Site	4
Murphy Site (CC:2:103 ASM)	1
Lippincott North Site	2
Yuma Wash Site	3
AZ CC:2:185 (ASM)	2
AZ CC:2:23 (BLM)	4
Buena Vista Ruin	3
AZ CC:2:33 (BLM)	1
Earven Flat Site	6
AZ CC:2:69 (ASM)	4
Fort Grant Silo Site	4
Fort Grant Pueblo	6
Richardson Orchard Site	6
P Ranch Canyon	6

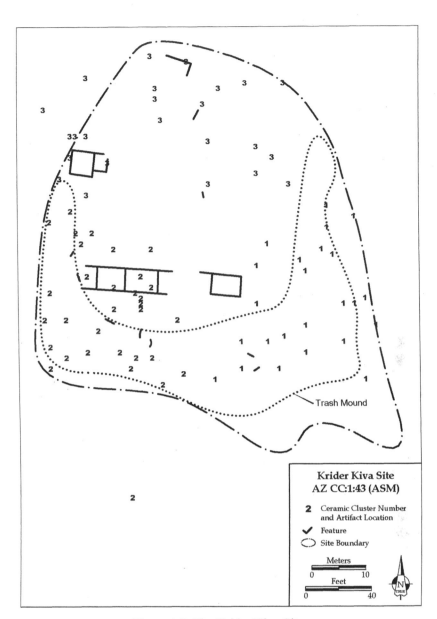

Figure 4.5. The Krider Kiva Site.

and AZ CC:2:33 (BLM), for which only one cluster was defined. In general, scaled values for richness and Brillouin statistics for the defined clusters are lower than 0.7, and most are between 0.2 and 0.5. These results mirror those richness and evenness statistics calculated on a site-wide basis. Several other patterns emerged in the cluster analysis (Table 4.4). First, several sites had temporally distinct ceramics clustered in different parts of each site, suggesting areas of the settlement were occupied sequentially, rather than contemporaneously. In contrast, at several sites ceramics dating to a restricted time interval were distributed evenly throughout the settlement, suggesting a single component occupation.

A third interesting pattern that emerged from these spatial clusters is the differential distribution of San Carlos Red-on-brown and Maverick Mountain Series ceramics. At four sites (Fischer, AZ CC:2:69 ASM, Fort Grant Silo, and Yuma Wash), San Carlos Red-on-brown ceramics and Maverick Mountain Series ceramics were spatially segregated and dominated different clusters. San Carlos Red-on-brown vessels were

Table 4.4. Patterns Evident in Spatial Clusters

Sites with evidence for temporal patterning in spatial clusters:	Haby Pueblo Wooten-Claridge Terrace Site Cluff Ranch Site Spear Ranch Site Krider Kiva Site Dewester Site Buena Vista Ruin Earven Flat Site Lippencott South Site Fort Grant Pueblo Richardson Orchard Site
Sites with evidence for single component occupation:	Pentagon Site AZ BB:3:22 (ASM) Rattlesnake Mesa Site Eagle Pass Site Crescent Ruin AZ CC:2:23 (BLM) Lippincott North Site
Sites with discrete clustering of Maverick Mountain Series or perforated plates and San Carlos Red-on-brown:	Krider Kiva Site Yuma Wash Site AZ CC:2:69 (ASM) Fischer Site Fort Grant Silo Site

probably produced by local groups (Lyons 2004), whereas Maverick Mountain Series vessels are clearly associated with Kayenta and Tusayan migrants, and both were produced in the late thirteenth and throughout the fourteenth centuries. Thus their spatial segregation at these settlements implies that migrant and local groups may have been living together but remained spatially segregated. A similar pattern appears in the spatially segregated distribution of San Carlos Red-on-brown and perforated plate fragments at the Krider Kiva Site, implying a sort of segregated coresidence of migrants and locals here as well.

Furthermore, at AZ CC:2:69 (ASM) and the Fischer Site, temporally later Roosevelt Red Ware sherds are relatively evenly distributed. Thus, the discrete spatial patterning of Maverick Mountain Series and San Carlos Red-on-brown at these two sites suggests that each group chose to maintain aspects of their premigration identity while reconfiguring other aspects in order to fit in with their new neighbors. Early in the occupation of these settlements (Fischer and AZ CC:2:69 ASM), the identities of these groups remained relatively separate as reflected in the distribu-

tion of Maverick Mountain Series and San Carlos Red-on-brown ceramics, but the dominance of later Roosevelt Red Ware pottery signifies that a transformation to a renegotiated uniform identity occurred soon afterward.

Measures of diversity and K-means cluster analyses of decorated ceramics show that diversity went up when the migrant groups arrived, and the spatial segregation of some ceramic types reveals that migrants and locals initially maintained separate identities which were later renegotiated into a new identity, visible in the prevalence of a new decorated pottery, Roosevelt Red Ware.

ARCHITECTURE AND SPACE SYNTAX

Space syntax is a method of understanding social behavior by quantifying differences in architecture and the use and structure of space. In other words, space syntax analyses highlight how the built environment structures and transforms space, and how the structure of space can shape the social dynamics of the people who utilize it (Hillier and Hanson 1984). The organization of space, both open space between structures and the structures themselves, is a function of social organization and integration (Chapman 1990; Hillier and Hanson 1984; Liebmann and others 2005; Potter 1998) wherein symmetrical spatial organization is a reflection of social integration. Although the idea that the built environment influences social dynamics, and vice versa, is not new, space syntax analysis operationalizes the theory behind this argument, providing a set of consistent and quantifiable methods that allow direct comparison of a variety of aspects of architecture. In this way, space syntax effectively links the theory of social interaction and space with the empirical material record.

In Hillier and Hanson's (1984) original formulation of space syntax theory, they developed a variety of measurements to quantify how spaces and buildings, and the spaces within buildings, influence social interaction. These measurements have been applied in numerous studies with results reaffirming the usefulness of these techniques (Chapman 1990; Dawson 2002; Elgohary and Hanson 1997; Ferguson 1996; Hillier and Penn 1992; Liebmann and others 2005; Oetelaar 2000). Because of the architectural focus of this study and the successful application of space syntax analy-

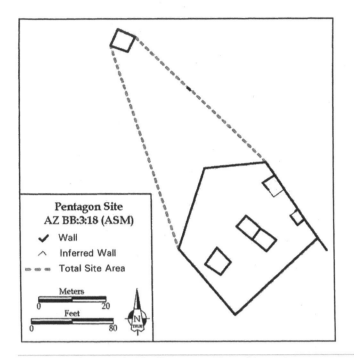

Figure 4.6. The Pentagon Site with total site area following Potter (1998).

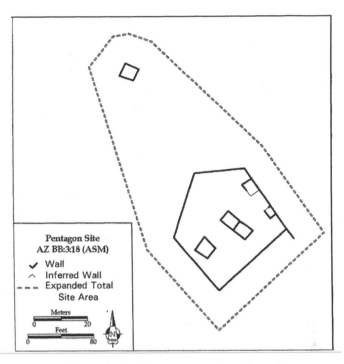

Figure 4.7. The Pentagon Site with total site area following Ferguson (1996).

ses in previous research, I used space syntax analyses to help quantify differences in architecture to examine how observed differences may help to better understand the expression of identity. Many of the analyses and measures created by Hillier and Hanson (1984), such as Gamma Analysis, require recognition of the interior configuration of rooms within a building. Because the analyses presented here use data from the surface remnants of unexcavated settlements, some of which have been heavily vandalized, the interior configuration of rooms, including the location of doorways and entrances, was not available.

Many of the measurements necessary for space syntax analyses hinge on the concept of convex space. Hillier and Hanson (1984:97) define convexity as a space (expressed as a polygon) in which "no tangent drawn on the perimeter passes through the space at any point." Socially, convexity can be interpreted as a space in which any one person standing at any point within that space can be seen by another person standing at any other point within that space (Ferguson 1996; Hillier and Penn 1992). Using convex space, several measurements can be calculated to look at the interaction of social dynamics and built space.

For the analyses performed here, I defined several sets of covex polygons describing open and enclosed

space for a subset of the 35 sites in the sample. Only 17 sites, those listed in Table 4.5, had surface architecture that was clear enough to be able to confidently determine site area and open and enclosed space. Total site area was defined in two ways. Following Potter (1998), total site area was first defined as the area of the buildings at the site plus the intervening space, with none of the surrounding area included. Second, total site area was defined as the area of the buildings at the site plus the intervening space surrounded by a 10–meter buffer of additional space (Figs. 4.6, 4.7), following Ferguson (1996). Open space was defined as the area of the site within the total site area boundary not occupied by architectural space, which included intervening space and the 10–meter buffer space in Ferguson's (1996) definition, and just the intervening space in Potter's (1998) definition. The open space at sites, with boundary configurations following both Potter (1998) and Ferguson (1996), was then divided into convex polygons, beginning with the largest convex polygon at each site. Defining convex polygons was difficult at several sites that contained circular architecture (either in the form of kivas or other circular structures), because a circle can be considered a polygon with an infinite number of vertices, creating infinitely small convex polygons and mathe-

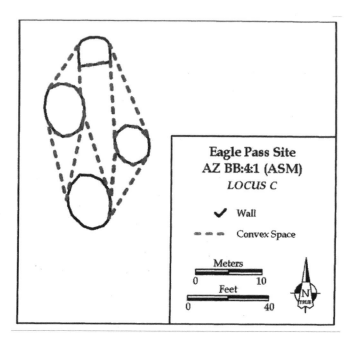

Figure 4.8. Locus C of the Eagle Pass Site with round structures transformed to create convex space.

matical problems in the analysis. In these cases the circular architecture was approximated as a polygon with a finite number of vertices (Fig. 4.8). Enclosed, or architectural space, was bounded by the walls of rooms or room blocks. For several of the analyses performed here, walls that were not part of rooms or room blocks, such as compound walls, were also included as architectural space. However, space inside compounds was considered open space and divided into convex polygons, similar to plazas enclosed by several room blocks.

Of the numerous possible measures of space syntax, I chose three for the analysis here, based on the architectural data available and their utility in looking at questions of identity. All three statistics, integration score, convex articulation, and grid convexity, provide measures of spatial integration of settlements based on the arrangements of buildings in relation to open space. With these measures, spatial organization can be used as a proxy for social integration (Ferguson 1996; Hillier and Hanson 1984). Such organization has meaningful implications for identity in postmigration environments, because the inhabitants of settlements with evidence of increased spatial and social integration are more likely to identify themselves as part of the same group. Thus, in situations where pre-

viously disparate migrant and indigenous populations lived side-by-side following migration, social integration apparently led to a renegotiation of migrant and indigenous identities. Spatial integration, quantified by these three measures, enhances our understanding of the consequences of migration on identity by determining how these disparate groups may have interacted.

Following Potter's (1998) analysis of Eastern and Western Puebloan sites in the northern Southwest, I conducted several calculations using the total site area, architectural space, open space, and convex space to arrive at an integration score for each site (Tables 4.5, 4.6). Potter (1998) used these measures to determine the level of social integration of the inhabitants of late Pueblo III and early Pueblo IV sites by looking at the structure of the total open space, including formal open space, such as plazas, and informal open space, such as the interstitial spaces among room blocks. Potter's (1998) integration score is calculated as follows:

$$A = \frac{\text{open space}}{\text{total site area}}$$

$$B = \frac{\text{area of three largest convex polygons}}{\text{open space}}$$

$$\text{Integration score} = \frac{B}{A}$$

Sites with a small proportion of their open space included in the three largest convex polygons exhibit a fragmented layout and a smaller integration score, whereas sites with a large proportion of their open space included in the three largest convex polygons exhibit a potentially more integrative layout and a larger integration score. This score therefore measures both the morphology, or arrangement of space, of a settlement, as well as the size of the settlement itself to determine spatial integration. From this measure of spatial integration, inferences can be made concerning how the inhabitants of the settlement interacted and whether they considered themselves part of a cohesive group.

I calculated integration scores for each of the 17 sites used in the space syntax analyses, first including the space occupied by walls not attached to rooms or room blocks (Table 4.5) and again without wall space included in the calculation of architectural space (Table 4.6). Total site area for these calculations followed

Table 4.5. Integration Score with Wall Space Included
(Sites Listed Early to Late; Area Measurements in Square Meters)

Site	Total Site Area	Enclosed Architectural Space	Wall Space	Total Architectural Area	Open Space	A (Open Space/ Total Area)	Area of Three Largest Convex Polygons	B (Area of Three Largest Convex Polygons/Open Space)	Integration Score (B/A)
Pentagon Site	2109.63	135.34	39.61	174.95	1934.68	0.92	1184.09	61.20	0.667
Lippencott South Site	293.06	38.65	13.61	52.26	240.80	0.82	199.26	82.75	1.007
Cluff Ranch Site	366.11	63.65	17.05	80.70	285.41	0.78	244.24	85.58	1.098
Crary Site	168.21	39.03	10.83	49.86	118.35	0.70	118.17	99.85	1.419
Sharon Site	1290.11	220.42	10.81	231.23	1058.88	0.82	880.21	83.13	1.013
Yuma Wash Site	2195.29	314.60	0.00	314.60	1880.69	0.86	1107.09	58.87	0.687
AZ CC:2:23 (BLM)	160.39	116.00	0.00	116.00	44.39	0.28	43.76	98.58	3.562
AZ CC:2:33 (BLM)	140.99	140.99	0.00	140.99	0.00	0.00	0.00	0.00	0.000
Goat Hill Site	804.92	339.16	0.00	339.16	465.76	0.58	283.80	60.93	1.053
Rattlesnake Mesa Site	2282.37	663.97	7.07	671.04	1616.33	0.71	746.18	46.17	0.652
AZ CC:2:185 (ASM)	8039.69	338.72	0.00	338.72	7700.97	0.96	4881.12	63.38	0.662
Dewester Site*	34.04	34.04	0.00	34.04	0.00	0.00	0.00	0.00	0.000
Eagle Pass Site	2938.02	727.39	9.18	736.57	2201.45	0.75	1174.01	53.33	0.712
Wooten-Claridge Terrace Site	98.77	98.77	0.00	98.77	0.00	0.00	0.00	0.00	0.000
Krider Kiva Site	937.29	142.66	0.00	142.66	794.63	0.85	670.08	84.33	0.995
Lippincott North Site	177.08	66.36	0.00	66.36	110.72	0.63	109.17	98.60	1.577
Marijilda Site	2699.08	971.13	23.69	994.82	1704.26	0.63	1259.37	73.90	1.170

*Deals only with the Safford phase component of this site.

Table 4.6. Integration Score with Wall Space Excluded
(Sites Listed Early to Late; Area Measurements in Square Meters)

Site	Total Site Area	Enclosed Architectural Space	Open Space	A (Open Space/ Total Area)	Area of Three Largest Convex Polygons	B (Area of Three Largest Convex Polygons/Open Space)	Integration Score (B/A)
Pentagon Site	2109.63	135.34	1974.29	0.94	1184.09	59.98	0.641
Lippencott South Site	293.06	38.65	254.41	0.87	199.26	78.32	0.902
Cluff Ranch Site	366.11	63.65	302.46	0.83	244.24	80.75	0.977
Crary Site	168.21	39.03	129.18	0.77	118.17	91.48	1.191
Sharon Site	1290.11	220.42	1069.69	0.83	880.21	82.29	0.992
Yuma Wash Site	2195.29	314.60	1880.69	0.86	1107.09	58.87	0.687
AZ CC:2:23 (BLM)	160.39	116.00	44.39	0.28	43.76	98.58	3.562
AZ CC:2:33 (BLM)	140.99	140.99	0.00	0.00	0.00	0.00	0.000
Goat Hill Site	804.92	339.16	465.76	0.58	283.80	60.93	1.053
Rattlesnake Mesa Site	2282.37	663.97	1618.03	0.71	746.18	46.12	0.651
AZ CC:2:185 (ASM)	8039.69	338.72	7700.97	0.96	4881.12	63.38	0.662
Dewester Site*	34.04	34.04	0.00	0.00	0.00	0.00	0.000
Eagle Pass Site	2938.02	727.39	2210.63	0.75	1174.01	53.11	0.706
Wooten-Claridge Terrace Site	98.77	98.77	0.00	0.00	0.00	0.00	0.000
Krider Kiva Site	937.29	142.66	794.63	0.85	670.08	84.33	0.995
Lippincott North Site	177.08	66.36	110.72	0.63	109.17	98.60	1.577
Marijilda Site	2699.08	971.13	1727.95	0.64	1259.37	72.88	1.138

*Deals only with the Safford phase component of this site.

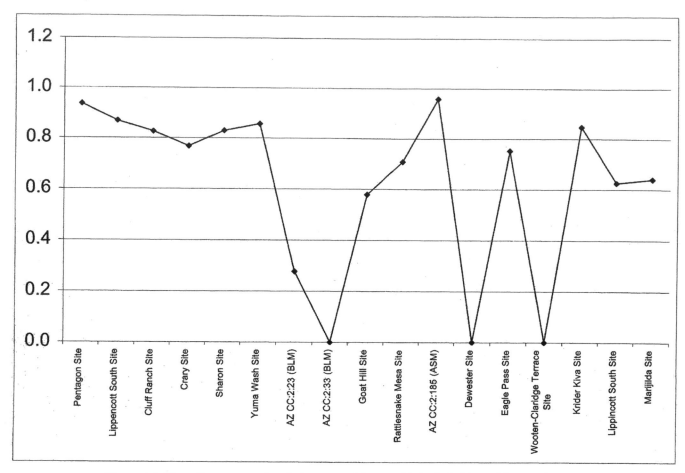

Figure 4.9. Plot of open space/total site area, without walls included in architectural space.

Potter (1998) and only included the space occupied by walls, rooms, and room·blocks and the intervening space between them. The list of sites in Tables 4.5 and 4.6 is ordered temporally, beginning with the earliest sites at the top and ending with the latest at the bottom.

Plots of selected values in Tables 4.5 and 4.6 are more informative. Figure 4.9 shows a plot of values of A (open space/total site area) without wall space included in architectural space. The first four sites in the plot (Pentagon, Lippencott South, Cluff Ranch, and Crary) are all dominated by Bylas phase (A.D. 1200–1275/1300) or earlier components and have relatively similar values for open space divided by total site area. However, in the subsequent Goat Hill or Middle Classic (A.D. 1275/1300–1325) and Safford or Fort Grant phases (1325–1450), values become much more variable, suggesting a similar increase in the variability of spatial integration and thus social integration of

settlements during this time. During the previous Bylas phase, site layout was much more consistent. This pattern is repeated when walls are included in the total architectural space at the site.

Integration score shows a similar, though more subtle, pattern of variability during and after the Goat Hill or Middle Classic phase (A.D. 1275/1300–1325). In Figure 4.10, sites to the right of the line date to the Goat Hill phase and after. In this case, the four earliest sites in the sample remain closely clustered in their integration scores. The variation in integration scores in later sites is not as dramatic as with values of A (open space/total site area; see Figure 4.9), but is still evident. Little change in integration scores is evident when walls are included in the calculation of architectural space. Integration score and values of A clearly demonstrate that spatial integration became much more variable after the arrival of Kayenta and Tusayan migrants in the area, as settlements occupied during

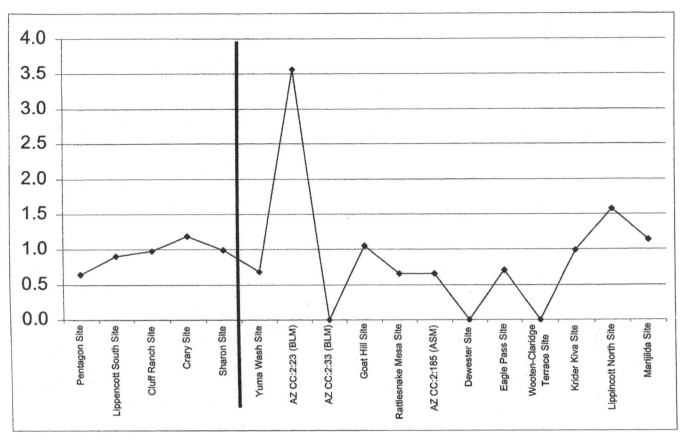

Figure 4.10. Plot of integration score, without walls included in architectural space.

and after this time show great disparities in their integration scores. Those sites known and suspected to be migrant enclaves, including Goat Hill, AZ CC:2:23 (ASM), and Marijilda had higher integration scores than most other sites, with the exception of the Lippincott North Site and the Krider Kiva Site, which also had high integration scores likely because of the small number of room blocks present and their compact arrangements. Settlements I suspect were occupied by both migrants and indigenous groups, such as AZ CC:2:185 (ASM), generally have lower integration scores than migrant enclaves. This suggests that migrant enclaves were more spatially and thus socially integrated than settlements that housed both migrant and indigenous groups. However, there is variability in the integration scores of settlements occupied by both groups, suggesting migrants and indigenous groups were more integrated at some sites, like Krider Kiva, than at other sites. Thus, it appears that migrants and indigenous groups were living together and were forming a new identity at this time.

I also calculated convex articulation and grid convexity for comparison with integration score. For both of these measures, I defined total site area as the space occupied by rooms, room blocks, and walls, the intervening space, and that space plus a 10–meter buffer, following Ferguson (1996). Convex articulation is the number of convex spaces divided by the number of buildings at a site. Lower values of convex articulation mean the site is more symmetrical and socially integrated, whereas higher values mean the site is more spatially fragmented and asymmetrical, and therefore, socially segregated. Grid convexity can be defined by the formula:

$$\text{grid convexity} = \frac{(\sqrt{I} + 1)^2}{C}$$

where I is the number of room blocks or rooms (discrete areas of architecture) at a site, and C is the number of convex spaces at a site. Grid convexity compares the convex space in an area to an orthogonal grid, and values of grid convexity denote how de-

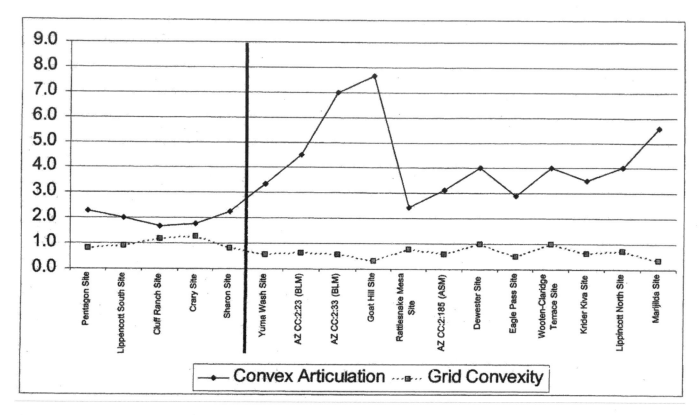

Figure 4.11. Plot of convex articulation and grid convexity, including walls
in architectural space and total site area following Ferguson (1996).

formed the convex space is in comparison to an orthogonal grid. Convex articulation and grid convexity are inversely proportional, such that high values of grid convexity indicate symmetry in space and, thus, increased social integration. Figure 4.11 and Tables 4.7 and 4.8 display the values of convex articulation and grid convexity for the sites in the sample.

Like integration scores, convex articulation and grid convexity become much more variable during and after the Goat Hill or Middle Classic phase (A.D. 1275/1300–1325; to the right of the line in Figure 4.11). Convex articulation is highest and grid convexity lowest at two of three sites that are known or suspected to be migrant enclaves (Goat Hill and Marijilda). This is not the case at the other suspected migrant enclave, AZ CC:2:23 (BLM), but convex articulation may be high and grid convexity low at this site because of the compact nature of the room block. Values of convex articulation are significantly lower and grid convexity higher for settlements that likely were inhabited by both Kayenta and Tusayan migrants and indigenous groups, implying more integration at

these settlements than at those that were occupied solely by migrants, which would have facilitated coresidence by these disparate groups. The values of convex articulation for Goat Hill or Middle Classic phase or later sites are higher and grid convexity lower overall than for earlier Eden and Bylas phase (A.D. 1100–1275/1300) sites, implying that settlements occupied earlier were more socially integrated than those occupied after migrants arrived. This result is not surprising, however, as these Eden and Bylas phase settlements were occupied by groups who were not as socially disparate as Kayenta and Tusayan migrants and populations indigenous to Safford. This level of integration indicated for settlements occupied by migrant and indigenous populations suggests migrant and indigenous groups who were living together formed a new identity during this time.

Interestingly, these results contradict those of Potter's (1998) integration score, which suggested that migrant enclave sites were, in general, better integrated than settlements occupied by both migrant and indigenous groups. This difference probably stems

Table 4.7. Convex Articulation and Grid Convexity, Total Site Area Following Potter (1998)
Sites Listed Early (*top*) to Late (*bottom*)

Site	Number of convex spaces	Number of buildings without walls	with walls	Convex Articulation without walls	with walls	Grid Convexity measure $(\sqrt{I} + 1)^2$ without walls	with walls	Grid Convexity without walls	with walls
Pentagon Site	12	5	7	2.40	1.71	10.45	13.27	0.87	1.11
Lippencott South Site	9	3	8	3.00	1.13	7.45	14.62	0.83	1.62
Cluff Ranch Site	5	3	6	1.67	0.83	7.45	11.86	1.49	2.37
Crary Site	2	2	4	1.00	0.50	5.81	9.00	2.91	4.50
Sharon Site	9	4	8	2.25	1.13	9.00	14.62	1.00	1.62
Yuma Wash Site	10	6	6	1.67	1.67	11.86	11.86	1.19	1.19
AZ CC:2:23 (BLM)	3	2	2	1.50	1.50	5.81	5.81	1.94	1.94
AZ CC:2:33 (BLM)	0	1	1	0.00	0.00	4.00	4.00	0.00	0.00
Goat Hill Site	12	3	3	4.00	4.00	7.45	7.45	0.62	0.62
Rattlesnake Mesa Site	11	5	7	2.20	1.57	10.45	13.27	0.95	1.21
AZ CC:2:185 (ASM)	13	7	7	1.86	1.86	13.27	13.27	1.02	1.02
Dewester Site*	0	1	1	0.00	0.00	4.00	4.00	0.00	0.00
Eagle Pass Site	33	19	21	1.74	1.57	28.67	31.15	0.87	0.94
Wooten-Claridge Terrace Site	0	1	1	0.00	0.00	4.00	4.00	0.00	0.00
Krider Kiva Site	5	4	4	1.25	1.25	9.00	9.00	1.80	1.80
Lippincott North Site	1	2	2	0.50	0.50	5.81	5.81	5.81	5.81
Marijilda Site	14	3	5	4.67	2.80	7.45	10.45	0.53	0.75

*Includes only the Safford phase component of this site.

Table 4.8. Convex Articulation and Grid Convexity, Total Site Area Following Ferguson (1996)
Sites Listed Early (*top*) to Late (*bottom*)

Site	Number of convex spaces	Number of buildings without walls	with walls	Convex Articulation without walls	with walls	Grid Convexity measure $(\sqrt{I} + 1)^2$ without walls	with walls	Grid Convexity without walls	with walls
Pentagon Site	16	5	7	3.20	2.29	10.45	13.27	0.65	0.83
Lippencott South Site	16	3	8	5.33	2.00	7.45	14.62	0.47	0.91
Cluff Ranch Site	10	3	6	3.33	1.67	7.45	11.86	0.75	1.19
Crary Site	7	2	4	3.50	1.75	5.81	9.00	0.83	1.29
Sharon Site	18	4	8	4.50	2.25	9.00	14.62	0.50	0.81
Yuma Wash Site	20	6	6	3.33	3.33	11.86	11.86	0.59	0.59
AZ CC:2:23 (BLM)	9	2	2	4.50	4.50	5.81	5.81	0.65	0.65
AZ CC:2:33 (BLM)	7	1	1	7.00	7.00	4.00	4.00	0.57	0.57
Goat Hill Site	23	3	3	7.67	7.67	7.45	7.45	0.32	0.32
Rattlesnake Mesa Site	17	5	7	3.40	2.43	10.45	13.27	0.61	0.78
AZ CC:2:185 (ASM)	22	7	7	3.14	3.14	13.27	13.27	0.60	0.60
Dewester Site*	4	1	1	4.00	4.00	4.00	4.00	1.00	1.00
Eagle Pass Site	61	19	21	3.21	2.90	28.67	31.15	0.47	0.51
Wooten-Claridge Terrace Site	4	1	1	4.00	4.00	4.00	4.00	1.00	1.00
Krider Kiva Site	14	4	4	3.50	3.50	9.00	9.00	0.64	0.64
Lippincott North Site	8	2	2	4.00	4.00	5.81	5.81	0.73	0.73
Marijilda Site	28	3	5	9.33	5.60	7.45	10.45	0.27	0.37

*Includes only the Safford phase component of this site.

from differing definitions of spatial integration used for the three calculated measures of space syntax.

Potter (1998) views integration as a measure of spatial cohesiveness, such that sites with large open areas, such as plazas, have more integration than sites with open space that is fragmented. However, Hillier and Hanson (1984) measure spatial symmetry, which leads to social integration, by the number and location of spaces that exist to facilitate interaction. These spaces are not necessarily large open spaces and can instead be common routes of travel from one part of a settlement to another, even if that settlement is fragmented. Although fragmentation of space does play a role, and highly fragmented space is generally considered less symmetrical, Hillier and Hanson's (1984) more nuanced approach takes other factors affecting spatial and the resulting social integration into account as well. It appears that the measures of convex articulation and grid convexity more accurately capture the degree of spatial symmetry and social integration present at the settlements in the sample.

From the data presented here, I conclude that social integration at settlements occupied during and after the Goat Hill or Middle Classic phase (A.D. 1275/ 1300–1325) was considerably more variable than in earlier phases, reflecting the diversity present in the population and the way they chose to live together. Measures of space syntax suggest that Eden and Bylas phase (A.D. 1100–1275/1300) settlements were structured to favor high social integration of their inhabitants. With the arrival of later Kayenta and Tusayan migrants, who appear to have lived alongside indigenous groups at all settlements (except those occupied strictly by migrants), measures of convex articulation and grid convexity indicate social integration decreased. However, ceramic evidence indicates that these two groups did live together and at settlements more socially integrative than those occupied solely by migrants. Furthermore, this lack of spatial integration at migrant settlements may reflect an overarching need for defensibility on the part of migrants (real or perceived), and communal structures such as kivas may have served to integrate the populations living there. Thus, the totality of evidence from decorated ceramics and space syntax measures indicates Kayenta and Tusayan migrants and indigenous groups lived together at settlements that were more integrated than those occupied solely by migrants and less integrated than those previously occupied by indigenous groups.

These new reconfigured settlements appear to have been a compromise in terms of the level of social integration on the part of both groups.

SETTLEMENT LOCATION ON THE LANDSCAPE

Archaeologists studying migration in the Greater Southwest have discerned that migrants, or newcomers to an area, are often marginalized by the indigenous groups or firstcomers already residing there, especially if migrants are a minority population (Clark 2001). This marginalization may have been spatial and economic, where migrants were relegated to living farther away from prime agricultural and resource gathering locations.

Social marginalization may have occurred hand-in-hand with economic marginalization, in which case migrants may not have been allowed entry into important social and religious societies or may have been left out of community decision making (Burmeister 2000). Social marginalization can be difficult to detect in the archaeological record, although physical spatial marginalization is evident in site location. Next I focus on the spatial marginalization of Kayenta and Tusayan migrant populations based on the location of settlements after they appeared in the Safford and Aravaipa valleys in the late thirteenth century.

Safford or Fort Grant and Goat Hill or Middle Classic phase (A.D. 1275/1300–1450) settlements are highly variable in their size and location. Room counts range from a low of two at the Dewester and Lippincott North sites to a high of 150 to 300 at Buena Vista Ruin. Previous research has suggested that groups in the Safford Basin might have moved down into the floodplain as they became increasingly aggregated in the Safford or Fort Grant phase (Neely 2004). However, upland locations may have been favorable as well, with numerous creeks and springs providing significant quantities of water in these areas. Therefore, not unexpectedly, site size does not appear to correlate with location (Fig. 4.12). Several large sites are located in upland areas, such as Spear Ranch and Marijilda, and at least one smaller site, Yuma Wash, is located immediately adjacent to the Gila River. Nor is there any evidence for such a distributional pattern along Aravaipa Creek where the distance between the floodplain and the upland areas of the Pinaleño, Galiuro, and Santa Teresa Mountains is compressed, and

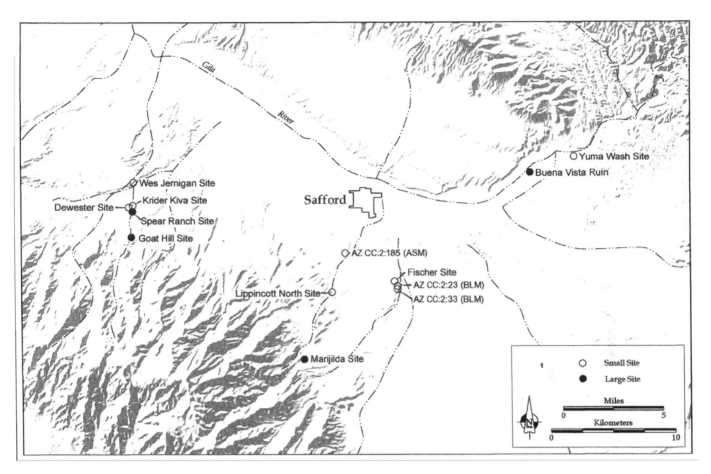

Figure 4.12. Large versus small Goat Hill and Safford phase sites.

sites of various sizes are adjacent to each other (Fig. 4.13). Clearly, settlement size does not determine location or proximity to major rivers.

There is some evidence, however, to indicate that migrant populations may have been marginalized upon their arrival in the Safford Valley (Fig. 4.14). The Goat Hill Site, the most conspicuous Kayenta and Tusayan migrant enclave in the Safford Valley, is located on a steep butte more than 14 km (9 miles) south of the Gila River. Although the inhabitants of Goat Hill likely utilized the creek in nearby Lefthand Canyon and the flat areas to the north and south of the settlement for agriculture (Neely 2005; Woodson 1995; see also Rinker 1998), they did not have ready access to as much agricultural land in the floodplain as did inhabitants of other settlements, and they may have had to supplement cultigens with wild resources or obtain them through other means such as exchange. Furthermore, it seems that the inhabitants of Goat Hill may have been physically isolated from many other

contemporaneous settlements, with the exception of Spear Ranch.

Another potential migrant enclave in the Safford Valley, AZ CC:2:23 (BLM), is also located atop a high mesa about 8 km (5 miles) south of Safford. Agricultural land would have been available at the base of the mesa around this site, which is located close to the confluence of the Stockton and Marijilda washes. Site AZ CC:2:23 (BLM) may have been somewhat less isolated than the Goat Hill Site, because AZ CC:2:33 (BLM), which also dates to the Goat Hill phase (1275/1300–1325), was located several hundred meters to the north on the same mesa. What is most interesting about CC:2:23 is its defensible location away from the Gila River floodplain, similar to the setting of the Goat Hill Site.

The Marijilda Site may be another migrant enclave dating mainly to the Safford phase (A.D. 1325–1450). Its location adjacent to a major wash well away from the Gila River is similar to that of the Goat Hill Site

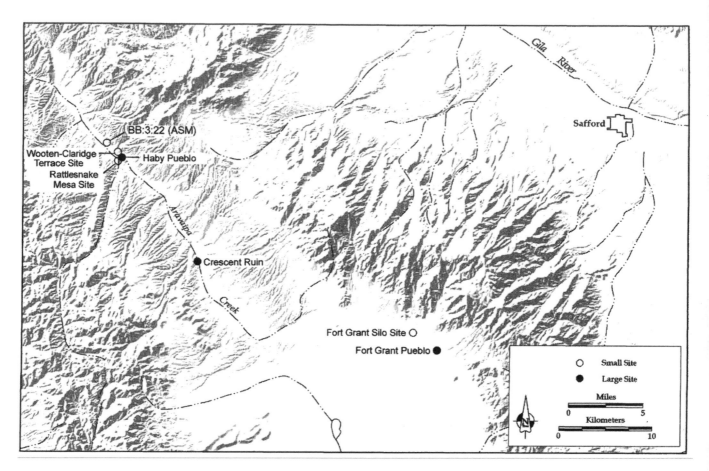

Figure 4.13. Large versus small Middle Classic and Fort Grant phase sites.

and AZ CC:2:23 (BLM), but it is not located in a defensible location. The inhabitants of Marijilda may have compensated for this by building one side of the room block on the edge of an embankment overlooking Marijilda Wash, combining the steep embankment with tall masonry walls and building a large wall on the other side of the settlement to promote defensibility. Although defensible locations of migrant enclaves do not necessarily suggest discord between migrant groups and the existing indigenous population, they do imply marginalization and at least concerns for security among these specific migrant groups.

Along Aravaipa Creek, most sites are located on terraces overlooking the creek. This positioning is particularly evident at the cluster of sites southeast of Klondyke, especially Haby Pueblo, Rattlesnake Mesa, and Pentagon, as well as at Crescent Ruin. However, considering the narrow floodplain along Aravaipa Creek, such prominent settlement locations may also have been a practical measure to avoid periodic flood-

ing. No sites along Aravaipa Creek appear to have been occupied solely by migrants.

Sites with perforated plates, considered a relatively reliable indicator of Kayenta and Tusayan migrants (Lyons and Lindsay 2006), do not present a clear pattern in their location on the landscape. However, since some of the settlements that have perforated plates in their assemblages were likely also inhabited by local groups, such as Buena Vista Ruin (Fig. 4.15), this arrangement is not surprising and follows the general pattern for sites post dating A.D. 1275. There is also no patterning in the location of sites with perforated plates along Aravaipa Creek, except that all are located close to major sources of water in addition to the Aravaipa, either springs or major washes. Several settlements with perforated plates, in both valleys, are located in close proximity to contemporaneous settlements without perforated plates.

From the current understanding of the arrival of Kayenta and Tusayan migrants in the Safford and

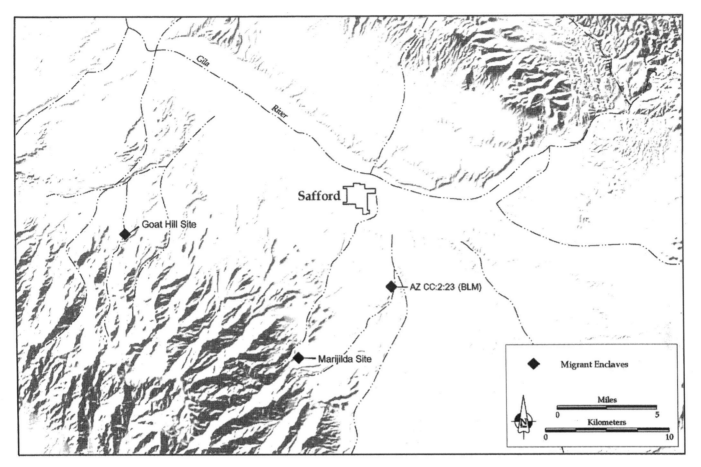

Figure 4.14. Potential migrant enclave sites.

Aravaipa areas, it appears that some migrant populations may have been physically, if not socially, marginalized upon their arrival. However, this marginalization did not continue for an extended period of time as many Safford or Fort Grant phase (A.D. 1325–1450) settlements, like Buena Vista Ruin and others, show evidence in ceramics and architecture of migrant and indigenous populations living together at socially integrated settlements.

SOCIAL INTEGRATION

After an initial brief separation in the Goat Hill and Middle Classic phase (A.D. 1275/1300–1325), when migrants confined themselves to a select few enclaves, Kayenta and Tusayan migrant groups and indigenous populations lived together at the same settlements and began to renegotiate their identity in the late Classic Period. Variability in decorated ceramic assemblages from this time can be attributed to diversity in the in-

habitants and exchange partners of Goat Hill or Middle Classic and Safford or Fort Grant phase populations. Spatial patterning in decorated ceramic wares and types, particularly those of the Maverick Mountain Series and San Carlos Red-on-brown at several sites, showed that although migrant and indigenous groups were living together at some settlements, they may have lived in discrete areas and maintained a degree of social separation.

The social integration shown in the diversity and spatial patterning of ceramics was also visible in the spatial patterning of architecture. In these analyses, spatial organization was viewed as a function of social integration (Ferguson 1996; Hillier and Hanson 1984), wherein architectural and spatial symmetry was used as a proxy for social integration. Analyses of space syntax showed variability in the integration score of postmigration settlements, likely inhabited by both groups. Measures of convex articulation and grid convexity suggested that settlements with both migrant

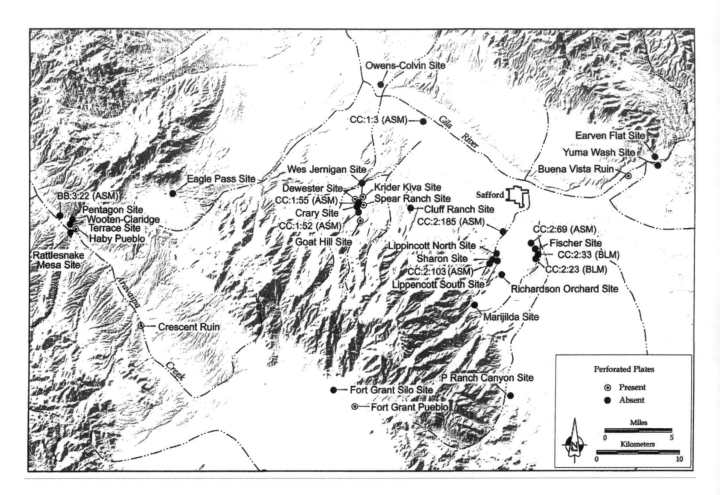

Figure 4.15. Sites with and without perforated plates.

and indigenous groups occupied during and after the Goat Hill or Middle Classic phase were not as spatially or socially integrated as previous Bylas phase settlements, but were more integrated than the migrant enclaves first settled by migrant populations, such as Goat Hill. These data support the proposition that Kayenta and Tusayan migrants coresided with indigenous groups after an initial separation and that these two disparate groups became increasingly socially integrated after the first wave of migrants arrived, resulting in the formation of a new identity that incorporated elements of both premigration identities.

CHAPTER FIVE

Differentiating Migration and Exchange Through Studies of Obsidian and Decorated Ceramics

Differences in enculturative background reflected in the technological style of utilitarian ceramics and architecture helped to detect distinct social groups in the archaeological record. Decorated ceramics identified the social ties of the inhabitants of Classic period sites, with decorated ceramic diversity (or lack thereof) being used as a proxy for the diversity among the inhabitants of Classic period settlements and their exchange partners. With evidence for distinct social groups and ceramic wares specifically associated with Kayenta and Tusayan migrants, these results demonstrated that migrants from the Kayenta and Tusayan areas were likely present at numerous Goat Hill or Middle Classic phase and later (A.D. 1275/1300–1450) settlements and that they appear to have substantially increased the diversity among the people present there.

I now evaluate evidence from obsidian and ceramic sourcing analyses to determine whether this diversity was in fact the result of an increasingly mixed population at Safford and Aravaipa valley settlements due to an influx of Kayenta and Tusayan migrants living alongside indigenous populations, or if such heterogeneity resulted from an increasingly varied exchange network of Classic period settlement inhabitants. Such information provides a more thorough evaluation of the effects of migration on identity during the Classic period in the Safford and Aravaipa valleys by contributing to our understanding of the groups that took part in the formation of this new identity.

OBSIDIAN

Obsidian is an essential part of Southwestern flaked stone assemblages. Fortunately for archaeologists, obsidian contains chemical signatures unique to each raw material source that can be securely identified,

tying each piece of flaked stone to its original provenance (Shackley 2005b). Several social mechanisms could have been used to obtain obsidian raw materials, including long distance exchange, down the line exchange, and primary procurement. Determining which of these social mechanisms accounts for the presence of obsidian in a given area can lend insight into social patterns and dynamics among that area's inhabitants and their exchange partners.

To get a better idea of how obsidian fit in to the larger Classic period social dynamics in the Safford and Aravaipa areas, I collected obsidian flakes, nodules, and tools at all of the sites in the study area where they appeared, and I submitted a representative sample of 197 pieces of obsidian for X-ray fluorescence (XRF) analysis to M. Stephen Shackley at the University of California at Berkeley (Table 5.1). Of the 197 samples submitted, five were either too small for analysis or were not obsidian, and were not analyzed. Table 5.2 summarizes the raw material source for each sample analyzed. The vast majority of obsidian collected from sites in the Safford and Aravaipa areas came from local sources, including the Blue or San Francisco rivers, Cow Canyon, and Mule Creek, which can be found in the Quaternary alluvium of the Gila River in the Safford Basin (Fig. 5.1; Shackley 2005b). Nodules from Cow Canyon have been found in the Gila River floodplain in the Safford Basin as far west as Geronimo (Shackley 2002). These sources account for 99 percent of all obsidian collected at Safford and Aravaipa area sites for this project, which mirrors the results of obsidian XRF analyses at other projects in the area (Shackley 2002). This prevalence of local obsidian suggests that the Classic period inhabitants of these areas engaged in very little exchange with groups outside the immediate area and instead procured obsidian directly (Shackley 2005b).

Table 5.1. Total Obsidian Collected and Sampled

Site	Total obsidian collected	Total obsidian sampled
Pentagon Site	2	2
P Ranch Canyon Site	2	2
Murphy Site (CC:1:52)	11	8
Earven Flat Site	34	28
Lippencott South Site	1	1
Owens-Colvin Site	2	2
Cluff Ranch Site	1	1
Richardson Orchard Site	1	1
Murphy Site (CC:2:103)	1	1
Crary Site	16	9
Sharon Site	3	3
Fort Grant Silo Site	2	2
Yuma Wash Site	2	1
AZ CC:2:23 (BLM)	1	1
Wes Jernigan Site	1	1
Rattlesnake Mesa Site	1	0
AZ CC:2:185 (ASM)	2	2
Crescent Ruin	37	28
Fort Grant Pueblo	50	37
Spear Ranch Site	4	2
Fischer Site	8	8
AZ CC:1:3 (ASM)	3	3
Dewester Site	1	1
Eagle Pass Site	1	1
Haby Pueblo	16	15
Wooten-Claridge Terrace Site	2	1
AZ BB:3:22 (ASM)	1	1
Lippincott North Site	1	1
AZ CC:2:69 (ASM)	22	13
Buena Vista Ruin	26	21
Total	255	197

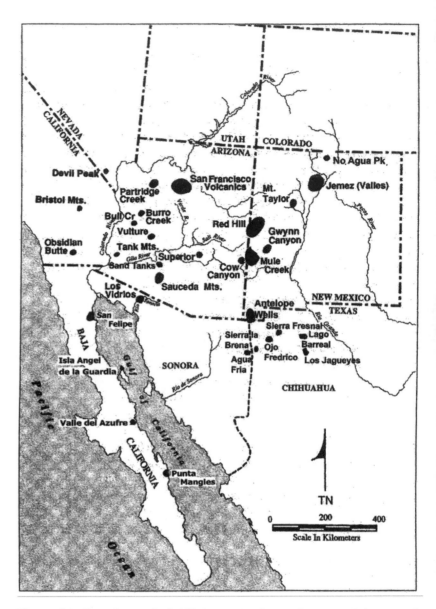

Figure 5.1. Locations of obsidian sources in southeastern Arizona and southwestern New Mexico. Map courtesy of M. Stephen Shackley (2005).

It is unclear, however, if this obsidian was collected out of the Gila River alluvium in the immediate local area or if it was procured from the primary sources near the Arizona-New Mexico border. Furthermore, there is no clear pattern suggesting that any of the local (or nonlocal) sources were used preferentially through time.

Assessing the data by phase does not distinguish any patterning, although it does make it clear that Cow Canyon and Mule Creek (Antelope Creek-Mule Mountains) were the most utilized sources through

time (Table 5.3). When viewing the data divided by sites occupied before and after migration, however, it becomes clear that obsidian was more prevalent at sites dating to the Goat Hill or Middle Classic (A.D.1275/1300–1325) and Safford or Fort Grant phases (A.D.1325–1450), even when taking the number of sites represented in each time period into account (Table 5.4). Table 5.2 shows that most sites where more than 10 pieces of obsidian were collected dated to the late Classic period (A.D.1275/1300–1450). Nonetheless, Cow Canyon and Mule Creek (Antelope

Table 5.2. Locations of Obsidian Sources by Site

Site	Blue/SF River	Cow Canyon	Probably Cow Canyon	Mule Creek AC/MM	Mule Creek N Sawmill Cr.	Sauceda Mountains	Superior	Total
Pentagon Site		2						2
P Ranch Canyon Site					1			1
Murphy Site (CC:1:52)	1	2	1	4				8
Earven Flat Site		11	3	12	1	1		28
Lippencott South Site		1						1
Owens-Colvin Site		1	1					2
Cluff Ranch Site				1				1
Richardson Orchard Site		1						1
Murphy Site (CC:2:103)				1				1
Crary Site	2	1	1	4			1	9
Sharon Site			1	2				3
Fort Grant Silo Site				2				2
Yuma Wash Site		1						1
AZ CC:2:23 (BLM)		1						1
Wes Jernigan Site		1						1
AZ CC:2:185 (ASM)				2				2
Crescent Ruin		6	1	20	1			28
Fort Grant Pueblo	5	4	1	25		1		36
Spear Ranch Pueblo				1				1
Fischer Site		2	1	4	1			8
AZ CC:1:3 (ASM)			1	1	1			3
Dewester Site				1				1
Eagle Pass Site			1					1
Haby Pueblo	2	2	1	9				14
Wooten-Claridge Terrace Site				1				1
AZ BB:3:22 (ASM)				1				1
Lippincott North Site		1						1
AZ CC:2:69 (ASM)		1	1	11				13
Buena Vista Site	1	6		11	2			20
Total	11	44	14	113	7	2	1	192

NOTE: Pearson chi-square = 158.632; df = 168; p = 0.686.
Results are suspect due to number of cells with a frequency less than five.

Table 5.3. Locations of Obsidian Sources by Dominant Phase

Dominant Phase	Blue/SF River	Cow Canyon	Probably Cow Canyon	Mule Creek AC/MM	Mule Creek N Sawmill Cr.	Sauceda Mountains	Superior	Total
Eden (3 sites)	1	4	1	4	1			11
Eden/Bylas (2 sites)		12	3	12	1	1		29
Bylas (5 sites)	2	3	2	6			1	14
Bylas/Goat Hill (1 site)			1	2				3
Goat Hill or Middle Classic (5 sites)		3		4				7
Safford or Fort Grant (13 sites)	8	22	7	85	5	1		128
Total	11	44	14	113	7	2	1	192

NOTE: Pearson chi-square = 39.379; df = 30; p = 0.117.
Results are suspect due to number of cells with a frequency less than five.

Table 5.4. Locations of Obsidian Sources Before or After Migration

Before or After Migration	Blue/SF River	Cow Canyon	Probably Cow Canyon	Mule Creek AC/MM	Mule Creek N Sawmill Cr.	Sauceda Mountains	Superior	Total
Before (10 sites)	3	19	6	22	2	1	1	54
Transitional (1 site)			1	2				3
After (18 sites)	8	25	7	89	5	1		135
Total	11	44	14	113	7	2	1	192

NOTE: Pearson chi-square = 17.594; df = 12; p = 0.129.
   Results are suspect due to number of cells with a frequency less than five.

Table 5.5. Locations of Obsidian Sources at Sites With and Without Perforated Plates

Sites With and Without Perforated Plates	Blue/SF River	Cow Canyon	Probably Cow Canyon	Mule Creek AC/MM	Mule Creek N Sawmill Cr.	Sauceda Mountains	Superior	Total
Without (23 sites)	3	26	11	46	4	1	1	92
With (6 sites)	8	18	3	67	3	1		100
Total	11	44	14	113	7	2	1	192

NOTE: Pearson chi-square = 13.034; df = 6; p = 0.043.
   Results are suspect due to number of cells with a frequency less than five.

Creek-Mule Mountains) remain the most prevalent raw material sources through time.

When the data are divided between sites with and without perforated plates, however, a provisional pattern does emerge (Table 5.5). Sites with perforated plates have more obsidian from the Mule Creek sources, whereas sites without perforated plates have more obsidian from the Cow Canyon source (including those artifacts that were sourced as likely being from Cow Canyon as well). It is unclear if this pattern is statistically significant when a Chi-square test is performed due to the high number of cells with a frequency of fewer than five. The pattern does suggest, however, that populations in the Safford and Aravaipa valleys present before the arrival of Kayenta and Tusayan migrants and those who did not live with these migrants may have preferred different sources of local obsidian or had different social networks of exchange to obtain obsidian than did migrants and the indigenous groups with whom they lived.

Three artifacts submitted for analysis are of particular interest. Two, from the Earven Flat Site and Fort Grant Pueblo, are from the Sauceda Mountains, a source widely used by Hohokam groups in the western Sonoran Desert southwest of the Phoenix Basin and west of the Tucson Basin. The presence of two artifacts from this source points to at least limited ties between inhabitants of the Safford and Aravaipa valleys and the nexus of the Hohokam culture area in the Phoenix Basin. Evidence of such ties is not surprising at the Earven Flat Site, which dates to the Eden and Bylas phase transition when Hohokam influence was relatively strong in the Safford area. The artifact found at Fort Grant Pueblo may have been curated from earlier occupations in the vicinity that show strong ties to the Hohokam core, and susequently reused. Another artifact from the Crary Site is from the Superior Picketpost Mountain source, also to the west. Although this source is closer to the Safford Basin, it also implies a relationship was maintained between the Safford Basin and the Globe-Superior area during the Bylas phase (A.D.1200–1275/1300; Shackley 2005b).

Evidence from obsidian sourcing analyses demonstrates that it is unlikely that Safford and Aravaipa valley Classic period populations engaged in long distance exchange to procure their obsidian. Instead, most obsidian was directly obtained from sources close by at the Arizona-New Mexico border or may have been obtained locally in alluvium along the Gila River. Obsidian use became more frequent during and after the arrival of Kayenta and Tusayan migrants (the

Goat Hill or Middle Classic and Safford or Fort Grant phases, A.D.1275/1300–1450). Because only one percent of the obsidian sampled came from sources far enough away that those items may have been brought into the region through exchange, it is clear that exchange did not play a large role in the procurement of obsidian.

CERAMIC COMPOSITIONAL ANALYSES

I conducted two types of compositional analyses on decorated ceramics from Safford and Aravaipa valley sites. First, oxidation analyses provided baseline data on the paste composition of various decorated wares. I used the results of this analysis to help choose a sample for petrographic analyses to get at a better understanding of ceramic composition and what it can tell us about the inhabitants of the Safford and Aravaipa valleys and their relationships to the surrounding regions.

Oxidation Analyses

Oxidation analysis is an expedient method to grossly characterize the chemical composition of the clays used to make ceramics. Specifically, oxidation analysis provides a qualitative measure of the iron content of clays based on the color of vessel paste after refiring and is most useful in geologically heterogeneous areas in which clays with different iron contents were available to potters (Mills and others 1999). Regardless of iron content, the color of ceramic pastes as found in the archaeological record can vary due to differences in firing conditions, firing atmosphere, duration of firing, and clay composition (Bubemyre and Mills 1993), as well as staining, leaching, burning, and carbon deposition from cooking (Shepard 1956). Oxidation analysis is useful as it eliminates the variability contributed by most of these components by maintaining constant firing conditions and emphasizing the variability due to differences in clay composition. Ceramics fired in precontact ceramic production are rarely fully oxidized because of low firing temperatures, and thus the color of the completely oxidized iron cannot be observed until the pottery is refired in an oxidizing atmosphere to at least 950° C (Rice 1987). Oxidation analysis can provide a general understanding of whether ceramics were made with clays from similar or different sources and, if geological clays are available for comparison, whether the ceramics could have been produced locally or not. In this study, oxidation analysis was a cost effective way to obtain a general picture of ceramic composition that could be enhanced later with more refined techniques.

I selected 117 sherds for oxidation analysis from sites in Lefthand Canyon, south of Pima, Arizona (Table 5.6). These settlements spanned a wide time range, from the Eden to the Safford phases (A.D.1100–1450) and were occupied early on by indigenous groups and later by both migrant and indigenous groups. Although these settlements were located in close proximity to one another and their inhabitants may have chosen to use clays from sources with similar geologic compositions, this sample provides an important preliminary study of ceramic composition that helps to refine research questions for further compositional analyses (see Petrography discussion below). Unfortunately, no sampling of geological clays has taken place in the Safford Basin to date, and therefore the archaeological samples cannot be meaningfully compared to the universe of useable clays that exists in the region.

Oxidation analysis methods for the analysis presented here follow those presented in Bubemyer and Mills (1993). First, the sample of 117 sherds chosen maximized the number of decorated wares represented and provided a comparison of wares among sites (Table 5.6). A small piece of each sherd was removed, and the two parts were each labeled with a unique number. The larger piece served as a control and the smaller piece was placed in a kiln for refiring for 30 minutes at 950° C, which is above the firing temperature for most precontact ceramic vessels. After refiring, I recorded the Munsell color of the paste of each refired sherd and of its complimentary control sherd under consistent lighting conditions. Munsell colors were then assigned to a general color category (such as red, orange, brown) to aid in the comparison of the data (Table 5.7).

Table 5.8 presents the results of these analyses. The paste color of all sherds was variable before refiring. However, refiring reduced the number of colors represented in the paste of each ceramic category. For example, San Simon Series ceramics refired mostly to orange and red and a few refired to brown and pink. No San Simon Series sherds refired to grey, tan, or white. Similarly, all Maverick Mountain Series sherds

Table 5.6. Ceramics Sampled for Oxidation Analysis by Site

Ceramics	Type	Spear Ranch	Krider Kiva	Murphy Site (CC: 1:52)	Crary Site	AZ CC: 1:55	Dewester Site	Total
Cibola White Ware	Snowflake Black-on-white				1			1
	Roosevelt Black-on-white				1			1
	Reserve or Tularosa Black-on-white		1					1
	Indeterminate Cibola White Ware		2		1			3
Maverick Mountain Series	Maverick Mountain Black-on-red	8						8
	Tucson Black-on-red	5						5
Mimbres Black-on-white	Style III					5		5
	Indeterminate Mimbres Black-on-white				2	5		7
Roosevelt Red Ware	Pinto Polychrome	4	1				2	7
	Gila Polychrome	7	9				4	20
	Cliff Polychrome						2	2
	Indeterminate Roosevelt Red Ware						2	2
San Simon Series	Encinas Red-on-brown		2	10		10	10	32
	Indeterminate San Simon Series		2					2
White Mountain Red Ware	Wingate Black-on-red				1			1
	St. Johns Polychrome			1	3			4
	Pinedale or Cedar Creek Polychrome				1			1
	Springerville Polychrome			1				1
	Indeterminate White Mountain Red Ware			4	5			9
Ancestral Zuni Glaze-decorated Ware	Heshotauthla Polychrome			1				1
	Kwakina Polychrome			1				1
	San Carlos Red-on-brown		2		1			3
Total		24	19	18	16	20	20	117

Table 5.7. General Color Categories with Corresponding Munsell Designations

Brown	Grey	Orange	Pink	Red	Tan	White
2.5 YR 3/4	Gley 1 3/2	2.5 YR 5/8	2.5 YR6/4	10 R 3/4	10 YR 7/6	Gley 1 8/N
2.5 YR 3/6	Gley 1 4/2	2.5 YR 6/8	2.5 YR 6/6	10 R 4/4	10 YR 8/4	Gley 2 8/5P
2.5 YR 4/4	Gley 1 5/N	2.5 YR 7/8	2.5 YR 7/4	10 R 4/6	7.5 YR 8/2	
5 YR 4/3	Gley 1 7/N	5 YR 5/8	2.5 YR 7/6	10 R 4/8	7.5 YR 8/3	
5 YR 4/6	Gley 2/5PB	5 YR 6/6	2.5 YR 8/4	10 R 5/6	7.5 YR 8/4	
5 YR 5/2	Gley 2 6/5P	5 YR 6/8	5 YR 7/1	10 R 5/8	7.5 YR 8/6	
5 YR 5/3	Gley 2 6/10	5 YR 7/6	5 YR 7/2	2.5 YR 4/6		
5 YR 5/4	Gley 2 7/5P	5 YR 7/8	5 YR 7/4	2.5 YR 4/8		
5 YR 5/6	Gley 2 7/10		5 YR 8/1	2.5 YR 5/6		
5 YR 6/4	10 YR 7/1		5 YR 8/2			
7.5 YR 4/4	10 R 4/1		5 YR 8/3			
7.5 YR 5/4	10 R 3/1		5 YR 8/4			
7.5 YR 6/2	5 YR 4/1		5 YR 8/7			
7.5 YR 6/3	5 YR 6/1		10 R 6/4			
7.5 YR 6/4	7.5 YR 4/1		10 R 6/8			
7.5 YR 6/6	5 YR 8/1		10 R 7/4			
7.5 YR 7/1	10 R 8/2		10 R 8/2			
7.5 YR 7/3	10 R 4/4					
7.5 YR 7/4	10 R 4/6					
10 YR 5/2	10 R 4/8					

Table 5.8. Results of Oxidation Analyses

Ceramics	Brown N	Brown %	Gray N	Gray %	Orange N	Orange %	Pink N	Pink %	Red N	Red %	Tan N	Tan %	White N	White %	Total N
Paste color before refiring															
Cibola White Ware	1	16.67					2	33.33					3	50.00	6
Maverick Mountain Series	2	15.38	2	15.38			2	15.38	7	53.84					13
Mimbres Black-on-white	1	8.33	9	75.00					1	8.33	1	8.33			12
Roosevelt Red Ware	11	35.48	5	16.13			2	6.45	13	41.93					31
San Carlos Red-on-brown	1	33.33					1	33.33	1	33.33					3
San Simon Series	16	47.06	1	2.94	4	11.76	9	26.47	4	11.76					34
White Mountain Red Ware	3	18.75	3	18.75			6	37.50			3	18.75	1	6.25	16
Ancestral Zuni Glaze-decorated Ware							1	50.00			1	50.00			2
Total	35	29.91	20	17.09	4	3.42	23	19.66	26	22.22	5	4.27	4	3.42	117
Paste color after refiring															
Cibola White Ware							2	33.33			3	50.00	1	16.67	10
Maverick Mountain Series							1	7.69	12	92.31					13
Mimbres Black-on-white	2	16.67			7	58.33	1	8.33	2	16.67					12
Roosevelt Red Ware							2	6.45	28	90.32	1	3.23			31
San Carlos Red-on-brown					1	33.33			2	66.67					3
San Simon Series	4	11.76			16	47.06	3	8.82	11	32.35					34
White Mountain Red Ware					5	31.25	4	25.00	1	6.25	6	37.50			16
Ancestral Zuni Glaze-decorated Ware					1	50.00	1	50.00							2
Total	6	5.13			30	25.64	14	11.96	56	47.86	10	8.55	1	0.85	117

refired to pink and red. Although not all sherds from the same categories refired to the same color, there are clear color groupings for each category, indicating that manufacturers of these items chose clay sources with similar geological properties. It is not possible with these data to determine whether producers chose the exact same source or whether all the sources in the local area of production had similar geological properties.

Several archaeologists have speculated that San Simon Series, San Carlos Red-on-brown, Roosevelt Red Ware, and Maverick Mountain Series ceramics were all locally produced in the Safford Valley (Brown 1973; Lyons 2004; Woodson 1995). There has been further speculation that San Simon Series and San Carlos Red-on-brown pottery was manufactured by groups indigenous to the area, whereas Roosevelt Red Ware and Maverick Mountain Series ceramics were manufactured by Kayenta and Tusayan migrants who moved into the area beginning in the late thirteenth century (Lyons 2004). If this were the case, differences may be apparent in the clay chosen

to produce these ceramics considering the geological heterogeneity present in the Safford and Aravaipa valleys (Wilson and Moore 1958). San Simon Series and San Carlos Red-on-brown vessels may have been manufactured from the same clays, as most of these sherds refired to orange or red, with only a few San Simon Series refiring to brown or pink. Roosevelt Red Ware and Maverick Mountain Series sherds also showed close similarities in their refired color, both being dominated by red and pink, with only one Roosevelt Red Ware sherd refiring to tan. Clearly, there is a good chance that Roosevelt Red Wares and Maverick Mountain Series ceramics were manufactured with the same raw clay source. Furthermore, vessels from these four categories all could have been manufactured from local sources, given the preponderance of sherds in all four that refired to a red color.

The similarity in the clays used for these four categories became particularly apparent when comparing them to the clays used for ceramics that likely were not produced locally, including Mimbres Black-on-white, Cibola White Ware, and White Mountain Red

Ware. Half of the Cibola White Ware and a third of the White Mountain Red Ware sherds refired to a tan color; the rest of the Cibola White Ware refired white and pink, and the rest of the White Mountain Red Ware refired orange, pink, and red. Although there is definitely some overlap in the refired color of purportedly local and nonlocal ceramics, the overall trends suggest that there are differences in the iron content of the clays used to produce San Simon Series, San Carlos Red-on-brown, Roosevelt Red Ware, and Maverick Mountain Series ceramics versus the clays used to produce Cibola White Ware and White Mountain Red Ware. This information supports the assumption that Cibola White Ware and White Mountain Red Ware were brought into the Safford and Aravaipa valleys through exchange.

The refired color of Mimbres Black-on-white sherds is more difficult to interpret, however. Most of the Mimbres Black-on-white sherds refired to orange or brown, which is clearly different from Cibola White Ware and White Mountain Red Ware, the other supposedly nonlocal wares present in the sample. This observation is not surprising, because Cibola White Ware and White Mountain Red Ware vessels were most likely manufactured in east-central Arizona and west-central New Mexico, whereas Mimbres Black-on-white vessels were most likely manufactured in the Mimbres area of southwestern New Mexico. The clays used to produce Mimbres Black-on-white vessels instead appear to be most similar to clays used to produce San Simon Series vessels, many of which also refired to brown and orange. These similarities do not necessarily indicate that Mimbres Black-on-white vessels were produced locally in the Safford Basin, rather the similarities seen here may be the result of geological homogeneity between the Safford and Aravaipa valleys and the Mimbres region to the east. Clearly, more detailed compositional analyses must be conducted to answer this question.

Obviously many of these results are not conclusive, but they do suggest that the ceramics thought to be locally produced were in fact locally produced, and vice versa. The most intriguing result is the ambiguity of the source of the clays used to produce Mimbres Black-on-white vessels. The possibility of a Mimbres migration from southwestern New Mexico to southeastern Arizona at the end of the Mimbres Classic period (A.D. 1150) has been suggested by John Smith (2005), but little research has been conducted to evaluate whether such a migration may have occurred (but see Nelson 1999 for a perspective from the Mimbres region). Production of Mimbres Black-on-white Style III vessels has been documented outside the Mimbres "heartland," but not as far west as the Safford and Aravaipa valleys (Gilman and others 1994). If the Mimbres Black-on-white ceramics found at sites in Lefthand Canyon were in fact produced with local clays, it is important that further research be conducted to examine whether migration, which may have been occurring over many centuries (the entire Mimbres ceramic sequence is present in the Safford Valley), could account for local production of these "nonlocal" wares.

Petrographic Analyses

Significant research has been conducted on the petrographic characterization of sands used to temper precontact ceramics in the Southwest (Abbott 2000; Abbott and Walsh-Anduze 1995; Habicht-Mauche 1995; Heidke 2004; Heidke and Miksa 2000; Heidke and others 2002; Judd 1954; Miksa and Heidke 1995; Stinson 1996). These studies have demonstrated that with the construction of petrographic models of specific geologically circumscribed areas, the source of the sand temper used in many ceramics throughout the Southwest can be identified with high accuracy at relatively low cost (Heidke 2004). The petrographic models I used here are part of a larger effort to accurately model the petrography of much of southern Arizona, led by geologists and archaeologists at Desert Archaeology, Inc. (Heidke 2004; Heidke and Miksa 2000; Heidke and Stark 1995; Miksa and Heidke 1995). Archaeologists have used these models to explore patterns of ceramic production and exchange throughout much of this region, now including the Safford and Aravaipa valleys.

As previous petrographic research has established, to determine the provenance of sands used in sand tempered ceramics it is imperative that the available universe of sands in the region is known and mineralogically characterized (Heidke 2004). Ceramics made with locally available sands are interpreted to have been locally manufactured, as ethnographic evidence has demonstrated that most potters travel less than 1 km (0.6 mile) to obtain tempering materials (Arnold 1985; Miksa and Heidke 1995). Conversely, ceramics made with nonlocally available sands, here termed extrabasinal, are interpreted to have been produced nonlocally and were more likely imported through exchange as finished products (Shepard 1956: 339). Thus, petrographic analyses characterizing the mineralogical content of sands used for tempering can provide important information on ceramic production and the exchange relationship between inhabitants of neighboring areas throughout much of the Southwest. Characterizing the "localness" of decorated ceramics at Safford and Aravaipa valley sites helps to determine whether the variety seen in the decorated ceramic assemblage is the result of exchange or is a reflection of the diversity of the inhabitants of these settlements.

The petrographic analyses described here were carried out by analysts Elizabeth Miksa and Carlos Lavayen, with help from intern Sam Duwe at Desert Archaeology in Tucson, Arizona. First, 85 samples of sands were collected from numerous washes throughout the Safford and Aravaipa valleys. Washes located in close proximity to Classic period settlements were targeted for sampling under the assumption that they would have served as likely temper sources for the nearby inhabitants. The characteristics of the sampling locations were recorded in the field, and sand samples were brought back to the lab in Tucson for further processing and sorting. Records of sand samples are available at Desert Archaeology. The sampling and sorting process is described in Miksa and Heidke (1995). From the sorted sands, an "actualistic petrofacies model" was built for the Safford and Aravaipa valleys (see Hiedke 2004: 85 for a flow chart describing the process). This technique differs from the key grain approach sometimes used by petrographers, in that the actualistic petrofacies model more accurately characterizes the quantities of specific minerals in each sample, whereas the key grain approach records their presence or absence. The actualistic petrofacies model provides a clearer region-wide picture and can differentiate more accurately among samples that may appear geologically homogenous in the key grain approach (Heidke 2004). Accuracy in other studies using an actualistic petrofacies model has been demonstrated to be greater than 93 percent (Heidke 2004; Heidke and Miksa 2000).

The model constructed for the Safford and Aravaipa valleys identified 17 distinct petrofacies, 8 in the Safford and San Simon valleys, and 9 along the Aravaipa Creek and Sulphur Springs Valley to the east (Fig. 5.2). A sample of 273 sherds from 34 Safford and Aravaipa area sites were submitted for analysis (Table 5.9) in order to compare the sands used in their temper to those available in the area. The sample targeted decorated and undecorated ceramics of interest (those associated with both migrant and local groups) and was chosen to maximize the number of sites represented in the sample. Sherds submitted for analysis were from collections made for this research, survey collections made by Gila Pueblo and now housed at the Arizona State Museum, and collections from the Coronado National Forest Office of the United States Forest Service. I augmented the sample by these existing collections to maximize sample diversity within sites and to include samples from as many Safford and Aravaipa valley sites as possible. Ceramics were examined under a binocular microscope. Their temper was identified as belonging to one or a group of the 17 petrofacies present in the Safford and Aravaipa valleys, as consisting of nonlocal, extrabasinal sands, or as consisting of sands that were not identifiable.

Table 5.9 summarizes the number of sherds submitted from each site and the local petrofacies available at each site. Out of the 273 samples submitted, 109 were assigned to specific local petrofacies (Table 5.10). Of the remaining 164 samples, 152 were assigned to a group of local petrofacies (such as A or B), 9 were found to have extrabasinal sands used as temper, and the source of the sands used for temper could not be identified in 3 sherds (Table 5.11). Clearly, these data show an overwhelming trend toward local Safford and Aravaipa valley production of all ceramics sampled, with less than five percent of the submitted sample showing extrabasinal or unknown sands used as temper. Although some of the samples were small, such as that for perforated plates and Safford Variety Middle Gila Buff Ware, data for both specific and general temper sources suggest substantial local production of all ceramics sampled.

Table 5.10 further demonstrates that local production was concentrated in a select few petrofacies: A and B in the Safford Valley and Hb in the Aravaipa Valley. In the Safford Valley, many Classic period settlements were concentrated in these two petrofacies (Fig. 5.2). In fact, 74 percent of the sites with sherds sampled for petrographic analysis in the Safford Valley are located within the boundaries of petrofacies A and B, suggesting that many of the ceramics made

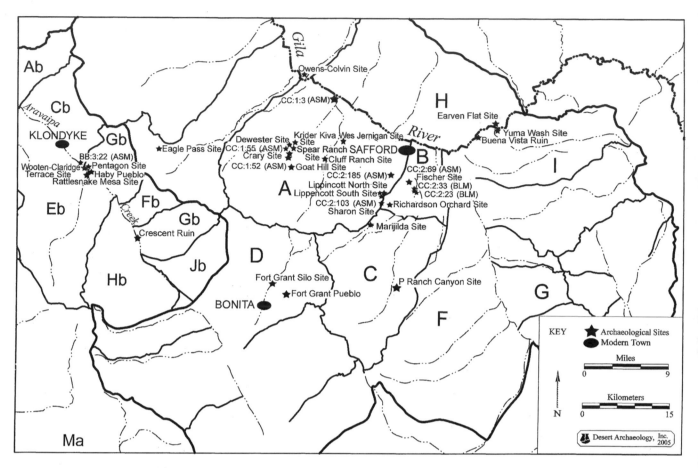

Figure 5.2. Locations of petrofacies in the Safford and Aravaipa valleys.

within these petrofacies were also utilized at settlements located within these petrofacies.

When the results are viewed by petrofacies, some interesting patterns suggesting local exchange among people using Safford Valley petrofacies emerge. It appears that the exchange of finished vessels may have occurred regularly among people using petrofacies A and B. Sherds from several vessels manufactured with sands from petrofacies B were found at sites within the boundaries of petrofacies A, such as a perforated plate and three Roosevelt Red Ware vessels at the Dewester Site. Vessels manufactured with sands from petrofacies A were found at sites within the boundaries of petrofacies B, such as Maverick Mountain Series vessels found at the Fischer Site and at site AZ CC:2:23 BLM (Tables 5.12–5.17).

Only three vessels (out of the 273 sampled) were definitively produced with sands from petrofacies C or D and then exchanged to settlements in other petrofacies (Tables 5.12, 5.14), and there is no evidence of

definitive production with sands from petrofacies H and I. Thus, ceramic production for local exchange appears to have been a significantly smaller part of the economy at settlements located in petrofacies C, D, H, and I, at least among the wares sampled here. This result is particularly interesting in light of the fact that Buena Vista Ruin appears to have been the largest and one of the latest, if not the latest, occupied settlements in the valley, and no definitive evidence for local ceramic production appeared in the sherds sampled from this site. Only five sherds could have been from vessels manufactured with sands from the petrofacies surrounding Buena Vista Ruin, and it is possible those were produced with sands from neighboring petrofacies G or H instead (Tables 5.16, 5.17).

The upper matrix in Figure 5.3 further summarizes how ceramics moved among Safford Valley settlements. Exchange was most prevalent among settlements in petrofacies A and B. Vessels manufactured with sands from petrofacies A were also found in set-

Table 5.9. Ceramics Sampled for Petrographic Analysis by Site and Petrofacies

Site	Petrofacies	Maverick Mountain Series	Safford Variety Middle Gila Buff Ware	Mimbres Black-on-white	Roosevelt Red Ware	San Carlos Red-on-brown	Perforated Plates	Total
Pentagon Site	Gb		1	1				2
P Ranch Site	C			5				5
AZ CC:1:55 (ASM)	A			2				2
Earven Flat Site	H		5	5				10
Owens-Colvin Site	Undefined		4			7		11
Cluff Ranch Site	A			1		2		3
Richardson Orchard Site	B	1	1	6				8
Murphy Site (CC:2:103)	A					9		9
Crary Site	A					1		1
Sharon Site	A		1			4		5
Fort Grant Silo Site	D		1					1
Yuma Wash Site	I	2						2
AZ CC:2:23 (BLM)	B	3						3
AZ CC:2:33 (BLM)	B	2						2
Goat Hill Site	A						1	1
Wes Jernigan Site	A					1		1
Rattlesnake Mesa Site	Eb	1			6			7
AZ CC:2:185 (ASM)	A					1		1
Crescent Ruin	Hb	1			36		2	39
Fort Grant Pueblo	D	4			44			48
Spear Ranch Site	A	4			11		2	17
Fischer Site	B	2			8	2		12
AZ CC:1:3 (ASM)	A					1		1
Dewester Site	A			3	4		3	10
Haby Pueblo	Eb				15		2	17
Wooten-Claridge Terrace Site	Gb				3			3
AZ BB:3:22 (ASM)	Cb	1		1	8	1		11
Krider Kiva Site	A				5		2	7
Marijilda Site	C	3			3			6
AZ CC:2:69 (ASM)	B	1			3	1		5
Buena Vista Ruin	I	6	2	2	8			18
Buena Vista Ruin (Gila Pueblo collection)	I	2						2
AZ L:1:15 (GP)*	Unknown				1			1
AZ L:6:2 (GP)*	Unknown				1			1
AZ L:6:4 (GP)*	Unknown						1	1
Total		33	15	26	156	30	13	273

*Temporal placement of these sites is unknown, but they likely date after A.D. 1275–1300, the Goat Hill phase.

tlements in petrofacies H, I, as well as the undefined petrofacies containing the Owens-Colvin Site, and vessels manufactured with sands from petrofacies B appeared in settlements in petrofacies C, I, and the undefined petrofacies containing the Owens-Colvin Site. Figure 5.3 (*bottom*) demonstrates that some vessels from every category analyzed were exchanged between production and final discard locations.

In the Aravaipa Valley, the pattern of local manufacture and exchange is different. The vast majority of pottery, particularly Roosevelt Red Ware, was produced in the Hb petrofacies. Only one Classic period site was recorded in this petrofacies (Crescent Ruin); however current evidence suggests it may have been the sole Classic period settlement in the area (but see Hartmann and Lee 2003 for a discussion of the Eureka Springs Ranch House Site, which may also be located in the Hb petrofacies). Furthermore, Roosevelt Red Ware ceramics tempered with sands from the Hb petrofacies were found approximately 25 km (15

Production petrofacies		Provenience (Recovery) Petrofacies: A	B	C	H	I	undefined
	A	Cluff Ranch Site AZ CC:1:3 (ASM) Spear Ranch Site Goat Hill Site Wes Jernigan Site Krider Kiva Site Sharon Site Murphy Site (CC:2:103) AZ CC:2:185(ASM)	AZ CC:2:23 (BLM) AZ CC:2:69 (ASM) Fischer Site Richardson Orchard Site		Earven Flat Site	Buena Vista Ruin	Owens-Colvin Site
	B	Cluff Ranch Site Krider Kiva Site Dewester Site Murphy Site (CC:2:103)	Fischer Site Richardson Orchard Site	Marijilda Site P Ranch Canyon Site		Buena Vista Ruin	Owens-Colvin Site
	C	Spear Ranch Site		Marijilda Site			
	D	Krider Kiva Site		Marijilda Site			

Shaded cells indicate where sherds were produced and found in the same petrofacies.

Production Petrofacies		Provenience (Recovery) Petrofacies: A	B	C	H	I	undefined
	A	• Perforated plates • Roosevelt Red Ware • San Carlos Red-on-brown	• Maverick Mountain Series • Middle Gila Buff Ware, Safford Variety • Mimbres Black-on-white • Roosevelt Red Ware		• Middle Gila Buff Ware, Safford Variety • Mimbres Black-on-white	• Maverick Mountain Series • Middle Gila Buff Ware, Safford Variety • Mimbres Black-on-white • Roosevelt Red Ware	• San Carlos Red-on-brown
	B	• Mimbres Black-on-white • Perforated plates • Roosevelt Red Ware • San Carlos Red-on-brown	• Mimbres Black-on-white • Roosevelt Red Ware	• Mimbres Black-on-white • Roosevelt Red Ware		• Mimbres Black-on-white	• San Carlos Red-on-brown
	C	• Perforated plates		• Maverick Mountain Series			
	D	• Perforated plates		• Roosevelt Red Ware			

Shaded cells indicate where sherds were produced and found in the same petrofacies.

Figure 5.3. Ceramic production and provenience matrices by site and ceramic category, Safford Valley.

Table 5.10. Temper Source, Specific (TSS) Summary of Analyzed Sherds

Temper Source, Specific	Maverick Mountain Series	Safford Variety Middle Gila Buff Ware	Mimbres Black-on-white	Roosevelt Red Ware	San Carlos Red-on-brown	Perforated Plates	Total
A	5	6	3	11	12	1	38
B		1	6	7	2	1	17
C	3					1	4
D				1		1	2
Cb				4			4
Gb				2			2
Hb				34		2	36
Jb				6			6
Total	8	7	9	65	14	6	109

Table 5.11. Unknown Temper Source, Specific (TSS) Summary of Analyzed Sherds

Temper Source, Specific	Maverick Mountain Series	Safford Variety Middle Gila Buff Ware	Mimbres Black-on-white	Roosevelt Red Ware	San Carlos Red-on-brown	Perforated Plates	Total
A, B, C, or D	14	2 (1 A?)	16 (4 B?, 3 A? 2 A or B?	14 (5 A?, 3 B?)	14 (5 A?, 3 B?, 1 A or B?)	2 (2 A?)	62
B or D		1		4		1	6
B or C	1			3		2 (1 C?)	6
E or F		1	1	1			3
G, H, or I		2 (2 H?)			1		3
G or I		2					2
Ab, Eb, Fb, or Hb				3 (1 Hb?)		1	4
Eb or Hb	3			23 (9 Hb?, 2 Eb?)			26
Cb, Gb, or Jb	1			22 (6 Jb?, 3 Cb?)			23
Gb or Jb	2			14 (8 Jb?)			16
Ea, Ba, or Ga (San Pedro)						1	1
Extrabasinal (mineralic)	4			3			7
Extrabasinal (mixed)				2			2
Unknown				2	1		3
Total	25	8	17	91	16	7	164

NOTE: Information in parentheses indicates the petrographer's inclination about the petrofacies source of some samples that could not be definitively assigned to a specific petrofacies.

miles) to the northwest in the settlement cluster around the modern town of Klondyke, and approximately 32 km (20 miles) to the southeast in the settlement cluster around the town of Bonita and the Fort Grant Prison complex (Table 5.14, Fig. 5.2). No ceramics definitively produced with sands from the petrofacies of the Klondyke (Cb, Eb, and Gb) and Fort Grant area (D) were found at the Crescent Ruin, the only site sampled in the Hb petrofacies. Thus, it appears that the inhabitants of the Crescent Ruin exported ceramics to many other contemporaneous settlements in the valley, and that many of the ceramic vessels used by Classic period inhabitants at settlements in the Aravaipa valley were not locally produced at those settlements but instead were obtained through exchange within the valley.

When looking at the data on a site level for the Aravaipa valley, some further interesting patterns

Table 5.12. Perforated Plate Petrofacies Summary

Site	Local Petrofacies	Hb	Ab, Eb, Fb, or Hb	A	B	C	D	A, B, C, or D	B or D	B or C	Extrabasinal
Haby Pueblo	Eb		1								(San Pedro) 1
Crescent Ruin	Hb	2									
Spear Ranch Site	A					1		1			
Goat Hill Site	A			1							
Krider Kiva Site	A						1		1		
Dewester Site	A				1					2	
Total		2	1	1	1	1	1	1	1	2	1

Table 5.13. Maverick Mountain Series Petrofacies Summary

Site	Local Petrofacies	Cb, Gb or Hb	Gb or Jb	Eb or Hb	A	C	A, B, C, or D	B or C	Extrabasinal
AZ BB:3:22 (ASM)	Cb	1							
Rattlesnake Mesa Site	Eb		1						
Crescent Ruin	Hb			1					
Fort Grant Pueblo	D		1	2					1
Spear Ranch Site	A						4		
AZ CC:2:23 (BLM)	B				2		1		
AZ CC:2:33 (BLM)	B						2		
AZ CC:2:69 (ASM)	B							1	
Fischer Site	B				1		1		
Richardson Orchard Site	B						1		
Marijilda Site	C					3			
Yuma Wash Site	I						2		
Buena Vista Ruin	I				2		3		3
Total		1	2	3	5	3	14	1	4

emerge. Most Roosevelt Red Ware and Maverick Mountain Series ceramics found at Aravaipa Valley sites were made with sands from petrofacies in the Aravaipa Valley (Tables 5.13, 5.14). Many of them were produced with sands from the Hb petrofacies, but still others were produced with sands from the Jb, Gb, Cb, and Eb petrofacies. Production with sands from the Cb, Gb, and Eb petrofacies is not surprising, considering the cluster of four Fort Grant phase sites in the area (Fig. 5.2). Vessels tempered with sands from the Jb petrofacies may have been produced at the 76 Ranch Ruin located between Crescent Ruin and Fort Grant Pueblo along the Aravaipa Creek, which was not sampled during this research. Interestingly, none of the sherds sampled from Fort Grant Pueblo, located in the D petrofacies, appear to be from vessels produced there with local sands. Almost all Maverick

Mountain Series and Roosevelt Red Ware vessels sampled from this site were produced with sands from the Hb, Cb, Jb, and Gb petrofacies, suggesting these vessels were imported from Middle Classic and Fort Grant phase settlements farther downstream along the Aravaipa Creek. This observation applies to both early (Pinto Polychrome) and late (Cliff Polychrome) types, suggesting that importing complete vessels was a pattern that continued throughout the life of the Fort Grant Pueblo occupation.

There is limited evidence for exchange between groups living at settlements along Aravaipa Creek and those in neighboring valleys. All Mimbres Black-on-white, Middle Gila Buff Ware, and San Carlos Red-on-brown vessels sampled from sites along Aravaipa Creek were produced with sands from the Safford area, suggesting these vessels were imported as fin-

Table 5.14. Roosevelt Red Ware Petrofacies Summary

Site	Local Petrofacies	Production Petrofacies							
		Cb	Gb	Hb	Jb	Eb or or Hb	Cb, Gb or Jb	Gb or Jb	Ab, Eb, Fb, or Hb
AZ BB:3:22 (ASM)	Cb			3		3	1		
Rattlesnake Mesa Site	Eb	1		3			2		
Haby Pueblo	Eb			8		4			1
Wooten-Claridge Terrace Site	Gb			2		1			
Crescent Ruin	Hb			12	5	6	6	7	
Fort Grant Pueblo	D	3	2	6	1	9	12	7	2
Total		4	2	34	6	23	21	14	3

Table 5.14. Roosevelt Red Ware Petrofacies Summary (*continued*)

Site	Local Petrofacies	Production Petrofacies								
		A	B	D	A, B, C, or D	B or D	B or C	E or F	Extra-basinal	Unknown
AZ BB:3:22 (ASM)	Cb									
Rattlesnake Mesa Site	Eb									
Haby Pueblo	Eb								1	1
Wooten-Claridge Terrace Site	Gb									
Crescent Ruin	Hb									
Fort Grant Pueblo	D								1	1
Spear Ranch Site	A	4			7					
Krider Kiva Site	A	1	2			2				
Dewester Site	A		3			1				
AZ CC:2:69 (ASM)	B	1			1	1				
Fischer Site	B	2	1		2		2	1		
Marijilda Site	C		1	1			1			
Buena Vista Ruin	I	3			4				1	
Total		11	7	1	14	4	3	1	3	2

ished products (Tables 5.15–5.17). Although the sample of sherds from these wares is small, this trend seems to continue through time, from the earliest sampled settlement in the Aravaipa Valley (the Pentagon Site) to later settlements in the area such as AZ BB:3:22 (ASM). Even though this sample size limits definitive conclusions, it appears these vessels arrived in the Aravaipa Valley through exchange as finished products and the existing population in the Aravaipa Valley was small prior to the arrival of migrants, probably from the Safford Valley, during the Middle Classic and Fort Grant phases (A.D.1275/1300–1450). However, the possibility that these vessels arrived with migrants or that the raw materials were imported cannot be fully ruled out (Shepard 1956: 339; Zedeño 1994: 19). In addition to the Mimbres Black-on-white, Middle Gila Buff Ware, Safford Variety, and San Carlos Red-on-brown ceramics that were imported from the Safford Valley, a perforated plate fragment that was found at Haby Pueblo was tempered with sands from the San Pedro Valley and likely was imported from there (Table 5.12). The evidence from this single sherd is not conclusive, but suggests that contact between Kayenta and Tusayan migrant groups in the Safford and Aravaipa Valleys and Kayenta and Tusayan migrant groups in the San Pedro River valley to the southwest was maintained after episodes of migration and that migration itself may not have been unidirectional.

Although the sample is small, there is evidence for local production of perforated plates and Maverick Mountain Series ceramics (Tables 5.12, 5.13), which are strongly associated with Kayenta and Tusayan migrants. The one perforated plate fragment examined

Table 5.15. Mimbres Black-on-white Petrofacies Summary

Site	Local Petrofacies	Production Petrofacies			
		A	B	A, B, C, or D	E or F
AZ BB:3:22 (ASM)	Cb			1	
Pentagon Site	Gb			1	
Cluff Ranch Site	A		1		
AZ CC:1:55 (ASM)	A			2	
Dewester Site	A			3	
Richardson Orchard Site	B	1	1	4	
P Ranch Canyon Site	C		2	2	1
Earven Flat Site	H	1		4	
Buena Vista Ruin	I	1	1		
Total		3	6	16	1

Table 5.16. Middle Gila Buff Ware, Safford Variety Petrofacies Summary

Site	Local Petrofacies	Production Petrofacies						
		A	B	B or D	A, B, C, or D	E or F	G, H, or I	G or I
Pentagon Site	Gb		1					
Fort Grant Silo Site	D			1				
Sharon Site	A				1			
Richardson Orchard Site	B	1						
Earven Flat Site	H	3			1	1		
Buena Vista Ruin	I	2						
Owens-Colvin Site	Undefined						2	2
Total		6	1	1	2	1	2	2

Table 5.17. San Carlos Red-on-brown Petrofacies Summary

Site	Local Petrofacies	Production Petrofacies				
		A	B	A, B, C, or D	G, H, or I	Unknown
AZ BB:3:22 (ASM)	Cb			1		
Cluff Ranch Site	A	1		1		
AZ CC:1:3 (ASM)	A	1				
Wes Jernigan Site	A	1				
Crary Site	A			1		
Sharon Site	A	2			1	1
Murphy Site (CC:2:103)	A	2	1	6		
AZ CC:2:185 (ASM)	A	1				
AZ CC:2:69 (ASM)	B			1		
Fischer Site	B			2		
Owens-Colvin Site	Undefined	4	1	2		
Total		12	2	14	1	1

from the Goat Hill Site was produced with sands local to this settlement. Perforated plates were also produced in petrofacies B, C, D, and Hb, suggesting some portion of the population in each of these petrofacies was composed of Kayenta and Tusayan migrants who manufactured this nonlocal vessel form with local raw materials (Table 5.12). Maverick Mountain Series ce-

ramics were produced locally in petrofacies A and C in the Safford Valley and in several of the petrofacies along Aravaipa Creek, although the evidence available is not definitive as to specifically which petrofacies (Table 5.13). Although Maverick Mountain Series ceramics are less tightly bound to settlements with migrant populations, the evidence of their production at many locales throughout the Safford and Aravaipa valleys does suggest that Kayenta and Tusayan migrants were present at many of the settlements located throughout these petrofacies.

The pattern of local production of Mimbres Black-on-white pottery in the Safford Valley, suggested by oxidation analyses and confirmed with petrographic analyses, may be evidence of an earlier migration of people from the Mimbres area to the Safford Valley during the Two Dog or Eden phase (A.D.1000–1200; Table 5.15). Although previous research has documented production of Mimbres Black-on-white outside the Mimbres "heartland" (Gilman and others 1994), production of Mimbres Black-on-white vessels has never been documented this far to the west (but see Smith 2005). Since these vessels appear to have been manufactured in the same style as those found in the Mimbres region and do not appear to be imitations of imported vessels by people indigenous to the Safford Valley, their presence implies that people from the Mimbres region migrated into the Safford Valley and continued to make Mimbres pottery using raw materials local to the Safford Valley (Shepard 1956: 339). Additional research must be undertaken to verify this conclusion, but all evidence presented here points toward a Mimbres migration to the Safford Valley during the eleventh or twelfth centuries, and probably earlier.

In sum, little ceramic exchange occurred between residents of the Safford and Aravaipa valleys and people who lived outside this larger region. Instead, the patterns in the petrographic results show that there was some exchange among local communities and exchange between contemporaneous settlements in the two valleys, especially with Mimbres Black-on-white, local varieties of Middle Gila Buff Ware, and San Carlos Red-on-brown pottery. Although the sample of sherds submitted for petrographic analyses was relatively small, the patterns they present are robust and suggest that interaction with people outside the Safford and Aravaipa valleys was limited during the Classic period. This observation is particularly important when examining ceramics associated with Kayenta and Tusayan migrant populations, such as perforated plates and Maverick Mountain Series vessels. The strong evidence for their production in many of the petrofacies in the Safford and Aravaipa valleys indicates that Kayenta and Tusayan migrant populations lived at many settlements in this region and had

a significant influence on ceramic production and distribution during this time.

LOCAL DIVERSITY

Classic period inhabitants of the Safford and Aravaipa valleys had relatively little contact with populations outside their immediate region through exchange of obsidian or decorated ceramics. The results of oxidation and petrographic analyses show that many of the decorated ceramics prevalent at Classic period settlements were manufactured with local raw materials and that various groups of people, including migrants from the Kayenta and Tusayan areas, were present in the Safford and Aravaipa valleys and manufactured diverse types of decorated ceramics with local raw materials. Obsidian sourcing analyses demonstrated that the vast majority of obsidian found at settlements occupied throughout the late Late Formative and Classic periods in the Safford and Aravaipa valleys was procured either locally in nodules found in the Gila River or at sources approximately 80 km (50 miles) to the east. Only 3 of the 197 obsidian samples submitted originated from sources distant enough that they were likely traded into the region. Thus, there is little evidence for exchange or regular interaction with outside populations at any of the sites sampled in the Safford and Aravaipa valleys.

The lack of evidence for widespread and prolonged interaction by the inhabitants of the Safford and Aravaipa valleys with outside groups via exchange indicates that the diversity evident in the ceramics and concurrent shifts in architectural layout and building materials at Classic period sites (Chapters 3 and 4) were instead local developments and that the material culture found at Classic period sites likely reflected the background of the inhabitants of these areas. The Safford Valley, in particular, seems to have been a destination for numerous migrants for several centuries beginning by at least A.D.1050/1100, likely earlier, based on evidence from Mimbres Black-on-white and corrugated ceramics. The material culture of Safford and Aravaipa valley settlements occupied after A.D.1275/1300 (Chapters 3 and 4) shows influences from both Kayenta and Tusayan migrant and indigenous groups. Maverick Mountain Series pottery, Roosevelt Red Ware, perforated plates, and shifts to room block layouts in habitation settlements are characteristics of migrants. Local populations remained part of the cultural mix as shown by the continuing presence of Middle Gila Buff Ware, Safford Variety, San Carlos Red-on-brown, and the use of cobble reinforced adobe architecture. This trend toward local diversity is supported by ceramic sourcing, which indicates that ceramic wares thought to be associated with both local and nonlocal groups were produced throughout the Safford Valley.

This totality of evidence illustrates that migrant and indigenous groups became increasingly spatially and socially integrated through time, as seen in changes in architecture and a shift toward the use of one kind of decorated pottery, Roosevelt Red Ware. Petrographic analyses demonstrated that decorated ceramics were exchanged locally within the Safford and Aravaipa valleys, adding to valley-wide interaction and cohesion. The inhabitants of these settlements formed a new inclusive identity in the late thirteenth century that incorporated elements from each group and reflected their diverse origins.

CHAPTER SIX

The Scale and Effect of Migration in the Safford and Aravaipa Valleys

Migrant and indigenous populations have been identified in the archaeological record in the Safford and Aravaipa valleys of southern Arizona through differences in the technological style of corrugated ceramics and domestic architecture. These two types of material culture demonstrated that diverse social groups were present at many Classic period sites in the area and that some of these groups were probably composed of Kayenta and Tusayan migrants. Based on the decorated ceramics they used and the way they structured the physical spaces they occupied, it is clear that these Kayenta and Tusayan migrant groups were initially segregated, whether by choice or because of deliberate exclusion, from the indigenous population. Shortly thereafter, however, these two groups appear to have lived together at the same settlements, interacting regularly. The exchange of decorated ceramics and obsidian was not widespread during the Classic period, suggesting that the diversity observed in decorated ceramic assemblages was a result of the diversity inherent in Classic period populations, not in their exchange partners. With this evidence it is possible to examine how migration affected the expression of identity by both migrant and indigenous populations before and after the arrival of migrants from the Kayenta and Tusayan areas of northeastern Arizona.

SOCIAL SCALE OF MIGRATION AND MIGRANT ENCLAVES

Previous to this research, archaeologists determined that the Goat Hill Site was occupied from about A.D. 1290 to 1315 by an enclave of Kayenta and Tusayan migrants (Woodson 1995, 1999). Material culture found foremost and present earlier in the Kayenta and Tusayan regions demonstrated the presence of migrants at the Goat Hill Site, including the dominance of Maverick Mountain Series ceramics, the presence of perforated

plates, a D-shaped kiva, entrybox complexes, coursed masonry room block architecture, small rooms comprising room suites, and the defensible location of the room block itself. There was no evidence that any of the occupants were indigenous to the Safford and Aravaipa valleys. Instead, this settlement is a clear example of a site-unit intrusion of people nonnative to the area (Rouse 1958; Wauchope 1956). Furthermore, the number of rooms at the settlement and the short duration of its occupation indicate it was occupied by multiple households. Hence, this particular group of migrants was likely a discrete and coherent social entity organized at the suprahousehold level that existed apart from the local population.

Two other sites in the Safford Valley also appear to have been migrant enclaves. AZ CC:2:23 (BLM), a small site located on top of a large mesa south of the town of Safford, dates to the Goat Hill phase and shares many characteristics of the Goat Hill Site. Although it does not conform to the edges of the mesa and has no restricted access, it is in a defensible location similar to the Goat Hill Site and is one of only a few sites located above the valley floor in the Safford Valley. The decorated ceramic assemblage of site AZ CC:2:23 (BLM) is dominated by Maverick Mountain Series ceramics, and at least some of these vessels were produced within the Safford Valley but curiously not with sands from the petrofacies local to the site. These vessels were likely transported as finished products, either through local exchange, or as the producers themselves moved through the valley and established a settlement at CC:2:23. In general, the decorated ceramic assemblage from this site was small and the overall surface scatter was light, suggesting a short occupation similar to the Goat Hill Site. Although several other decorated wares were represented in the assemblage (Table 6.1), Maverick Mountain Series pottery was by far the most ubiquitous. Additionally, the location, size, and shape of a

Table 6.1. Decorated Ceramic Assemblage from Site AZ CC:2:23 (BLM)

Ceramics	Types	N	% of decorated
Cibola White Ware	Indeterminate Cibola White Ware	1	4.55
Maverick Mountain Series	Maverick Mountain Black-on-red	1	4.55
	Tucson Polychrome	1	4.55
	Indeterminate Maverick Mountain Series	11	50.00
Mimbres Black-on-white	Mimbres Black-on-white Style II/III	1	4.55
	Indeterminate Mimbres Black-on-white	1	4.55
White Mountain Red Ware	Indeterminate White Mountain Red Ware	1	4.55
	Indeterminate White Mountain Red Ware, no paint	1	4.55
	Unidentified red slipped	4	18.18
Total		22	

large circular depression south of the room block indicate a kiva may have been part of this settlement.

Two characteristics of AZ CC:2:23 (BLM) clearly set it apart from the Goat Hill Site. Its small room block (which has been heavily impacted by vandalism) was constructed of cobble reinforced adobe, a local construction technique, rather than masonry. The domestic living space, however, was arranged into a room block instead of a compound or isolated rooms. Although disturbance to the room block has obscured the arrangement of walls within it, the four to six rooms present would have held no more than two households simultaneously (Hill and others 2004; Lowell 1991). Therefore, the migrants living at AZ CC:2:23 (BLM) were likely organized on a household level, differing from the social scale of the group that occupied the Goat Hill Site.

The Marijilda Site, dating to the late Goat Hill and Safford phases (A.D. 1275/1300–1450) was also likely a migrant enclave in the Safford Valley. The strongest indicator of a migrant population at the Marijilda Site is the use of masonry architecture arranged into a compact contiguous room block fully or almost fully enclosing three associated plazas. Rooms here were smaller than average for the Safford and Aravaipa valleys, as was the case at the Goat Hill Site. Current knowledge of the ceramic assemblage from the site is based on private collections from excavated rooms (Brown 1973) and collections made from backdirt from vandalized rooms (William Gillespie, personal communication 2004), but obviously Maverick Mountain Series ceramics were common. Some of the Maverick Mountain Series sherds found at the Marijilda

Site were produced with sands from the local petrofacies and were thus likely produced by the inhabitants of Marijilda. No perforated plates have yet been found at the Marijilda Site. Brown (1973) recorded slab lined hearths, which also appear to be associated with Puebloan migrant populations, in three of the vandalized rooms he recorded. Current evidence provides no indication of a kiva, but no professional excavations have been carried out in any of the 40 or more rooms or the 3 plazas, one or more of which may have been or contained a kiva. It is also possible that the plazas may have taken the place of kivas in ritual activities, as was the case with some other settlements dating to this time period around the Southwest. The number of rooms clearly indicates that social organization at the Marijilda Site was at the suprahousehold level if these rooms were occupied contemporaneously.

From the evidence available at the Goat Hill Site, a definitive migrant enclave, and at site AZ CC:2:23 (BLM) and the Marijilda Site, both potential migrant enclaves, it appears that migrants from the Kayenta and Tusayan areas arrived in the Safford Valley as suprahousehold groups, and possibly as household level groups as well. These groups established their own settlements and initially appear to have lived segregated from the remainder of the indigenous population already inhabiting the Safford Valley. The Goat Hill Site, dating from A.D. 1290 to 1315 according to Woodson (1999), and AZ CC:2:23 (BLM), which was occupied for a short time during the Goat Hill phase, were likely inhabited by some of these first groups of migrants.

SOCIAL SCALE OF MIGRATION AND NONENCLAVE SETTLEMENTS

In addition to the three settlements occupied exclusively by migrant populations from the Kayenta and Tusayan areas who began arriving after A.D. 1275, many other settlements in the Safford and Aravaipa valleys inhabited during the Goat Hill and Safford phases (A.D.1275/1300–1450) also exhibited both intrusive and indigenous technological styles. These sites were not enclaves occupied solely by migrants, but instead were occupied by both migrants and local groups (Fig. 6.1).

Four of these sites stand out as having at least five of the nine indicators of migrant populations listed in Figure 6.1, including Fort Grant Pueblo at the eastern end of the Aravaipa Valley, the Spear Ranch Site and the Krider Kiva Site in Lefthand Canyon southwest of the town of Pima, and Buena Vista Ruin near the eastern end of the Safford Valley. Current chronological resolution dates their occupation to the A.D. 1275–1450 period. These four sites have some of the strongest indicators of migration: all contained perforated plates and the Krider Kiva Site contained a kiva (Jernigan 1993) virtually identical to one excavated at Davis Ranch Ruin, a Kayenta and Tusayan migrant enclave in the San Pedro River valley (Di Peso 1958: 14). Migrants undoubtedly made up a significant portion of the population at these four settlements. However, other evidence, including the presence of locally produced Safford Variety Middle Gila Buff Ware and cobble reinforced adobe construction techniques, reveal that local populations were living at these settlements as well.

The presence of a mixed population is not surprising at the Buena Vista Ruin, which is one of the largest and longest occupied settlements in the Safford Valley. Unfortunately, much of the late occupation has been severely impacted by vandalism, which included the use of backhoes and bulldozers. Ceramics identified an occupation that extended back at least into the Two Dog phase (A.D. 1000–1100), if not earlier, showing that local populations had established a settlement at Buena Vista Ruin before Kayenta and Tusayan migrants arrived in the area in the late thirteenth century. These migrants likely chose or were invited to live alongside the local populations at this large settlement located at the head of the Gila River floodplain in the Safford Valley. Ceramic spatial clusters defined at Buena Vista Ruin contained concentrations of Safford Variety Middle Gila Buff Ware and Mimbres Black-on-white pottery in the northern part of the settlement and concentrations of later ceramics like Roosevelt Red Ware and St. Johns and Pinedale polychromes (White Mountain Red Ware) in the southern part. This patterning suggests that the northern part of Buena Vista Ruin was occupied before the arrival of Kayenta and Tusayan migrants, and that the settlement expanded southward, perhaps to accommodate the influx of population due to the arrival of migrants. Petrographic data indicate that both Maverick Mountain Series and Safford Variety Middle Gila Buff Ware ceramics at Buena Vista Ruin were produced in the western Pueblo Viejo Safford Basin and transported to the settlement as finished products, indicating that the inhabitants of Buena Vista Ruin had social relationships with both Kayenta and Tusayan migrants and indigenous groups in the valley and that both groups were probably living there during the Goat Hill and Safford phases (A.D. 1275–1450).

Coresidence is not as apparent at the other three sites, Fort Grant Pueblo, the Spear Ranch Site, and the Krider Kiva Site. The proximity of the Spear Ranch and Krider Kiva sites suggests they were likely part of the same settlement. The main indicator of indigenous populations at these sites is the presence of San Carlos Red-on-brown and Safford Variety Middle Gila Buff Ware ceramics. We do not know if these vessels were made on site or were obtained through local exchange; none were submitted for petrographic analyses. Considering the patterns of local production of these wares in the Safford Valley, it is probable that San Carlos Red-on-brown and Safford Variety Middle Gila Buff Ware were made at the Krider Kiva and Spear Ranch sites, and perhaps at Fort Grant Pueblo as well. Portions of these sites have been excavated but poorly reported (but see Crary 1997; Jernigan 1993; Neuzil 2005b: 521–531), and the presence of pit houses with Maverick Mountain Series ceramic assemblages at Fort Grant Pueblo and the Spear Ranch Site would suggest that these two settlements were founded by migrant populations, as was the case at Point of Pines (Lindsay 1986).

Furthermore, since the Krider Kiva Site and the Spear Ranch Site can probably be considered part of the same settlement, the presence of a kiva at the former (one of only two confirmed kivas in the Safford Valley) indicates that Puebloan migrants made up a

Site	Architecture — Migrant					Location — Migrant	Ceramics — Migrant			Ceramics — Indigenous
	Kiva	Smaller than average habitation rooms	Room block architecture	Underlying pit houses	Masonry architecture	Defensible location	Maverick Mountain ceramics	Perforated plates	Differences in corrugated ceramics	San Carlos Red-on-brown or Middle Gila Buff Ware
Cluff Ranch Site		P					P			P*
Richardson Orchard Site			?				P			P*
Crary Site		P								P*
Sharon Site			P							P*
Fort Grant Silo Site		P	?				P		P	P
Yuma Wash Site		P	P				P			P
AZ CC:2:33 (BLM)			P			P	P*			P
Wes Jernigan Site			?			?	P		P	P*
Rattlesnake Mesa Site		P	P			?	P			P
AZ CC:2:185 (ASM)			P			?	P		P	P*
Crescent Ruin			?			?	P		P	P
Fort Grant Pueblo			P	P			P*	P	P	P
Spear Ranch Site		P	P	P			P*	P		P
Fischer Site			?				P*	P	P	P*
AZ CC:1:3 (ASM)			?				P			P*
Dewester Site		P	P				P			P
Eagle Pass Site			P			?		P		P
Haby Pueblo			P		P		P	P		P
Wooten-Claridge Terrace Site			P		P		P			P
AZ BB:3:22 (ASM)			?				P			P
Krider Kiva Site	P		P		P		P	P		P
Lippincott North Site							P*			P
AZ CC:2:69 (ASM)			?				P*			P
Buena Vista Ruin			P	P			P*		P	P*

P = present; ? = indeterminate; P* = ceramics with evidence of local production present.

Figure 6.1. Migrant and indigenous features at Goat Hill or Middle Classic and Safford or Fort Grant phase sites.

Table 6.2. Selected Ceramic Counts for Fort Grant Pueblo, the Spear Ranch Site, and the Krider Kiva Site

Ceramics	Fort Grant Pueblo		Spear Ranch Site		Krider Kiva Site	
	N	%	N	%	N	%
Maverick Mountain Series	87	17.02	55	31.97	3*	1.05*
Safford Variety Middle Gila Buff Ware	1	0.20			1	1.12
San Carlos Red-on-brown	1	0.20	9	5.23	3	3.37

NOTE: Percent is of total decorated ceramics from the site.
*These numbers come from Jernigan's (1993) counts from excavations in the kiva. No Maverick Mountain Series ceramics were collected at the Krider Kiva Site in the collections made for the research discussed here.

large percentage of the inhabitants there as well. Maverick Mountain Series ceramics generally far outnumber San Carlos Red-on-brown and Safford Variety Middle Gila Buff ware at these sites, suggesting that migrants constituted the bulk of the population, although there was a local component present as well (Table 6.2). Local and migrant ceramics were distributed relatively evenly at the Spear Ranch Site and Fort Grant Pueblo, but not at the Krider Kiva Site, where San Carlos Red-on-brown sherds were concentrated on the south side of the site and perforated plates were concentrated on the north side.

The rest of the sites listed in Figure 6.1, all of which postdate A.D. 1275, have one to three definite indicators of migrant populations present. Material culture from these sites denotes a less substantial migrant presence than at the sites discussed above. Migrants certainly influenced some aspects of material culture, such as the room block arrangement of those settlements mainly occupied during the late thirteenth and early fourteenth century (Goat Hill or Middle Classic phases), but local populations clearly influenced decorated ceramic assemblages and construction techniques used to build residences. Such mixed patterns portray residence by both migrants and local groups. More fine grained studies are necessary to fully characterize these populations and how they interacted at the intrasettlement level.

As with the migrant enclave sites discussed above, the evidence from these nonenclave sites suggests that migrants arrived and settled in the valley in both household and suprahousehold level groups. The four sites with the strongest indicators of migration (Fort Grant Pueblo, Spear Ranch, Krider Kiva, and Buena Vista Ruin) are all large enough that they could have been occupied simultaneously by multiple households, particularly if the Krider Kiva Site is considered part

of the same settlement as the Spear Ranch Site. Such a determination depends on how many rooms were occupied contemporaneously, which cannot be accurately ascertained without excavations. Differences in the technological attributes of corrugated ceramics at Fort Grant Pueblo and Buena Vista Ruin (Chapter 3) lend support to the idea that multiple households resided at these settlements.

Several smaller sites in the Safford and Aravaipa valleys suggest migrants may have arrived and settled in household level groups as well. These sites contained a small number of habitation rooms and material culture associated with both migrant and indigenous groups. Site AZ CC:2:33 (BLM) contained six to nine rooms with Maverick Mountain Series, Safford Variety Middle Gila Buff Ware, and San Carlos Red-on-brown ceramics present, although Maverick Mountain Series sherds outnumbered Safford Variety Middle Gila Buff Ware and San Carlos Red-on-brown by about three to one (Table 6.3). Petrographic evidence indicated that some of the Maverick Mountain Series ceramics at CC:2:33 were manufactured with sands local to the area, but perhaps not by inhabitants of CC:2:33 itself, and the vessels may have been obtained through exchange. Habitation rooms were constructed in a single contiguous room block, a migrant spatial configuration, using cobble reinforced adobe, a local construction technique. Thus, CC:2:33 contained indicators of both migrant and indigenous groups but was not large enough to have housed several households of each. Similar situations are present at several other locations, including the Fort Grant Silo Site, the Wes Jernigan Site, and AZ BB:3:22 (ASM). Household level migrant groups also may have been present at the rest of the sites listed in Figure 6.1, but current data do not indicate whether only one or multiple households were present.

Table 6.3. Decorated Ceramic Assemblage from Site AZ CC:2:33 (BLM)

Ceramics	Types	N	% of decorated
Cibola White Ware	Tularosa Black-on-white	1	1.22
	Tularosa/Pinedale Black -on-white	2	2.44
	Indeterminate Cibola White Ware	1	1.22
	Indeterminate Cibola White Ware, no paint	2	2.44
Maverick Mountain Series	Maverick Mountain Black-on-red	10	12.20
	Maverick Mountain Black-on-red interior, polychrome exterior	1	1.22
	Indeterminate Maverick Mountain Series	25	30.49
	Indeterminate Maverick Mountain Series, white line exterior design	2	2.44
Middle Gila Buff Ware Safford Variety	Sacaton-Rincon Red-on-buff	1	1.22
	Indeterminate Middle Gila Buff Ware	3	3.66
Roosevelt Red Ware	Pinto/Gila/Cliff Polychrome	1	1.22
White Mountain Red Ware	St. Johns Polychrome	3	3.66
	Indeterminate White Mountain Red Ware	6	7.32
	Indeterminate White Mountain Red Ware, no paint	3	3.66
Ancestral Zuni Glaze- decorated Ware	Heshotauthla Polychrome	2	2.44
	San Carlos Red-on-brown, nonphyllite sand temper	4	4.88
	San Carlos Red-on-brown, sherd temper	3	3.66
	Unidentified decorated	1	1.22
	Unidentified red slipped	11	13.41
Total		82	

Thus, migrants from the Kayenta and Tusayan areas arrived in the Safford and Aravaipa valleys during the late thirteenth and fourteenth centuries as both household and suprahousehold level groups. Migrant enclaves and settlements occupied primarily, but perhaps not exclusively, by migrants apparently were settled by suprahousehold level groups. Household level migrant groups settled predominantly within settlements already inhabited by local groups, resulting in coresidence, or interacted closely with the residents of these settlements, indicating that the size of the migrant group may have, in part, influenced whether migrants chose to establish a settlement removed from the local population. Although the pattern among migrant enclaves suggests that the initial wave of Kayenta and Tusayan migrants arrived and settled as suprahousehold level groups, it is still unclear whether subsequent migrants arrived in the Safford and Aravaipa valleys as larger suprahousehold level groups that then fissioned into constituent households, or arrived as individual households. Evidence of both household level and suprahousehold level migrant groups is present at earlier and later migrant settle-

ments along the proposed migration route (Di Peso 1958; Haury 1958; Mills 1998; Slaughter and Roberts 1996).

EXTENT OF MIGRATION DURING THE THIRTEENTH AND FOURTEENTH CENTURIES A.D.

Migration was widespread in both the Safford and Aravaipa valleys after about A.D. 1275. At least one and as many as three locations in the Safford Valley were settled and occupied exclusively by migrants from the Kayenta and Tusayan areas. As Figure 6.1 demonstrates, every site with a late thirteenth and fourteenth century (Goat Hill or Middle Classic and Safford or Fort Grant phase) component exhibited at least one ceramic or architectural attribute suggesting migrants may have lived at these settlements. The evidence is clearly stronger at some sites, such as Spear Ranch and Buena Vista Ruin than at others, such as Lippincott North or AZ CC:1:3 (ASM). Figure 6.2 shows the location of all sites with components postdating A.D. 1275 ranked by the number of migrant in-

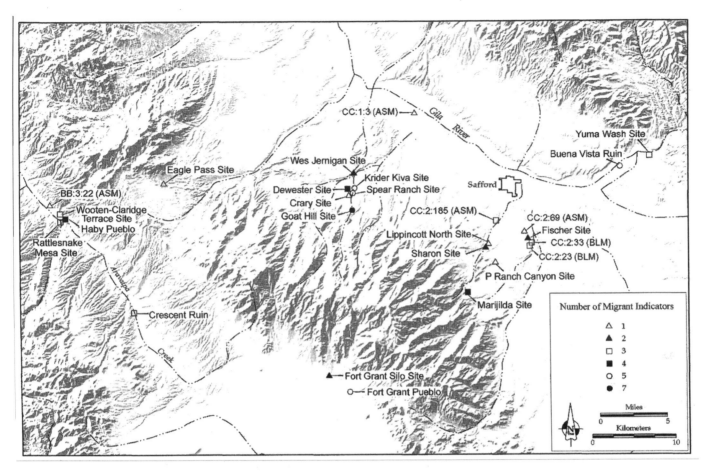

Figure 6.2. Sites with components postdating A.D. 1275 ranked by the number of migrant indicators present.

dicators present at each site. The trend is readily apparent; migrant populations from the Kayenta and Tusayan areas quickly became widespread throughout the Safford and Aravaipa valleys after their initial segregation at migrant enclave settlements. The rise and prevalence of Roosevelt Red Ware and universal changes in architecture highlight this trend.

Figure 6.2 also reveals that migrant enclaves and settlements with five indicators of migrants were generally located away from the Gila River floodplain next to large drainages originating in the foothills of the Pinaleño Mountains. This positioning may be indicative of a social boundary that existed between migrant and indigenous groups, but current information does not indicate that such a boundary existed, particularly since settlements on the floodplain not investigated in the research presented here (the Daley Site and the Methodist Church Site) hold substantial evidence for migrant populations (Brown 1973; Hall and Clark 2004). One exception to this rule is the Buena Vista Ruin, which was undoubtedly established by local groups long before the appearance of Kayenta and Tusayan migrants, and locals probably made up a significant portion of its population throughout its occupation. Petrographic evidence (Chapter 5) demonstrated that ceramic manufacture was exceptionally limited at Buena Vista Ruin. All categories of ceramics tested, those associated both with migrants (Maverick Mountain Series) and locals (Middle Gila Buff Ware and San Carlos Red-on-brown), were made with sands from petrofacies found elsewhere in the Safford Valley, implying that many ceramic vessels were obtained through local exchange. However, the presence of a perforated plate at this site (Mills and Mills 1978; not analyzed petrographically here), a vessel form generally found only at settlements with Kayenta and Tusayan migrants present, and the presence of Maverick Mountain Series ceramics indicate migrants did live at Buena Vista at some time during its occupation.

Recent research into Classic period agriculture of the Safford Valley has revealed that upland areas were farmed extensively using a system of canals carrying runoff from upland areas and small fields (Doolittle and Neely 2004; Neely 2005; Rinker 1998). Establishing settlements in these upland areas may not have been a result of forcible social, economic, and spatial marginalization, as was the case for Puebloan migrants in other areas of the Southwest (Clark 2001; Clark and Lyons 2008), but rather a conscious choice intended to maximize the combined potential of upland and lowland areas. Regardless of the logic behind settlement location choices, Kayenta and Tusayan migrants were widespread throughout the Safford and Aravaipa areas through the late thirteenth and much of the fourteenth centuries (Fig. 6.2).

THE EFFECT OF MIGRATION ON IDENTITY

The first groups of migrants to the Safford and Aravaipa areas who arrived during the late thirteenth century (Goat Hill or Middle Classic phase) initially remained physically and socially separated from the local population. Excavations have demonstrated that the people living at the isolated and defensible Goat Hill Site were almost exclusively migrants, based on the ceramics and architectural elements (Woodson 1995, 1999). Other potential migrant enclaves (AZ CC:2:23 BLM and the Marijilda Site) exhibited many of the same characteristics of physical isolation in their locations and social isolation in their material culture, specifically ceramics and architecture. Immediately after migration, migrants undoubtedly still identified themselves as being socially distinct from the local population in the area, and vice versa.

After the initial arrival and settlement of these migrant enclaves, this separation slowly became less pronounced. Settlements that were occupied at this time, such as the Yuma Wash and Wes Jernigan sites, showed evidence of an integration of migrant and indigenous populations. Decorated ceramic assemblages from these sites contained a mixture of both ceramics associated with migrants (particularly Maverick Mountain Black-on-red and Polychrome) and ceramics associated with local populations (particularly San Carlos Red-on-brown and Safford Variety Middle Gila Buff Ware). Measures of diversity in ceramic assemblages revealed a definite increase in the variability of ceramic assemblages from the Goat Hill phase (A.D. 1275/1300–1325) in comparison to the earlier Eden (A.D. 1100–1200) and Bylas (A.D. 1200–1275/1300) phase assemblages. In many cases, a greater number of ceramic wares and types were represented at these Goat Hill phase sites than at earlier sites, implying at least more interaction with a wider variety of people practicing different stylistic and technological traditions, if not embracing coresidence, during this time.

Architecture from these sites showed a similarly mixed pattern. Some sites are laid out in room blocks, a puebloan form differing from earlier compound layouts, but constructed with local techniques like cobble reinforced adobe. Furthermore, several measures of space syntax, particularly the ratio of open space to total site area and measures of convex articulation and grid convexity, showed greater diversity during the late thirteenth and early fourteenth century (Goat Hill or Middle Classic phase) than previously. This variety implies that settlements were constructed and laid out with more diversity than before, which may be related to the new cultural heterogeneity among their inhabitants. Interestingly, these ceramic and architectural patterns were repeated in the small number of settlements investigated in the Aravaipa Valley as well, even though current evidence suggests the valley may have been nearly depopulated during the Early Classic phase (A.D. 1200–1275/1300). Perhaps both Kayenta and Tusayan migrants, as well as people local to the Safford Valley or the San Pedro River Valley to the west, moved into the Aravaipa Valley simultaneously during the late thirteenth and early fourteenth centuries. It appears that each group maintained some differences, seen in a continuation of distinct decorated ceramic traditions side-by-side at many of the sites during this interval. Migrant and indigenous groups renegotiated their identity and redefined their social space in order to facilitate coresidence, but likely would not have characterized themselves as a single cohesive social group at this time.

The pattern in architectural layout and construction technique endured through the later fourteenth century (Safford and Fort Grant phases). Variability in measures of space syntax continued to reflect the diversity in the way the inhabitants chose to structure their surroundings to create ways to live with a recently diversified population. Also during this time, settlements in the Safford and Aravaipa valleys became significantly larger as fewer new settlements were constructed, and those that were built and occupied became increasingly nucleated. The overall layout of settlements also changed somewhat, as the larger sites were constructed as contiguous and compact room blocks, often surrounding plazas. An increase in settlement nucleation, coupled with an increase in the number of people in residence, undoubtedly required the development of new integrative institutions, such as plazas, that would ensure the inhabitants could live together peacefully and functionally. Such sweeping social changes clearly had an impact on identity and its expression during this time.

In the fourteenth century, diversity measures for ceramic wares and types were overall lower than in previous late thirteenth and early fourteenth century settlements. There is still variability in this measure, but the trend in diversity is clear: ceramic type and ware diversity decreased from the late thirteenth to the fourteenth century and Roosevelt Red Ware ceramics were the most ubiquitous during this time. At Crescent Ruin and the Eagle Pass Site, Roosevelt Red Ware ceramics dominated the decorated assemblage with 87 and 90 percent, respectively. At other sites dating to the fourteenth century, Roosevelt Red Ware outnumbered all other decorated wares present. This overall increase in the ubiquity of a single ware means it must have been used by an increasing number of people and that other local and nonlocal decorated wares became less important.

The Safford and Aravaipa valleys are not the only locales in which Roosevelt Red Ware ceramics became prevalent after A.D. 1300. Roosevelt Red Ware vessels were initially produced by migrants from the Kayenta and Tusayan northlands in many areas of the Southwest for exchange because of their limited access to resources and good agricultural land as latecomers to the areas in which they settled (Crown 1994: 213; Lyons 2003: 66). Production of these vessels spread to other social groups thereafter, and Roosevelt Red Ware vessels are found at sites with no strong indicators of Kayenta and Tusayan migrants (Crown 1994: 209; Lyons 2003: 66). Therefore, the dominance of this ware at fourteenth-century sites suggests that almost all settlements dating to this time were either inhabited at least in part by Kayenta and Tusayan migrants or they were involved in regular exchange or interaction with Kayenta and Tusayan migrants. Considering the increase in settlement size

and the decrease in number of settlements as they became increasingly nucleated in the Safford and Aravaipa valleys, alongside evidence for coresidence in material culture, it is most likely that Kayenta and Tusayan migrants and indigenous groups were living together at the same settlements. However, the number of migrants in relation to indigenous groups at each settlement may not have been equal, establishing a power differential between these two groups. Evidence from late thirteenth century and early fourteenth century sites indicates that migrant and local groups began living together shortly after the arrival of the migrants, and undoubtedly some of the social boundaries between these groups steadily became increasingly permeable through intermarriage and daily social interaction, eventually resulting in the expression of an entirely new identity that incorporated elements from both migrants and locals.

Along with a decrease in measures of diversity of ceramic assemblages at these fourteenth century (Safford or Fort Grant phase) sites, ceramic assemblages also showed variability in their measures of evenness during this time. Some sites had assemblages with several wares and types evenly represented, whereas other sites had assemblages dominated by only one or two wares and types. This pattern of dominance of two wares or types can be partially explained in some cases by the small size of several fourteenth-century sites, such as Wooten-Claridge Terrace and Dewester, which had so few rooms that each likely contained only one household group. However, this diversity in decorated ceramics among settlements also suggests that there was some variability in the social networks of the inhabitants; the available decorated vessels were not universally accepted by all.

Kayenta and Tusayan migrants became increasingly integrated into the local population after A.D. 1325 (Safford and Fort Grant phases), although each group still maintained social networks and exchange patterns established before migrants arrived in the Safford and Aravaipa valleys. Settlements became larger and more nucleated, but continued to demonstrate a mixture of puebloan room block layout built with local cobble reinforced adobe construction techniques. Measures of space syntax remained variable during this time, suggesting that social integration across this region of the Southwest was still not uniform. The measures of evenness of ceramic assemblages remained variable through the fourteenth century, demonstrating maintenance of previous social networks for the production and exchange of ceramics. Despite this fact, overall social integration had most certainly increased since the arrival of migrants in the area in the late thirteenth century, as shown by the decrease in diversity among decorated ceramic assemblages at later fourteenth century sites. Settlements became larger and more nucleated, bringing more people than ever before to live together at the same location. In this unique situation where the structure underlying the expression of the social identities of both migrant and indigenous groups was challenged, individuals in each of these groups chose to alter this structure of identity expression by accepting and integrating new types of material culture to fit in, socially, with their new neighbors.

A MODEL OF MIGRATION AND IDENTITY REFINED

Most migration research undertaken in the past has focused mainly on detecting migrants in the archaeological record (Di Peso 1958; Haury 1958; Reid 1997; Slaughter and Roberts 1996; Woodson 1999). The model predicting the effect of different scales of migration on the identity of local and migrant groups presented in Chapter 1 (Table 1.2) helped to refine our understanding of the totality of the migration process. In this model, three factors highlight the driving forces affecting the outcome of migration on the expression of identity. First, the scale or level of organization of migrant groups influences how readily they may attempt to integrate into existing social groups. Community level migrant groups, which are of sufficient size to form independent settlements and communities, may be more able to fully function without help from local groups, whereas household level migrant groups may be compelled to interact closely with local groups to obtain sufficient resources for daily living. Second, the size of the indigenous population in relation to the size of the migrant group affects the power relationships that emerge between the two groups upon the arrival of migrants. If local groups substantially outnumber migrant groups, the former may have a distinct advantage in both numbers of people as well as knowledge of and access to better land and resources. If migrant groups outnumber indigenous groups, their numbers may put them on more equal footing with

local groups, and they may be able to acquire access to optimal agricultural land and resources more easily. Third, the physical distance traveled by the migrant population may affect their willingness to alter the structure behind their identity to fit into their new social group. People who migrate long distances may be less likely to return home and thus may be more willing to integrate with the existing local population. These factors may also be influenced by the predisposition of migrant and indigenous groups to integrate, by what they considered to be long distance, by whether they stopped and established other settlements along the path of migration from the homeland, and by the original motivations for migration from the homeland.

The last column of Table 1.2 proposes four options as the social consequences of migration. First, migrant and indigenous groups may maintain their premigration identities and the social structure that helps to shape them, resulting in indigenous settlements associated with indigenous enculturative and high visibility local material culture and migrant settlements associated with migrant enculturative and high visibility intrusive material culture. Second, the identities of migrant and indigenous groups may be renegotiated such that the structure that creates and maintains identity is altered through practice, and the enculturative backgrounds of each group, reflected in material culture, are maintained and appear alongside each other in the archaeological record along with new forms of high visibility material culture that reflects the formation of a new identity for both migrant and indigenous groups. Third, migrant populations may adopt the identity of the local population, in which case the structure of the migrant group that maintains identity alters radically in the face of substantial challenges incurred by new actions on the part of migrants. In this case, there would be very few high visibility material culture indicators of migrant populations and migrants could only be detected through subtle differences in the technological styles of particular items. Fourth, indigenous populations may adopt the identity of the migrant population and local populations could only be identified in the archaeological record through subtle differences in the technological styles of particular items.

In light of the evidence presented here concerning changes in the expression of identity of migrant and indigenous groups in the Safford and Aravaipa valleys

Table 6.4. Refined Scale of Migration Model

Scale	Size of Indigenous Population	Distance Traveled by Migrants	Length of Occupation following Migration	Consequences for Identity
Household				
	Smaller	—	—	—
	Larger	Long	Less than one generation	Migrants adopt indigenous identity
			More than one generation	Identities are renegotiated
		Short	Less than one generation	Identities are maintained
			More than one generation	Identities are renegotiated
Suprahousehold or Community				
	Smaller	Long	Less than one generation	Identities are maintained
			More than one generation	Indigenous population adopt migrant identity
		Short	Less than one generation	Identities are maintained
			More than one generation	Indigenous population adopt migrant identity
	Larger	Long	Less than one generation	Identities are maintained
			More than one generation	Identities are renegotiated
		Short	Less than one generation	Identities are maintained
			More than one generation	Identities are renegotiated

after an influx of Kayenta and Tusayan migrants in the late thirteenth century, I propose two alterations to the basic structure of the original model (Table 1.2), as presented in Table 6.4. Based on this case study, the model can be both simplified and expanded. The consequences of migration on identity at the scale of suprahousehold and community level groups, composed of multiple households, are largely the same. These two categories are similar in that they represent groups large enough that they can act as autonomous social units, although they may interact with other groups as a matter of choice. They differ from household scale migrants, who need to interact with other household level groups to maintain social and economic viability. An additional variable, length of occupation following migration, reflects the different consequences of migration observed in the Safford Valley when comparing those settlements occupied immediately after migration for less than one generation (the Goat Hill Site) with those occupied for more than one generation following migration (Buena Vista Ruin). The length of time available for migrant and indigenous people to interact greatly influences whether or not they will renegotiate their identities to fit in with the surrounding population. These changes are reflected in Table 6.4.

Although this model accommodates the coarse resolution of the archaeological record and can be used to help predict the outcomes of migration, understanding why it may not work in some cases is also insightful. For example, what if a suprahousehold or community level group migrated a long distance into an area with a smaller local population, stayed for less than one generation, and adopted the local identity as opposed to maintaining their own premigration identity? Clearly, other social factors challenging the structure underlying the way they defined their identity would have to be considered, such as differences in social complexity, ritual elaboration, and technological levels between groups. In cases such as this, the fact that the expectations of the model were not borne out is in itself an interesting outcome, requiring additional study. With this new information, the model of the social consequences of migration could be expanded and refined even further.

SOCIAL CONSEQUENCES OF MIGRATION IN THE SAFFORD AND ARAVAIPA VALLEYS

Migrants from the Kayenta and Tusayan areas arrived in the Safford and Aravaipa valleys in both household and suprahousehold level groups. When they arrived, they found the local population was similarly organized at household and suprahousehold levels, based on the size and quantity of settlements dating to the earlier thirteenth century (Bylas phase, A.D. 1200–1275/1300). Immediately after the arrival of the first suprahousehold level migrant groups, who settled at the Goat Hill Site and probably also at AZ CC:2:23 (BLM) and the Marijilda Site, migrants and indigenous populations maintained their separate social identities and lived spatially segregated from each other. These results are consistent with the model in Table 6.4. Shortly thereafter, household level migrant groups began settling in the valleys and chose to live alongside local populations who were organized into larger or comparably sized social groups.

Material culture remains, which reflect the structure and practice used to define and maintain social identity, demonstrate that the new social situation created by migration and subsequent coresidence challenged the existing structure such that both of these groups changed the structure and practice that guided their daily lives. Thus, the manner in which each of these groups expressed their identities shifted to reflect a newly defined structure delineated by the social realities of the postmigration environment. In this way, the duality of structure, the dialectical interplay between structure and agency, played out in the archaeological record. Each group lived within their existing structure until new social situations arose that challenged this structure and led migrant and indigenous groups to reevaluate and alter the structure of their identity to accommodate this unprecedented social situation. Select items from the material record, particularly architecture and ceramics, reflect these social changes.

A logical next step for research on migration in the Safford and Aravaipa areas would be to explore why migrant and indigenous populations became spatially and socially integrated in the aftermath of migration. In a strictly environmental sense, sufficient land and resources were available so that migrant and local groups should not have felt forced to live and work together in order to survive, as was the case in the Tonto Basin (Lyons and others 2005). Agricultural resources in the Safford Valley were plentiful, and populations utilized both the floodplain and the upland areas for wild resources and cultivated crops (Doolittle and Neely 2004; Neely 2005). Although the floodplain was much more limited in the Aravaipa Valley, agriculture there was certainly possible. Therefore, other social factors must have played a role in the decision to live in nucleated villages alongside

people with whom each group previously had no experience.

In other regions of the Southwest, aggregation was often a response to a hostile social environment, such that people joined together to protect themselves (Cordell 1996). Although warfare has never been discussed in the context of the Safford and Aravaipa valleys, it is certainly not out of the realm of possibility. Aggregation is known to have been an adaptive strategy that was difficult to maintain, leading to decreased sanitary conditions, a greater impact on the local environment, and a scarcity of resources in the local area (Cordell 1996). Aggregation was common, however, if key resources were localized and required a large labor investment (Cordell 1996). Labor requirements may have been the root stimulus for aggregation in the Safford Valley, where canals similar to those built at Hohokam settlements have been found (Nials and others 2004). If these canals and the water control they entailed constituted a key resource, they could have required aggregation, stimulating integration of socially disparate groups. However, several researchers have pointed out that aggregation is ultimately a social process (Dean and others 1985; Longacre 1966; Plog 1983), and could have been brought on by the emergence of ideological trends or advances in technology. Macroregional processes and demographic trends, which eventually led to coalescence in much of the Southwest, also likely played a role in the decision to aggregate (Hill and others 2004). However, given the previous experience the inhabitants of the Safford Valley had in incorporating migrants into the local social fabric, (Chapter 5; Clark and Lengyel 2002), aggregation and coresidence of migrant and indigenous groups easily led to fundamental changes in structure and changes in identity of both groups during the late thirteenth and fourteenth centuries.

MIGRATION RESEARCH IN THE GREATER SOUTHWEST

Migration has been a common research theme in understanding the precontact social dynamics of the Greater Southwest because archaeologists have clear evidence for substantial mobility across much of the area through time (Bernardini 2005; Cameron 1995a; Clark 2001; Duff 2002; Ennes 1999; P. Fish and others 1994; Hegmon and others 2000; Herr 2001; Herr and Clark 1997; Lindsay 1987; Lyons 2003; Spielmann 1998; Woodson 1999). Migration can be identified in the archaeological record through robust patterns in multiple lines of evidence from material culture. Early investigations into migration in the Southwest focused on trait list approaches and site-unit intrusions that left the clearest signatures of migration in the archaeological record (Di Peso 1958; Haury 1958; Lindsay 1987), but recent refinements in method and theory have brought a more nuanced approach to the subject that can identify smaller groups and move beyond simply detecting migrant groups in the archaeological record (Clark 2001; Duff 2002; Herr 2001; Mills 1998; Stark and others 1995; Stark and others 1998). These analyses follow a technological style approach to combine evidence from ceramics, architecture, foodways, and other domestic items to build a complete picture of migration.

I used these more subtle indicators of migration to understand the full process of population movement into the Safford and Aravaipa valleys and to trace the connections between areas where Kayenta and Tusayan migrants are known to have settled in the thirteenth century. North of these valleys, excavations at the Point of Pines Site revealed evidence of Kayenta and Tusayan migrants south of their homeland, based on evidence from ceramics, architecture, and foodways (Haury 1958; Lindsay 1987). To the south and west, recent investigations into the Classic period in the lower San Pedro River valley have confirmed early archaeological inquiries in the area that suggested a substantial influx of migrants to a cluster of sites in the valley, including Reeve Ruin and the Davis Ranch Site (Clark and Lyons 2008; Di Peso 1958). The Safford and Aravaipa valleys lie intermediate between these two regions, and the evidence presented here suggests that migrants who traveled to the Point of Pines region then continued south to the Safford Valley, settling at Goat Hill and other locations in the late thirteenth century. From there, Kayenta and Tusayan migrants continued their journey, settling at several places along Aravaipa Creek before moving on to the San Pedro River valley.

So far, there as been little research devoted to assessing the actual routes of migration, but anecdotal evidence provides some possibilities. Eagle Creek and Bonita Creek flow from north to south from the modern San Carlos Indian Reservation past the eastern end of the Gila Mountains to join the Gila River in the Gila Box Riparian area (Neuzil 2006; Wasley 1962;

Welch 1995). Cliff dwellings along these creeks contain substantial evidence of migrant groups, primarily Maverick Mountain Series ceramics and a suite of artifacts resembling those found in the Sunflower Cave Cache (Kidder and Guernsey 1919), suggesting that these canyons may have been used as natural pathways between the Point of Pines region and the Safford Valley. Migrants may also have traveled to the Safford Valley from settlements in the Duncan area to the east, although so little research has been completed in this area it is difficult to evaluate this possibility. From the Safford Valley, migrants may have traveled along the east side of the Pinaleño Mountains, then headed west to Aravaipa Creek through Stockton Pass, or they may have traveled around the Pinaleño Mountains to the west through Eagle Pass and then south to Aravaipa Creek. Neither route has clear evidence of migrant enclave settlements that might have been occupied by migrants on their journey, but the Eagle Pass Site, located in Eagle Pass on the west side of the Pinaleño Mountains, does have a modicum of evidence for occupation by migrant populations. No migrant enclaves have been found between Aravaipa Creek and the San Pedro River, but several ranchers and long time inhabitants of the area view Rattlesnake Canyon through the Galiuro Mountains as a logical migration route.

Based on migration research in many other areas of the Southwest, the level of apparent spatial and social integration of migrant and indigenous groups in the Safford and Aravaipa valleys is somewhat surprising. In most other documented instances of migration, migrant populations stayed separate from the existing local population (Clark 2001; Di Peso 1958). Some of the results described herein may be due to the scale at which these analyses were undertaken. For example, trait list approaches are best at identifying large scale groups, which are more likely to remain independent, even after migration. However, considering the precedent for migration in the Safford and Aravaipa valleys, with two previous influxes coming in the twelfth and thirteenth centuries (Clark and Lenyel 2002; Neuzil 2005b), the local populations there may have had the social mechanisms to incorporate outsiders more readily available than local populations in other areas. This level of diversity inherent in the local population in the Safford and Aravaipa valleys may have made traces of migrants easier to see in the archaeological record. Because the local population was already somewhat "multicultural," migrants may not have felt as much pressure to conform to fit in and may have been able to outwardly express aspects of their identity more freely than if they had moved to other areas with a more uniform population.

This study also reconfirms that migration and population movement were important social forces in the thirteenth and fourteenth centuries across much of the Greater Southwest. Significant thought has gone into understanding population shifts that occurred during this time period (Ahlstrom and others 1995; Clark 2001; Dean and others 1985; Dean and others 1994; Doelle 2000; Duff 1998; Hill and others 2004; Lekson and others 2002), concluding that migration, aggregation, and coalescence of populations all played large roles. Numerous explanations have been posited to explain why people engaged in such movement and reorganization, including social conflict, environmental changes and degredation, disease, and resource depletion. In reality, no single reason can fully account for these population movements, and the motivation to move and reorganize socially was likely the result of a combination of these factors.

This approach differs from other research on migration and the resulting settlement nucleation of the late thirteenth through fifteenth centuries, which has focused more on large scale regional differences rather than on small scale differences among social groups (Adams and Duff 2004). The work presented by Adams and Duff (2004) looks at changes in the Pueblo IV period and characterizes them at a regional scale, emphasizing village and settlement cluster level expressions of identity. This approach has validity in viewing larger scale social organization and interaction, but it is difficult to assess the effects of population coalescence on identity at this scale, as identity is often primarily expressed at the individual or small social group level (Jenkins 1996). It is at these levels that large scale population movements would have the

most profound effects. Research on identity and migration in all regions of the Southwest would benefit from following the approach presented here, because similar cultural changes took place across much of the Southwest during the thirteenth and fourteenth centuries. By combining the information gained from low visibility material culture (Clark 2001; Stark and others 1998) with that gained from high visibility material culture (Bernardini and Brown 2004; Duff 2004; Graves 2004; Huntley and Kintigh 2004), the full consequences of population movements, on both the groups that move and those with whom they ultimately settle, can be better understood.

In sum, the evidence presented in previous chapters provides a unique opportunity to examine the process of migration, particularly its consequences for identity, in the past. This research demonstrated that ancestral Puebloan migrants moved into the Safford and Aravaipa valleys in the late thirteenth and fourteenth centuries as household and suprahousehold level groups, and settled alongside the local population after an initial separation. Thereafter, these groups became socially integrated and changed the way they expressed their identity through material culture, particularly ceramics and architecture, to reflect this integration. Thus, this research adds to the growing body of knowledge about ancient migrations in the Greater Southwest, as well as the understanding of migration in the past and how it may be recognized at a variety of scales in the archaeological record. With this information, a model of the effects of migration on identity was created and refined for use in future research. The research presented here has greatly advanced the study of migration and its impact on the expression of identity. Furthermore, the methods and model employed have helped to characterize the process of migration in its entirety, and are applicable not only in the Greater Southwest, but in numerous other cases of migration in the past and present around the world as well.

References

Abbott, David R.

2000 *Ceramics and Community Organization Among the Hohokam.* University of Arizona Press, Tucson.

Abbott, David R., and Mary-Ellen Walsh-Anduze

1995 Temporal Patterns Without Temporal Variation: The Paradox of Hohokam Red Ware Ceramics. In *Ceramic Production in the American Southwest*, edited by Barbara J. Mills and Patricia L. Crown, pp. 88–114. University of Arizona Press, Tucson.

Adams, E. Charles

1998 Late Prehistory in the Middle Little Colorado River Area: A Regional Perspective. In "Migration and Reorganization: The Pueblo IV Period in the American Southwest," edited by Katherine A. Spielmann, pp. 53–63. *Arizona State University Anthropological Research Papers* 51. Arizona State University, Tempe.

Adams, E. Charles, and Andrew I. Duff (editors)

2004 *The Protohistoric Pueblo World:* A.D. *1275–1600.* University of Arizona Press, Tucson.

Ahlstrom, Richard V. N., David P. Doak, and Gregory R. Seymour

1997 Introduction and Cultural Setting. In "The Sanchez Copper Project: Volume I: Archaeological Investigations in the Safford Valley, Graham County, Arizona," edited by Gregory R. Seymour, Richard V. N. Ahlstrom, and David P. Doak, pp. 1-1-1-16. *SWCA Archaeological Report* 94–82. SWCA, Inc., Tucson.

Ahlstrom, Richard V. N., Carla R. Van West, and Jeffrey S. Dean

1995 Environmental and Chronological Factors in the Mesa Verde-Northern Rio Grande Migration. *Journal of Anthropological Archaeology* 14(2): 125–142.

Aldenderfer, Mark S., and Charles Stanish

1993 Domestic Architecture, Household Archaeology, and the Past in the South-Central Andes. In *Domestic Architecture, Ethnicity, and Complementarity in the South-Central Andes*, edited by Mark S. Aldenderfer, pp. 1–12. University of Iowa Press, Iowa City.

Anthony, David W.

1990 Migration in Archaeology: The Baby and the Bathwater. *American Anthropologist* 92: 895–914.

1994 Prehistoric Migration as Social Process. Paper presented at the 59th Annual Meeting of the Society for American Archaeology, Anaheim.

1997 Prehistoric Migration as Social Process. In "Migrations and Invasions in Archaeological Explanation," edited by John Chapman and Helena Hamerow, pp. 21–32. *BAR International Series* 664. Hadrian Books, Oxford, England.

Anyon, Roger, and Steven A. LeBlanc

1984 *The Galaz Ruin: A Prehistoric Mimbres Village in Southwestern New Mexico.* Maxwell Museum of Anthropology and University of New Mexico Press, Albuquerque.

Arnold, Dean E.

1985 *Ceramic Theory and Cultural Process.* Cambridge University Press, Cambridge.

1989 Patterns of Learning, Residence and Descent among Potters in Ticul, Yucatan, Mexico. In *Archaeological Approaches to Cultural Identity*, edited by S. J. Sherman, pp. 174–184. Unwin Hyman, London.

Bagwell, Elizabeth A.

2004 Architechtural Patterns Along the Rio Taraises, Northern Sierra Madre Occidental, Sonora. *Kiva* 70(1): 7–30.

Baldwin, Stuart J.

1987 Roomsize Patterns: A Quantitative Method for Approaching Ethnic Identification in Architecture. In *Ethnicity and Culture: Proceedings of the Eighteenth Annual Conference of the Archaeological Association of the University of Calgary*, edited by Réginald Auger, Margaret F. Glass, Scott MacEachern, and Peter H. McCartney, pp. 163–174. University of Calgary Archaeological Association, Calgary.

Bandelier, Adolph F.

1890 *Final Report of Investigations Among the Indians of the Southwestern United States, Carried on Mainly in the Years from 1880 to 1885, Part I.*

Bandelier, Adolph F. (*continued*)
    Reprint. Papers of the Archaeological Institute of America, American Series. Kraus Reprint Co., Millwood. 1976.

Barrett, John C.
    2001   Agency, the Duality of Structure, and the Problem of the Archaeological Record. In *Archaeology Theory Today*, edited by Ian Hodder, pp. 141–164. Polity Press, Cambridge.

Barth, Fredrik
    1969   Introduction: Ethnic Groups and Boundaries. In *Ethnic Groups and Boundaries: The Social Organization of Culture Difference*, edited by Fredrik Barth, pp. 9–38. Little, Brown, and Co., Boston.
    1994   Enduring and Emerging Issues in the Analysis of Ethnicity. In *The Anthropology of Ethnicity: Beyond 'Ethnic Groups and Boundaries'*, edited by Hans Vermeulen and Cora Govers, pp. 11–32. Het Spinhuis, Amsterdam.
    2000   Boundaries and Connections. In *Signifying Identities: Anthropological Perspectives on Boundaries and Contested Values*, edited by Anthony P. Cohen, pp. 17–36. Routledge, London.

Bayman, James M., and M. Guadalupe Sanchez
    1998   The Surface Archaeology of Classic Period Hohokam Community Organization. In *Surface Archaeology*, edited by Alan P. Sullivan, III, pp. 75–88. University of New Mexico Press, Albuquerque.

Bentley, G. Carter
    1987   Ethnicity and Practice. *Comparative Studies in Society and History* 29(1): 24–55.

Bernardini, Wesley
    1998   Conflict, Migration, and the Social Environment: Interpreting Architectural Change in Early and Late Pueblo IV Aggregations. In "Migration and Reorganization: The Pueblo IV Period in the American Southwest," edited by Katherine A. Spielmann, pp. 91–114. *Arizona State University Anthropological Research Papers* 51, Arizona State University, Tempe.
    2002   *The Gathering of the Clans: Understanding Ancestral Hopi Migration and Identity, A.D. 1275–1400*. Doctoral dissertation, Department of Anthropology, Arizona State University, Tempe. University Microfilms, Ann Arbor.
    2005   Reconsidering Spatial and Temporal Aspects of Prehistoric Cultural Identity: A Case Study from the American Southwest. *American Antiquity* 70(1): 31–54.

Bernardini, Wesley, and Gary M. Brown
    2004   The Formation of Settlement Clusters on Anderson Mesa. In *The Protohistoric Pueblo World: A.D. 1275–1600*, edited by E. Charles Adams and Andrew I. Duff, pp. 108–118. University of Arizona Press, Tucson.

Bierer, Susan B.
    1995   Plan of Work for Limited Archaeological Data Recovery at AZ CC:2:72(ASM) and AZ CC:2:185(ASM), Graham County, Arizona. SWCA Environmental Consultants, Inc., Tucson.

Bierer, Susan B., and Thomas N. Motsinger
    1994   Revised: A Cultural Resource Survey of An Overhead Powerline Easement South of Safford, Graham County, Arizona. SWCA Archaeological Report No. 94–172. SWCA Environmental Consultants, Inc., Tucson.

Black, Andrew T., and Margerie Green, eds.
    1995   *The San Carlos Reservoir Cultural Resources Survey*. Cultural Resources Report No. 87. Archaeological Consulting Services, Ltd., Tempe.

Bourdieu, Pierre
    1977   *Outline of a Theory of Practice*. Cambridge University Press, Cambridge.

Breternitz, David A.
    1966   An Appraisal of Tree-Ring Dated Pottery in the Southwest. *Anthropological Papers of the University of Arizona* 10. University of Arizona Press, Tucson.

Brettell, Caroline B., and James F. Hollifield
    2000   Migration Theory: Talking Across Disciplines. In *Migration Theory: Talking Across Disciplines*, edited by Caroline B. Brettell and James F. Hollifield, pp. 1–26. Routledge, New York.

Bronitsky, Gordon, and James D. Merritt
    1986   The Archaeology of Southeast Arizona: A Class I Cultural Resource Inventory. *Cultural Resource Series* 2. Bureau of Land Management, Phoenix.

Brown, Jeffrey L.
    1973   The Origin and Nature of Salado: Evidence from the Safford Valley, Arizona. Doctoral dissertation, Department of Anthropology, University of Arizona, Tucson.
    1974   Pueblo Viejo Salado Sites and Their Relationship to Western Pueblo Culture. *The Artifact* 12(2).

Bubemyre, Trixi, and Barbara J. Mills
    1993   Clay Oxidation Analyses. In *Across the Colorado Plateau: Anthropological Studies for the Transwestern Pipeline Expansion Project, Volume XVI: Interpretation of Ceramic Artifacts*, edited by Barbara J. Mills, Christine E. Goetze, and Maria Nieves Zedeño, pp. 235–277. Office of Contract Archaeology and Maxwell Museum of Anthropology, Albuquerque.

Bugocki, Peter
    1987   The Establishment of Agrarian Communities on the North European Plain. *Current Anthropology* 28(1): 1–24.

Burmeister, Stefan
2000   Archaeology and Migration: Approaches to an Archaeological Proof of Migration. *Current Anthropology* 41(4): 539–567.

Cameron, Catherine M.
1998   Coursed Adobe Architecture, Style, and Social Boundaries in the American Southwest. In *The Archaeology of Social Boundaries*, edited by Miriam T. Stark, pp. 183–207. Smithsonian Institution Press, Washington D.C.
1995a   (Editor) Migration and the Movement of Southwestern Peoples. *Journal of Anthropological Archaeology* 14(2).
1995b   Migration and the Movement of Southwestern Peoples. *Journal of Anthropological Archaeology* 14(2): 104–124.

Carlson, Roy L.
1970   White Mountain Redware: A Pottery Tradition of East-Central Arizona and Western New Mexico. *Anthropological Papers of the University of Arizona* 19. University of Arizona Press, Tucson.

Chapman, John
1990   Social Inequality on Bulgarian Tells and the Varna Problem. In *The Social Archaeology of Houses*, edited by Ross Samson, pp. 49–92. Edinburgh University Press, Edinburgh.

Chilton, Elizabeth S.
1998   The Cultural Origins of Technical Choice: Unraveling Algonquian and Iroquoian Ceramic Traditions in the Northeast. In *The Archaeology of Social Boundaries*, edited by Miriam T. Stark, pp. 132–160. Smithsonian Institution Press, Washington D.C.

Clark, Jeffery J.
2001   Tracking Prehistoric Migration: Pueblo Settlers Among the Tonto Basin Hohokam. *Anthropological Papers of the University of Arizona* 65. University of Arizona Press, Tucson.
2004   (Editor) Ancient Farmers of the Safford Basin: Archaeology of the U.S. 70 Safford-to-Thatcher Project. *Anthropological Papers* 39. Center for Desert Archaeology, Tucson.

Clark, Jeffery J., and Stacey Lengyel
2002   "Mogollon" Migrations into Southeastern Arizona. Paper Presented at the 12th Annual Mogollon Conference, Las Cruces.

Clark, Jeffery J., and Patrick D. Lyons, Editors
2008   Migrants and Mounds: Classic Period Archaeology of the Lower San Pedro Valley. *Anthropological Papers* 45. Center for Desert Archaeology, Tucson.

Clark, Jeffery J., Anna A. Neuzil, and Patrick D. Lyons
2004   Safford Basin Past and Present. In "Ancient Farmers of the Safford Basin: Archaeology of the U.S. 70 Safford-to-Thatcher Project," edited by Jeffery J. Clark, pp. 181–198. *Anthropological Papers* 39. Center for Desert Archaeology, Tucson.

Clark, Jeffery J., Fred L. Nials, and James M. Vint
2004   Introduction. In "Ancient Farmers of the Safford Basin: Archaeology of the U.S. 70 Safford-to-Thatcher Project," edited by Jeffery J. Clark, pp. 1–22. *Anthropological Papers* 39. Center for Desert Archaeology, Tucson.

Colton, Harold S.
1953   Potsherds: An Introduction to the Study of Prehistoric Southwestern Ceramics and Their Use in Historic Reconstruction. *Museum of Northern Arizona Bulletin* 25. The Northern Arizona Society of Science and Art, Flagstaff.

Comas d'Argemir, Dolors, and Joan J. Pujadas
1999   Living In/On the Frontier: Migration, Identities, and Citizenship in Andorra. *Social Anthropology* 7(3): 253–264.

Conrad, Geoffrey W.
1993   Domestic Architecture of the Estuquiña Phase: Estuquiña and San Antonio. In *Domestic Architecture, Ethnicity, and Complementarity in the South-Central Andes*, edited by Mark S. Aldenderfer, pp. 1–12. University of Iowa Press, Iowa City.

Cordell, Linda S.
1996   Big Sites, Big Questions: Pueblos in Transition. In *The Prehistoric Pueblo World, A.D. 1150–1350*, edited by Michael A. Adler, pp. 228–240. University of Arizona Press, Tucson.

Craib, Ian
1992   Structuration Theory. In *Anthony Giddens*, pp. 33–72. Routledge, London.

Craig, Douglas B.
2001   Preface. In "The Grewe Archaeological Research Project, Volume 2: Material Culture, Part I: Ceramic Studies," edited by David R. Abbott, pp. xiii–xvii. *Anthropological Papers* 99–1. Northland Research, Inc., Flagstaff.

Crary, Joseph H.
1995   Previous Research. In *The San Carlos Reservoir Cultural Resources Survey, Vol. 1*, edited by Andrew T. Black and Margerie Green, pp. 5–24. Archaeological Consulting Services, Ltd., Tempe.
1997   The Chronology and Culture of Upper (Northern) Southeast Arizona: The Formative and Classic Periods. Paper presented at the seminar "Between the Hohokam and the Mimbres: Archaeology of a Land Between," Amerind Foundation, Dragoon.

Crown, Patricia L.
1994   *Ceramics and Ideology: Salado Polychrome Pottery*. University of New Mexico Press, Albuquerque.

Cuba, Lee, and David M. Hummon
1993   Constructing a Sense of Home: Place Affiliation and Migration Across the Life Cycle. *Sociological Forum* 8(4): 547–572.

Dale, Jacqueline M.
2005   A Cultural Resources Survey of Bureau of Land Management Land near Yuma Wash, Safford, Graham County, Arizona. *Technical Report* 2005–102. Center for Desert Archaeology, Tucson.

Dart, Allen
1999   Cultural Resources Survey of 3.6 Acres for Cluff Ranch Road Widening and Webster Road Realignment in the Cluff Ranch Wildlife Area, South of Pima in Graham County, Arizona. Letter Report No. 99028. Old Pueblo Archaeology Center, Tucson.

David, Nicholas, Kodzo Gavua, A. Scott MacEachern, and Judy Sterner
1991   Ethnicity and Material Culture in North Cameroon. *Canadian Journal of Archaeology* 15: 171–177.

Dawson, Peter C.
2002   Space Syntax Analysis of Central Inuit Snow Houses. *Journal of Anthropological Archaeology* 21: 464–480.

Dean, Jeffrey S.
1996   Kayenta Anasazi Settlement Transformations in Northeastern Arizona: A.D. 1150–1350. In *The Prehistoric Pueblo World: A.D. 1150–1350*, edited by Michael A. Adler, pp. 29–47. University of Arizona Press, Tucson.

Dean, Jeffrey S., William H. Doelle, and Janet D. Orcutt
1994   Adaptive Stress: Environment and Demography. In *Themes in Southwest Prehistory*, edited by George J. Gumerman, pp. 53–86. School of American Research Press, Santa Fe.

Dean, Jeffrey S., Robert C. Euler, George J. Gumerman, Fred Plog, Richard H. Hevly, and Thor N.V. Karlstrom
1985   Human Behavior, Demography, and Paleoenvironment on the Colorado Plateau. *American Antiquity* 50(3): 537–554.

Dietler, Michael and Ingrid Herbich
1998   *Habitus*, Techniques, Style: An Integrated Approach to the Social Understanding of Material Culture and Boundaries. In *The Archaeology of Social Boundaries*, edited by Miriam T. Stark, pp. 232–263. Smithsonian Institution Press, Washington D.C.

Di Peso, Charles C.
1958   The Reeve Ruin of Southeastern Arizona: A Study of a Prehistoric Western Pueblo Migration into the Middle San Pedro Valley. *Amerind Foundation* 8. The Amerind Foundation, Dragoon.

Doak, David P., and Richard V.N. Ahlstrom
1995   Archaeological Data Recovery on Three Sites North of Safford, Arizona: The Sanchez Supplemental Data Recovery Project. *Archaeological Report* 95–197. SWCA, Inc., Tucson.

Doelle, William H.
2000   Tonto Basin Demography in a Regional Perspective. In "Salado," edited by Jeffrey S. Dean, pp. 81–105. *Amerind Foundation New World Studies Series* 4. Amerind Foundation, Dragoon, and University of New Mexico Press, Albuquerque.

Doolittle, William E., and James A. Neely, Editors
2004   The Safford Valley Grids: Prehistoric Cultivation in the Southern Arizona Desert. *Anthropological Papers of the University of Arizona* 70. University of Arizona Press, Tucson.

Downum, Christian E., and Gregory Burrell Brown
1998   The Reliability of Surface Artifact Assemblages as Predictors of Subsurface Remains. In *Surface Archaeology*, edited by Alan P. Sullivan III, pp. 111–123. University of New Mexico Press, Albuquerque.

Duff, Andrew I.
1998   The Process of Migration in the Late Prehistoric Southwest. In "Migration and Reorganization: The Pueblo IV Period in the American Southwest," edited by K. A. Spielmann, pp. 231–278. *Arizona State University Anthropological Research Papers* 51. Arizona State University, Tempe.

2002   *Western Pueblo Identities: Regional Interaction, Migration, and Transformation.* University of Arizona Press, Tucson.

2004   Settlement Clustering and Village Interaction in the Upper Little Colorado Region. In *The Protohistoric Pueblo World: A.D. 1275–1600*, edited by E. Charles Adams and Andrew I. Duff, pp. 75–84. University of Arizona Press, Tucson.

Duffen, William A.
1937   Some Notes on a Summer's Work near Bonita, Arizona. *The Kiva* 2(4): 13–16.

Duffen, William A., and William K. Hartmann
1997   The 76 Ranch Ruin and the Location of Chichilticale. In *The Coronado Expedition to Tierra Nueva: The 1540–1542 Route Across the Southwest*, edited by Richard Flint and Shirley Cushing Flint, pp. 190–211. University Press of Colorado, Boulder.

Duwe, Samuel Gregg
2005   Communities of Practice and Ancient Apprenticeship in the American Southwest: Pigment Analyses of Pueblo IV Period Ceramics from Bailey Ruin, East-Central Arizona. Master's thesis, Department of Anthropology, University of Arizona, Tucson.

Elgohary, Amr F., and Julienne Hanson
1997   In Search of a Spatial Culture. In *Tradition, Location, and Community: Place-making and Development*, edited by Adenrele Awotona and Necdet Teymur, pp. 81–120. Avebury, Aldershot.

Elson, Mark D., Miriam T. Stark,
and David A. Gregory, Editors
1995   The Roosevelt Community Development Study: New Perspectives on Tonto Basin Prehistory. *Anthropological Papers* 15, Center for Desert Archaeology, Tucson.

Emory, W. H.
1848   Notes of a Military Reconnoissance, from Fort Leavenworth, in Missouri, to San Diego, in California, including part of the Arkansas, Del Norte, and Gila Rivers. *Executive Document* 41. Wendell and Van Benthuysen, Washington, D.C.

Enciso, Graciela Freyermuth, and Mariana
Fernandez Guerrero
1995   Migration, Organization, and Identity: The Case of a Women's Group from San Cristobal de las Casas. *Signs* 20(4): 970–995.

Ennes, Mark J.
1999   Evidence for Migration in the Eastern Mimbres Region, Southwestern New Mexico. In *Sixty Years of Mogollon Archaeology, Papers from the Ninth Mogollon Conference*, edited by Stephanie M. Whittlesey, pp. 127–134. SRI Press, Tucson.

Esse, Douglas L.
1992   The Collared Pithos at Megiddo: Ceramic Distribution and Ethnicity. *Journal of Near Eastern Studies*. 51(2): 81–103.

Farrell, Mary M., Peter M. Taylor,
and William B. Gillespie
2002   An Archaeological Investigation of Proposed Maintenance of the Graham County Electrical Cooperative Power Line, Safford Ranger District, Coronado National Forest. Report 2002–05–019. MS on file, Coronado National Forest Office, Tucson, Arizona.

Fenn, Thomas R., Barbara J. Mills, and Maren Hopkins
2006   The Social Contexts of Glaze Paint Ceramic Production and Consumption in the Silver Creek Area. In *The Social Life of Pots*, edited by Judith Habicht-Mauche, Suzanne Eckert and Deborah Huntley. University of Arizona Press, Tucson.

Ferguson, T. J.
1996   Historic Zuni Architecture and Society: An Archaeological Application of Space Syntax. *Anthropological Papers of the University of Arizona* 60. University of Arizona Press, Tucson.
2004   Academic, Legal, and Political Contexts of Social Identity and Cultural Affiliation Research in the Southwest. In *Identity, Feasting, and the Archaeology of the Greater Southwest*, edited by Barbara J. Mills, pp. 27–41. University Press of Colorado, Boulder.

Fewkes, Jesse W.
1898   A Preliminary Account of Archaeological Field Work in Arizona in 1897. In *Annual Report of the Smithsonian Institution for 1897*, pp. 601–623. Government Printing Office, Washington D.C.
1904   Two Summers Work in Pueblo Ruins. In *The Twenty-Second Annual Report of the Bureau of American Ethnology*, pp. 3–196. Government Printing Office, Washington D.C.

Fish, Paul R., Suzanne K. Fish, George J. Gumerman,
and J. Jefferson Reid
1994   Toward an Explanation for Southwestern "Abandonments." In *Themes in Southwest Prehistory*, edited by George J. Gumerman, pp. 135–163. School of American Research Press, Santa Fe.

Fish, Suzanne K., Paul R. Fish,
and John H. Madsen, Editors
1992   The Marana Community in the Hohokam World. *Anthropological Papers of the University of Arizona* 56. University of Arizona Press, Tucson.

Fitting, J. E.
1977   *Mitigation of Adverse Effects to Archaeological Resources on the Foote Wash Conservation and Development Project, Graham County, Arizona.* Report Number 1786. Commonwealth Associates, Inc., Jackson, Michigan.

Foster, Michael S.
1994   Intrusive Ceramics. In "The Pueblo Grande Project: Material Culture," edited by Michael S. Foster, pp. 119–165. *Publications in Archaeology* 20. Soil Systems, Inc., Phoenix.

Frayne, Bruce, and Wade Pendelton
2001   Home is Where the Heart Is: Namibians on Cross-Border Migration and Regional Integration. *African Studies* 60(2): 205–224.

Gardner, Andrew
2002   Social Identity and the Duality of Structure in late Roman-period Britain. *Journal of Social Archaeology* 2(3): 323–351.

Gauntlett, David
2002   *Media, Gender, and Identity: An Introduction.* Routledge, London.

Gerald, Rex E.
1957   Haby Site Dig – Field Notes. Manuscript on file, Amerind Foundation, Dragoon.
1975   Drought Correlated Changes in Two Prehistoric Pueblo Communities in Southeastern Arizona. Doctoral dissertation, Department of Anthropology, University of Chicago, Chicago.

Giddens, Anthony
1979   *Central Problems in Social Theory: Action, Structure and Contradiction in Social Analysis.* University of California Press, Berkeley.

Giddens, Anthony (*continued*)
1984   *The Constitution of Society*. University of California Press, Berkeley.

Gifford, James C.
1980   Archaeological Explorations in Caves of the Point of Pines Region, Arizona. *Anthropological Papers of the University of Arizona* 36. University of Arizona Press, Tucson.

Gifford, James C., and Watson Smith
1978   Gray Corrguated Pottery from Awatovi and Other Jeddito Sites in Northeastern Arizona. Reports of the Awatovi Expedition, Report No. 10. *Papers of the Peabody Museum of Archaeology and Ethnology,* Vol. 69. Peabody Museum of Archaeology and Ethnology, Cambridge.

Gillespie, William B., and Chris Schrager
2002   Inspection and Evaluation of Prehistoric Sites, Oak Draw Archaeological District, Safford Ranger District, Coronado National Forest. Cultural Resources Report 2003–05–14. MS on file Coronado National Forest Office, Tucson, Arizona.

Gilman, Patricia, and Barry Richards
1975   An Archaeological Survey in Aravaipa Canyon Primitive Area. Report prepared for the Bureau of Land Management. Cultural Resource Management Section, Arizona State Museum, University of Arizona.

Gilman, Patricia L., and Peter Sherman
1975   An Archaeological Survey of the Graham-Curtis Project: Phase II. Report prepared for the Cultural Resource Management Section, Arizona State Museum, University of Arizona, Tucson.

Gilman, Patricia A., Valetta Canouts, and Ronald L. Bishop
1994   The Production and Distribution of Classic Mimbres Black-on-white Pottery. *American Antiquity* 59(4): 695–709.

Gladwin, Harold Sterling
1957   *A History of the Ancient Southwest*. Bond Wheelwright Company, Portland, Maine.

Gosselain, Olivier
1998   Social and Technical Identity in a Clay Crystal Ball. In *The Archaeology of Social Boundaries*, edited by Miriam T. Stark, pp. 78–106. Smithsonian Institution Press, Washington D.C.
2002   Materializing Identities: An African Perspective. *Journal of Archaeological Method and Theory* 7(3): 187–218.

Graves, William M.
2004   Social Identity and the Internal Organization of the Jumanos Pueblos Settlement Cluster in the Salinas District, Central New Mexico. In *The Protohistoric Pueblo World: A.D. 1275–1600*, edited by E. Charles Adams and Andrew I. Duff, pp. 43–52. University of Arizona Press, Tucson.

Gregory, David A.
1995   A Chronological Framework for the Prehistory of the Safford Basin. In *The San Carlos Reservoir Cultural Resources Survey*, edited by Andrew T. Black and Margerie Green, pp. 123–136. Cultural Resources Report 87. Archaeological Consulting Services, Ltd., Tempe.

Gutierrez, Anastacia E., and David B. Tucker
2003   The 76 Ranch Access Road Survey: A Cultural Resource Survey of Approximately 3 Miles of a 20-foot-wide Access Road Right-of-way and Proposed Reroute for the 76 Ranch, Northwest of Bonita, Graham County, Arizona. *SWCA Cultural Resources Report* 03–108. SWCA, Inc., Tucson.

Habicht-Mauche, Judith A.
1995   Changing Patterns of Pottery Manufacture and Trade in the Northern Rio Grande Region. In *Ceramic Production in the American Southwest*, edited by Barbara J. Mills and Patricia L. Crown, pp. 167–199. University of Arizona Press, Tucson.

Hadley, Diana, Peter Warshall, and Don Bufkin
1991   Environmental Change in Aravaipa, 1870–1970: An Ethnoecological Suvery. *Cultural Resources Series* 7. Bureau of Land Management, Phoenix.

Hadley, Diana, Richard V.N. Ahlstrom, and Scott Mills
1993   El Rio Bonito: An Ethnoecological Study of the Bonita Creek Watershed, Southeastern Arizona. *Cultural Resources Series* 8. Bureau of Land Management, Phoenix.

Hagenbuckle, Kristen Angela
2000   Ritual and the Individual: An Analysis of Cibicue Painted Corrugated Pottery from Grasshopper Pueblo, Arizona. Master's thesis, Department of Anthropology, University of Arizona, Tucson.

Hall, Susan D., and Jeffery J. Clark
2004   AZ CC:2:289 (ASM). In "Ancient Farmers of the Safford Basin: Archaeology of the U.S. 70 Safford-to-Thatcher Project," edited by Jeffery J. Clark, pp. 23-41. *Anthropological Papers* 39. Center for Desert Archaeology, Tucson.

Hamilton, Patrick
1884   *The Resources of Arizona*. A. L. Bancroft and Co., San Francisco.

Hardin, Margaret Anne
1977   Individual Style in San José Pottery Painting: The Role of Deliberate Choice. In *The Individual in Prehistory: Studies of Variability in Style in Prehistoric Technologies*, edited by J. H. Hill and J. Gunn, pp. 109–136. Academic Press, New York.

Hartmann, William K., and Betty Graham Lee
2003   Chichilticale: A Survey of Candidate Ruins in Southeastern Arizona. In *The Coronado Expedition: From the Distance of 460 Years*, edited by

Richard Flint and Shirley Cushing Flint, pp. 81–108. University of New Mexico Press, Albuquerque.

Haug, Ruth
2002 Forced Migration, Processes of Return and Livelihood Construction among Pastoralists in Northern Sudan. *Disasters* 26(1): 70–84.

Haury, Emil W.
1936 Some Southwestern Pottery Types: Series IV. *Medallion Papers* 19. Gila Pueblo, Globe.
1958 Evidence at Point of Pines for a Prehistoric Migration from Northern Arizona. In "Migrations in New World Culture History," edited by Raymond H. Thompson, pp. 1–6. *University of Arizona Social Science Bulletin* 27. University of Arizona, Tucson.
1985 *Mogollon Culture in the Forestdale Valley, East-Central Arizona.* University of Arizona Press, Tucson.

Haury, Emil W., and Lisa W. Huckell, Editors
1993 A Prehistoric Cotton Cache From the Pinaleño Mountains, Arizona. *Kiva* 59(2): 95–145.

Heckman, Robert A.
2000a The San Simon Tradition. In "Prehistoric Painted Pottery of Southeastern Arizona," edited by Robert A. Heckman, Barbara K. Montgomery, and Stephanie M. Whittlesey, pp. 63–74. *Technical Series* 77. Statistical Research, Inc., Tucson.
2000b The Trincheras Tradition. In "Prehistoric Painted Pottery of Southeastern Arizona," edited by Robert A. Heckman, Barbara K. Montgomery, and Stephanie M. Whittlesey, pp. 75–81. *Technical Series* 77. Statistical Research, Inc., Tucson.

Hegmon, Michelle
1989 Social Integration and Architecture. In "The Architecture of Social Integration in Prehistoric Pueblos," edited by William D. Lipe and Michelle Hegmon, pp. 5–14. *Occasional Paper* 1. Crow Canyon Archaeological Center, Cortez.

Hegmon, Michelle, Margaret C. Nelson, and Mark J. Ennes
2000 Corrugated Pottery, Technological Style, and Population Movement in the Mimbres Region of the American Southwest. *Journal of Anthropological Research* 56(2): 217–240.

Heidke, James M.
2004 Utilitarian Ceramic Production and Distribution in the Prehistoric Tonto Basin. In "2000 Years of Settlement in the Tonto Basin: Overview and Synthesis of the Tonto Creek Archaeological Project," edited by Jeffery J. Clark and James M. Vint, pp. 77–138. *Anthropological Papers* 25. Center for Desert Archaeology, Tucson.

Heidke, James M., and Elizabeth J. Miksa
2000 Ceramic Temper Provenance Studies. In "Tonto Creek Archaeological Project: Artifact and Environmental Analyses, Volume 1: A Tonto Basin Perspective on Ceramic Economy," edited by James M. Vint and James M. Heidke, pp. 95–146. *Anthropological Papers* 23. Center for Desert Archaeology, Tucson.

Heidke, James M., and Miriam T. Stark
1995 Ceramic Chronology, Technology, and Economics in the Roosevelt Community Development Study Area. In "The Roosevelt Community Development Study, Volume 2: Ceramic Chronology, Technology, and Economics," edited by James M. Heidke and Miriam T. Stark, pp. 395–407. *Anthropological Papers* 14. Center for Desert Archaeology, Tucson.

Heidke, James M., Elizabeth J. Miksa, and Henry D. Wallace
2002 A Petrographic Approach to Sand-Tempered Pottery Provenance Studies: Examples from Two Hohokam Local Systems. In "Ceramic Production and Circulation in the Greater Southwest: Source Determination by INAA and Complementary Mineralogical Investigations," edited by Donna M. Glowacki and Hector Neff, pp. 152–178. *Cotsen Institute Monograph* 44. Cotsen Institute of Archaeology, University of California, Los Angeles.

Heleniak, Timothy
2004 Migration of the Russian Diaspora After the Breakup of the Soviet Union. *Journal of International Affairs* 57(2): 99–117.

Hendrickson, Mitch J.
2003 Design Analysis of Chihuahuan Polychrome Jars from North American Museum Collections. *BAR International Series* 1125. Archaeopress, Oxford.

Herr, Sarah A.
2001 Beyond Chaco: Great Kiva Communities on the Mogollon Rim Frontier. *Anthropological Papers of the University of Arizona* 66. University of Arizona Press, Tucson.

Herr, Sarah, and Jeffrey J. Clark
1997 Patterns in the Pathways: Early Historic Migrations in the Rio Grande Pueblos. *Kiva* 62(4): 365–389.

Hill, J. Brett, Jeffery J. Clark, William H. Doelle, and Patrick D. Lyons
2004 Prehistoric Demography in the Southwest: Migration, Coalescence, and Hohokam Population Decline. *American Antiquity* 69(4): 689–716.

Hillier, Bill, and Julienne Hanson
1984 *The Social Logic of Space.* Cambridge University Press, Cambridge.

Hillier, Bill, and Alan Penn
1992 Dense Civilisations: The Shape of Cities in the 21st Century. *Applied Energy* 43: 41–66.

Hodge, H. C.
1875   Old Ruins – Rich Land – Large Products – Telegraph Building. *Arizona Citizen*, 9 October.

Hough, Walter
1907   Antiquities of the Upper Gila and Salt River Valleys in Arizona and New Mexico. *Bureau of American Ethnology Bulletin* 35. Government Printing Office, Washington D.C.

Huntley, Deborah L., and Keith W. Kintigh
2004   Archaeological Pattering and Organizational Scale of Late Prehistoric Settlement Clusters in the Zuni Region of New Mexico. In *The Protohistoric Pueblo World: A.D. 1275–1600*, edited by E. Charles Adams and Andrew I. Duff, pp. 62–74. University of Arizona Press, Tucson.

Jenkins, Richard
1992   *Pierre Bourdieu*. Routledge, London.
1996   *Social Identity*. Routledge, London.

Jernigan, E. Wesley
1990   Letter Report to Paul Fish concerning a survey in Graham County. Letter on file at the Arizona State Museum Site Files Office, Tucson, Arizona.
1993   Krider Kiva site, AZ CC:1:43 (ASM) site card, site map, ceramic counts, and kiva plan and profile maps. On file, Arizona State Museum Site Files Office, Tucson, Arizona.

Jett, Stephen C.
1964   Pueblo Indian Migrations: An Evaluation of the Possible Physical and Cultural Determinants. *American Antiquity* 29: 281–300.

Johnson, Alfred E., and William W. Wasley
1966   Archaeological Excavations Near Bylas, Arizona. *The Kiva* 31(4): 205–253.

Johnston, A. R.
1848   Journal of Captain A. R. Johnston, First Dragoons. In "Notes of a Military Reconnoissance, from Fort Leavenworth, in Missouri, to San Diego, in California, including part of the Arkansas, Del Norte, and Gila Rivers," by Lieutenant Colonel W. H. Emory, pp. 567–614. *Executive Document* 41. Wendell and Van Benthuysen, Washington D.C.

Jones, Gill
1999   'The Same People in the Same Places'? Socio-Spatial Identities and Migration in Youth. *Sociology* 33(1): 1–22.

Jones, Jeffrey T.
1996   Mapping of AZ CC:5:16 (ASM) Archaeological Features Within 200-Foot Corridor for Fort Grant Prison Irrigation Project Pipeline. Letter Report No. 96-13. Old Pueblo Archaeology Center, Tucson.
2000   Cultural Resources Survey of a 3,000 Square Foot Water Tower Improvement Area and Approximately 1,200 Linear Feet of Proposed Fencing Courses Around a Barn and Equipment Storage Area on the Cluff Ranch Wildlife Area South of Pima, Graham County, Arizona. Letter Report No. 2000.020. Old Pueblo Archaeology Center, Tucson.

Jones, Sîan
1997   *The Archaeology of Ethnicity: Constructing Identities in the Past and Present*. Routledge, London.

Judd, Neil M.
1954   The Material Culture of Pueblo Bonito. *Smithsonian Miscellaneous Collections*, Vol. 124. Smithsonian Institution, Washington D.C.

Kaldahl, Eric J., and Allen Dart
2002   Cultural Resources Survey of the 4,600–ft Fort Grant Landfill Perimeter and 34 Proposed Soil Test Sites on Arizona State Trust Lands at Fort Grant, Arizona (ASLD Institutional Lease No. 89–94333). Letter Report No. 2001.070. Old Pueblo Archeology Center, Tucson, Arizona.

Kidder, Alfred Vincent
1924   *An Introduction to the Study of Southwestern Archaeology with a Preliminary Account of the Excavations at Pecos, and a Summary of Southwestern Archaeology Today*. Yale University Press, New Haven.

Kidder, Alfred Vincent, and Samuel J. Guernsey
1919   Archaeological Explorations in Northeastern Arizona. *Bureau of American Ethnology Bulletin* 65. Smithsonian Institution. Government Printing Office, Washington D.C.

Kintigh, Keith W.
1989   Sample Size, Significance, and Measures of Diversity. In *Quantifying Diversity in Archaeology*, edited by Robert D. Leonard and George T. Jones, pp. 25–36. Cambridge University Press, Cambridge.
2002   *Tools for Quantitative Archaeology: Programs for Quantitative Analysis in Archaeology*. Manual accompanying computer programs. Department of Anthropology, Arizona State University, Tempe.

Kohler, Timothy A., George J. Gumerman, and Robert G. Reynolds
2005   Simulating Ancient Societies: Computer Model is Helping Unravel the Archaeological Mysteries of the American Southwest. *Scientific American* 293(1): 76–84.

Lascaux, Annick, and Barbara K. Montgomery, Editors
2008   Archaeological Investigations along U.S. 70 and State Route 75 from Solomon to Apache Grove, Graham and Greenlee Counties, Southeast Arizona, Vol. 2, Epley's Ruin (AZ CC:2:64 [ASM]): A Long-Lived Irrigation Community in the Safford Basin from 200 B.C. to A.D. 140. *Tierra Archaeological Report* 2005–94. Tierra Right of Way Services, Ltd., Tucson.

LeBlanc, Chris, Peter M. Taylor, William Gillespie,
and Sarah Cowie
2003 Heritage Resource Report: Stockton Pass Prescribed Burn, Safford Ranger District, Coronado National Forest. Cultural Resources Report 2002-04-025. MS on file at Coronado National Forest Office, Tucson, Arizona.

Lechtman, Heather
1977 Style in Technology – Some Early Thoughts. In *Material Culture: Styles, Organization and Dynamics of Technology*, edited by Heather Lechtman and R. S. Merrill, pp. 3–20. West Publishing, St. Paul.

Lee, Betty Graham
1981 (Editor) The Daley Site: An Archaeological Salvage Report. *Eastern Arizona College Museum of Anthropology Publication* 1. Eastern Arizona College, Thatcher.
1996 The Eagle Pass Site: An Integral Part of the Province of Chichilticale. *Eastern Arizona College Museum of Anthropology Publication* 5. Eastern Arizona College, Thatcher.

Lekson, Stephen H.
2002 Salado Archaeology of the Upper Gila, New Mexico. *Anthropological Papers of the University of Arizona* 67. University of Arizona Press, Tucson.

Lekson, Stephen H., and Catherine M. Cameron
1995 The Abandonment of Chaco Canyon, the Mesa Verde Migrations, and the Reorganization of the Pueblo World. *Journal of Anthropological Archaeology* 14(2): 184–202.

Lekson, Stephen H., Curtis P. Nepstad-Thornberry,
Brian E. Yunker, Toni S. Laumbach, David P. Cain,
and Karl W. Laumbach
2002 Migrations in the Southwest: Pinnacle Ruin, Southwestern New Mexico. *Kiva* 68(2): 73–101.

Lemonnier, Pierre
1986 The Study of Material Culture Today: Toward an Anthropology of Technical Systems. *Journal of Anthropological Archaeology* 5: 147–186.
1989 Bark Capes, Arrowheads and Concorde: On Social Representations of Technology. In *The Meaning of Things: Material Culture and Symbolic Expressions*, edited by Ian Hodder, pp. 156–171. Unwin Hyman, London.
1992 Elements for an Anthropology of Technology. *Museum of Anthropology Anthropological Papers* 88. University of Michigan Museum of Anthropology, Ann Arbor.

Levy, Thomas E., and Augustin F. C. Holl
2002 Migrations, Ethnogenesis, and Settlement Dynamics: Israelites in Iron Age Canaan and Shuwa-Arabs in the Chad Basin. *Journal of Anthropological Archaeology* 21: 83–118.

Liebmann, Matthew, T. J. Ferguson,
and Robert W. Preucel
2005 Pueblo Settlement, Architecture, and Social Change in the Pueblo Revolt Era, A.D. 1680 to 1696. *Journal of Field Archaeology* 30(1): 45–60.

Lilley, Ian
2004 Diaspora and Identity in Archaeology: Moving Beyond the Black Atlantic. In *A Companion to Social Archaeology*, edited by Lynn Meskell and Robert W. Preucel, pp. 287–312. Blackwell Publishing, Malden.

Lindsay, Alexander Johnston, Jr.
1986 Late Thirteenth Century Pit House and Pueblo Occupations at the Point of Pines Ruin, Arizona. Paper presented at the 51st Annual Meeting of the Society for American Archaeology, New Orleans, Louisiana.
1987 Anasazi Population Movements to Southern Arizona. *American Archaeology* 6(3): 190–198.
1992 Tucson Polychrome: History, Dating, Distribution, and Design. In "Proceedings of the Second Salado Conference," edited by Richard C. Lange and Stephen Germick, pp. 230–237. *Arizona Archaeological Society Occasional Paper*. Arizona Archaeological Society, Phoenix.

Lipe, William D.
1995 The Depopulation of the Northern San Juan: Conditions in the Turbulent 1200s. *Journal of Anthropological Archaeology* 14(2): 143–169.

Longacre, William A.
1966 Changing Patterns of Social Integration: A Prehistoric Example from the American Southwest. *American Anthropologist* 68(1): 94–102.

Lowell, Julie C.
1991 Prehistoric Households at Turkey Creek Pueblo, Arizona. *Anthropological Papers of the University of Arizona* 54. University of Arizona Press, Tucson.

Lucassen, Jan, and Leo Lucassen
1997a (Editors) *Migration, Migration History, History: Old Paradigms and New Perspectives*. Peter Lang, Bern.
1997b Migration, Migration History, History: Old Paradigms and New Perspectives. In *Migration, Migration History, History: Old Paradigms and New Perspectives*, edited by Jan Lucassen and Leo Lucassen, pp. 9–38. Peter Lang, Bern.

Lyon, Jerry D., Danielle Desruisseaux,
and Richard V. N. Ahlstrom
1999 Class III Archaeological Inventory of 4,600 Acres North of Safford in Graham County, Arizona: The Phelps Dodge Water Exploration Survey. *SWCA Cultural Resources Report* 99–200. SWCA, Inc., Tucson.

Lyons, Patrick D.
2003   Ancestral Hopi Migrations. *Anthropological Papers of the University of Arizona* 68. University of Arizona Press, Tucson.
2004   Ceramics. In "Ancient Farmers of the Safford Basin: Archaeology of the U.S. 70 Safford-to-Thatcher Project," edited by Jeffery J. Clark, pp. 95–126. *Anthropological Papers* 39. Center for Desert Archaeology, Tucson.

Lyons, Patrick D., and Alexander J. Lindsay, Jr.
2006   Perforated Plates and the Salado Phenomenon. *Kiva* 72(1): 5–54.

Lyons, Patrick D., Elizabeth J. Miksa, Sergio F. Castro-Reino, and Carlos Lavayen
2005   Using Petrography to Demonstrate the Link Between Roosevelt Red Ware and Ancient Immigrants. Paper presented at the 70th Annual Meeting of the Society for American Archaeology, Salt Lake City, Utah.

Mabry, Jonathan B.
2003   *Las Capas: An Early Agricultural Site in a Southwestern Floodplain.* Manuscript on file, Desert Archaeology, Inc., Tucson, Arizona.

Marshall, Joan, and Natalie Foster
2002   "Between belonging": *Habitus* and the Migration Experience. *The Canadian Geographer* 46(1): 63–84.

Martin, Paul S., John B. Rinaldo, Elaine Bluhm, Hugh C. Culter, and Roger Grange, Jr.
1952   Mogollon Cultural Continuity and Change: The Stratigraphic Analysis of Tularosa and Cordova Caves. *Fieldiana: Anthropology* 40. Chicago Natural History Museum, Chicago.

Mauer, Michael David
1970   Cibicue Polychrome, A Fourteenth Century Ceramic Type from East-Central Arizona. Master's thesis, Department of Anthropology, University of Arizona, Tucson.

McCall, John C.
1999   Structure, Agency, and the Locus of the Social: Why Poststructural Theory is Good for Archaeology. In "Material Symbols: Culture and Economy in Prehistory," edited by John E. Robb, pp. 16–20. *Center for Archaeological Investigations Occasional Paper* 26. Southern Illinois University, Carbondale.

McGregor, John C.
1965   *Southwestern Archaeology.* University of Illinois Press, Urbana.

Meskell, Lynn
2001   Archaeologies of Identity. In *Archaeology Theory Today*, edited by Ian Hodder, pp. 187–213. Polity Press, Cambridge.
2002   The Intersections of Identity and Politics in Archaeology. In *Annual Reviews in Anthropology* 31: 279–301.

Meyer, Daniel
1999   Masonry and Social Variability in the Chaco System. Doctoral dissertation, Department of Archaeology, University of Calgary, Calgary.

Miksa, Elizabeth, and James M. Heidke
1995   Drawing a Line in the Sands: Models of Ceramic Temper Provenance. In "The Roosevelt Community Development Study, Volume 2: Ceramic Chronology, Technology, and Economics," edited by James M. Heidke and Miriam T. Stark, pp. 133–205. *Anthropological Papers* 14. Center for Desert Archaeology, Tucson.

Mills, Barbara J.
1998   Migration and Pueblo IV Community Reorganization in the Silver Creek Area, East-Central Arizona. In "Migration and Reorganization: The Pueblo IV Period in the American Southwest," edited by Katherine A. Spielmann, pp. 65–80. *Arizona State University Anthropological Research Papers* 51. Arizona State University, Tempe.
1999   Ceramic Ware and Type Systematics. In "Living on the Edge of the Rim: Excavations and Analysis of the Silver Creek Archaeological Research Project 1993–1998," edited by Barbara J. Mills, Sarah A. Herr, and Scott Van Keuren, pp. 243–268. *Arizona State Museum Archaeological Series* 192. University of Arizona Press, Tucson.
2004   Identity, Feasting, and the Archaeology of the Greater Southwest. In *Identity, Feasting, and the Archaeology of the Greater Southwest*, edited by Barbara J. Mills, pp. 1–23. University Press of Colorado, Boulder.

Mills, Barbara J., and Sarah A. Herr
1999   Chronology of the Mogollon Rim Region. In "Living on the Edge of the Rim: Excavations and Analysis of the Silver Creek Archaeological Research Project 1993–1998," edited by Barbara J. Mills, Sarah A. Herr, and Scott Van Keuren, pp. 269–293. *Arizona State Museum Archaeological Series* 192. University of Arizona Press, Tucson.

Mills, Barbara J., Sarah A. Herr, Susan L. Stinson, and Daniela Triadan
1999   Ceramic Production and Distribution. In "Living on the Edge of the Rim: Excavations and Analysis of the Silver Creek Archaeological Research Project 1993–1998," edited by Barbara J. Mills, Sarah A. Herr, and Scott Van Keuren, pp. 295–324. *Arizona State Museum Archaeological Series* 192. University of Arizona Press, Tucson.

Mills, Jack P., and Vera M. Mills
1978   *The Curtis Site: A Pre-historic Village in the Safford Valley.* Independently published.

Minar, C. Jill
2001 Motor Skills and the Learning Process: The Conservation of Cordage Final Twist Direction in Communities of Practice. *Journal of Anthropological Research* 57: 381–405.

Minar, C. Jill, and Patricia L. Crown
2001 Learning and Craft Production: An Introduction. *Journal of Anthropological Research* 57: 369–380.

Morris, Ann Axtell
1934 *Digging in the Southwest.* Doubleday, Doran and Co., Garden City.

Munson, Jessica L., Charles R. Riggs, and Scott Van Keuren
2005 Social Integration of Puebloan Architecture in the Mogollon Rim Region: An Open Space Analysis. Paper presented at the 70th Annual Meeting of the Society for American Archaeology, Salt Lake City, Utah.

Nash, Roy
2003 Social Explanation and Socialization: On Bourdieu and the Structure, Disposition, Practice Scheme. *The Sociological Review* 51(1): 43–62.

Neely, James A.
1997 Foothill Irrigation and Domestic Water Systems of the Safford Valley, Southeastern Arizona. Paper presented at the 62nd Annual Meeting of the Society for American Archaeology, Nashville, Tennessee.

2001 Prehistoric Agricultural Fields and Water Management Technology of the Safford Valley, southeastern Arizona. *Antiquity* 75: 681–682.

2004 Paleoclimatic and Archaeological Contexts. In "The Safford Valley Grids: Prehistoric Cultivation in the Southern Arizona Desert," edited by William E. Doolittle and James A. Neely, pp. 18–30. *Anthropological Papers of the University of Arizona* 70. University of Arizona Press, Tucson.

2005 Prehistoric Agricultural and Settlement Systems in Lefthand Canyon, Safford Valley, Southeastern Arizona. In "Inscriptions: Collected Papers in Honor of Richard B. and Nathalie F. S. Woodbury," edited by Regge N. Wiseman, Thomas C. O'Lauglin, and Cordelia T. Snow, pp. 145–169. *Papers of the Archaeological Society of New Mexico* 31. Archaeological Society of New Mexico, Albuquerque.

Neely, James A., and Joseph S. Crary
1998 The Marijilda Canyon Canal: A Complex Irrigation and Domestic Water System in the Safford Valley, Southeastern Arizona. Paper presented at the 63rd Annual Meeting of the Society for American Archaeoology, Seattle, Washington.

Neily, Robert B., Joseph S. Crary, Gay M. Kinkade, and Stephen Germick
1993 The Owens-Colvin Site Revisited: A Preliminary Report of the Excavations of a Bylas Phase Settlement near Eden, Arizona. Paper presented at the 66th Annual Pecos Conference, Springerville, Arizona.

Nelson, Margaret C.
1999 *Mimbres During the Twelfth Century: Abandonment, Continuity, and Reorganization.* University of Arizona Press, Tucson.

Neuzil, Anna A.
2001 Ceramics and Social Dynamics: Technological Style and Corrugated Ceramics During the Pueblo III to Pueblo IV Transition, Silver Creek, Arizona. Master's thesis, Department of Anthropology, University of Arizona, Tucson.

2005a Corrugated Ceramics and Migration in the Pueblo III to Pueblo IV Transition, Silver Creek, Arizona. *Kiva* 71(1): 101–124.

2005b *In the Aftermath of Migration: Assessing the Social Consequences of Late 13th and 14th Century Population Movements into Southeastern Arizona.* Doctoral dissertation, Department of Anthropology, University of Arizona, Tucson. University Microfilms, Inc., Ann Arbor.

2006 Ten Sites in the Gila Box Riparian National Conservation Area, Northeast of Safford, Graham County, Arizona. *Technical Report* No. 2006–106. Center for Desert Archaeology, Tucson.

Newcomb, Joanne M.
1999 Silver Creek Settlement Patterns and Paleodemography. In "Living on the Edge of the Rim: Excavations and Analysis of the Silver Creek Archaeological Research Project 1993–1998," edited by Barbara J. Mills, Sarah A. Herr, and Scott Van Keuren, pp. 31–52. *Arizona State Museum Archaeological Series* 192. University of Arizona Press, Tucson.

Nials, Fred L., James P. Holmlund, and Susan D. Hall
2004 Prehistoric and Historic-Period Canals. In "Ancient Farmers of the Safford Basin: Archaeology of the U.S. 70 Safford-to-Thatcher Project," edited by Jeffery J. Clark, pp. 59–83. *Anthropological Papers* 39. Center for Desert Archaeology, Tucson.

Oetelaar, Gerald A.
2000 Beyond Activity Areas: Structure and Symbolism in the Organization and Use of Space Inside Tipis. *Plains Anthropologist* 45(171): 35–61.

Olson, Alan P.
1959 An Evaluation of the Phase Concept in Southwestern Archaeology: As Applied to the Eleventh and Twelfth Century Occupations at Point of Pines, East Central Arizona. Doctoral dissertation, Department of Anthropology, University of Arizona, Tucson.

Ortner, Sherry B.
  1996   Making Gender: Toward a Feminist, Minority, Postcolonial, Subaltern, etc., Theory of Practice. In *Making Gender: The Politics and Erotics of Culture*, pp. 1–20. Beacon Press, Boston.
  2001   Commentary: Practice, Power, and the Past. *Journal of Social Archaeology* 1(2): 271–278.

Owens, Rex
  1990   Owens Colvin Site, AZ CC:1:19 (ASM), Eden, AZ: A Surface Structure. MS on file, Bureau of Land Management, Safford District Office.
  1992   Excavations at the Fischer Site AZ CC:2:100 in the Safford Area, Southeastern Arizona. MS on file, Bureau of Land Management, Safford District Office.
  1993   Two Dog Site: AZ W:13:14 (ASM). MS on file, Bureau of Land Management, Safford District Office.

Pauketat, Timothy R.
  2001   Practice and History in Archaeology. *Anthropological Theory* 1(1): 73–98.

Phillips, Jr., David A.
  1984   Prehistory and History of the Upper Gila River, Arizona and New Mexico: An Archaeological Overview. *Western Division Report of Investigations* 2. New World Research, Inc., Tucson.

Pierce, Christopher
  1999   Explaining Corrugated Pottery in the American Southwest: An Evolutionary Approach. Doctoral dissertation, Department of Anthropology, University of Washington, Seattle.

Plog, Fred
  1983   Political and Economic Alliance on the Colorado Plateau, A.D. 400–1450. *Advances in World Archaeology* 2: 289–330.

Potter, James M.
  1998   The Structure of Open Space in Late Prehistoric Settlements in the Southwest. In "Migration and Reorganization: The Pueblo IV Period in the American Southwest," edited by Katherine A. Spielmann, pp. 137–163. *Arizona State University Anthropological Research Papers* 51. Arizona State University, Tempe.

Purcell, David E.
  2004   (Editor) Formative Settlements on the Pinaleño Mountains Bajada: Results of Phases Archaeological Treatment of Sites AZ CC:6:40 and AZ CC:6:43 (ASM) within the U.S. Highway 191 Right-on-way Between Mileposts 110.40 and 117.60 South of Safford, Graham County, Arizona. *Archaeological Research Services Project Report* 2001:076. Archaeological Research Services, Inc., Tempe.
  2006   Dynamics of Safford Basin Prehistory: Cultural Affiliation at the Artesia Site and Roadrunner Village, Southeastern Arizona. In *Mostly Mimbres: A Collection of Papers from the 12th Biennial Mogollon Conference*, edited by Marc Thompson, Jason Jurgena, and Lora Jackson, pp. 69–82. El Paso Museum of Archaeology, El Paso.

Purcell, David E., and Terry L. Coriell
  2004   The Cultural Identity of Pinaleño Bajada Villagers and Analysis of their Physical Remains. In "Formative Settlements on the Pinaleño Mountains Bajada: Results of Phases Archaeological Treatment of Sites AZ CC:6:40 and AZ CC:6:43 (ASM) within the U.S. Highway 191 Right-on-way Between Mileposts 110.40 and 117.60 South of Safford, Graham County, Arizona," edited by David E. Purcell, pp. 11.1–11.17. *Archaeological Research Services Project Report* 2001:076. Archaeological Research Services, Inc., Tempe.

Reid, J. Jefferson
  1997   Return to Migration, Population Movement, and Ethnic Identity in the American Southwest. In *Vanishing River: Landscapes and Lives of the Lower Verde River*, edited by Stephanie M. Whittlesey, Richard Ciolek-Torrello, and Jeffrey H. Altschul, pp. 629–638. SRI Press, Tucson.

Reid, J. Jefferson, and Barbara K. Montgomery
  1998   The Brown and the Gray: Pots and Population Movement in East-Central Arizona. *Journal of Anthropological Research* 54(4): 447–459.

Rice, Prudence M.
  1987   *Pottery Analysis: A Sourcebook*. University of Chicago Press, Chicago.

Riggs, Charles R.
  2001   *The Architecture of Grasshopper Pueblo*. University of Utah Press, Salt Lake City.

Rinker, Jennifer R.
  1998   The Bryce-Smith Project: Irrigated Agriculture and Habitation from A.D. 1000 to 1450, Lefthand Canyon, Safford Valley, Arizona. Master's thesis, Department of Anthropology, University of Texas, Austin.

Rockman, Marcy, and James Steele, Editors
  2003   *The Colonization of Unfamiliar Landscapes*. Routledge, London.

Rohn, Arthur H.
  1971   Wetherill Mesa Excavations: Mug House, Mesa Verde National Park – Colorado. *Archaeological Research Series* Number Seven-D. National Park Service, U.S. Department of the Interior, Washington, D.C.

Roth, Barbara J.
  1993   An Archaeological Assessment of a U.S. West Communications Buried Cable Alignment in the Cluff Ranch Wildlife Area, Graham County, Arizona. Tierra Right of Way Services, Ltd., Tucson.

Rouse, Irving
1958 The Inference of Migrations from Anthropological Evidence. In "Migrations in New World Culture History," edited by Raymond H. Thompson, pp. 63–68. *University of Arizona Social Science Bulletin* 27. University of Arizona, Tucson.

Rule, Pam
1993 The Owens-Colvin Site of the Safford Valley. *Eastern Arizona College Museum of Anthropology Publication* 3. Eastern Arizona College, Thatcher.

Sahlins, Marshall
1981 Historical Metaphors and Mythical Realities: Structure in the Early History of the Sandwich Islands Kingdom. *Association for Social Anthropology in Oceania Special Publications* 1. University of Michigan Press, Ann Arbor.

Sassaman, Kenneth E., and Wictoria Rudolphi
2001 Communities of Practice in the Early Pottery Traditions of the American Southeast. *Journal of Anthropological Research* 57: 407–425.

Sauer, Carl, and Donald Brand
1930 Pueblo Sites in Southeastern Arizona. *University of California Publications in Geography* 3(7): 415–458.

Sayles, E. B.
1936 Some Southwestern Pottery Types: Series V. *Medallion Papers* 21. Gila Pueblo, Globe.

Schiffer, Michael B.
1987 *Formation Processes of the Archaeological Record.* University of New Mexico Press, Albuquerque.

Schmidt, Kari M.
2005 The Faunal Assemblage from McEuen Cave, Southeastern Arizona. Paper presented at the 70th Annual Meeting of the Society for American Archaeology, Salt Lake City, Utah.

Schnapper, Dominique
1994 The Debate on Immigration and the Crisis of National Identity. *West European Politics* 17(2): 127–139.

Schriwer, Charlotte
2002 Cultural and Ethnic Identity in the Ottoman Period Architecture of Cyprus, Jordan, and Lebanon. *Levant* 34: 197–218.

Schwartz, Douglas W.
1970 The Postmigration Culture: A Base for Archaeological Inference. In *Reconstructing Pueblo Societies*, edited by William A. Longacre, pp. 174–193. University of New Mexico Press, Albuquerque.

Sewell, William H., Jr.
1992 A Theory of Structure: Duality, Agency, and Transformation. *American Journal of Sociology* 98(1): 1–29.

Seymour, Gregory R.
1992 A Class III Archaeological Resource Inventory of Approximately 1440 Acres for the Sanchez Copper Project Area, Graham County, Arizona. *SWCA Archaeological Report* 92–2. SWCA Environmental Consultants, Inc., Tucson.

Seymour, Gregory R., Richard V.N. Ahlstrom, and David P. Doak (editors)
1997 The Sanchez Copper Project: Volume I: Archaeological Investigations in the Safford Valley, Graham County, Arizona. *SWCA Archaeological Report* 94–82. SWCA, Inc., Tucson.

Shackley, M. Steven
2002 Source Provenance of Obsidian Artifacts from Prehistoric Sites Along US HWY 70, Safford Valley, Southeastern Arizona. MS, report prepared for and on file at Desert Archaeology, Inc., Tucson.

2005a Chronometry and Geochemistry at McEuen Cave: The Radiocarbon and Obisidan Geochemical Data. Paper Presented at the 70th Annual Meeting of the Society for American Archaeology, Salt Lake City, Utah.

2005b Source Provenance of Obsidian Artifacts from Late Period Sites from Aravaipa Canyon and Safford Valley, Southeastern Arizona. MS, report prepared for and on file at the Center for Desert Archaeology, Tucson.

Shapiro, Jason S.
1999 New Light on Old Adobe: A Space Syntax Analysis of the Casa Grande. *Kiva* 64(4): 419–446.

Shepard, Anna O.
1956 *Ceramics for the Archaeologist.* Carnegie Institution of Washington, Washington, D.C.

Slaughter, Mark C., and Heidi Roberts, Editors
1996 Excavation of the Gibbon Springs Site: A Classic Period Village in the Northeastern Tucson Basin. *SWCA Report* 94–87. SWCA, Inc., Tucson.

Smith, John W.
2005 Ceramic Composition and Ancient Social Networks in the San Simon Valley of Southeastern Arizona. Master's thesis, Department of Anthropology, University of Oklahoma, Norman.

Spielmann, Katherine A., Editor
1998 Migration and Reorganization: The Pueblo IV Period in the American Southwest. *Arizona State University Anthropological Research Papers* 51. Arizona State University, Tempe.

Stark, Miriam T.
1998 Technical Choices and Social Boundaries in Material Culture Patterning. In *The Archaeology of Social Boundaries*, edited by Miriam T. Stark, pp. 1–11. Smithsonian Institution Press, Washington, D.C.

Stark, Miriam T., Jeffery J. Clark, and Mark D. Elson
1995 Social Boundaries and Cultural Identity in the Tonto Basin. In "The Roosevelt Community

Stark, Miriam T., Jeffery J. Clark,
and Mark D. Elson (*continued*)
   Development Study: New Perspectives on Tonto
   Basin Prehistory, edited by Mark D. Elson, Mir-
   iam T. Stark, and David A. Gregory, pp. 343–368.
   Anthropological Papers 15. Center for Desert
   Archaeology, Tucson.
Stark, Miriam T., Mark D. Elson, and Jeffery J. Clark
   1998   Social Boundaries and Technical Choices in Tonto
          Basin Prehistory. In *The Archaeology of Social
          Boundaries*, edited by Miriam Stark, pp. 208–231.
          Smithsonian Institution Press, Washington, D.C.
Stinson, Susan L.
   1996   Roosevelt Red Ware and the Organization of
          Ceramic Production in the Silver Creek Area.
          Master's thesis, Department of Anthropology,
          University of Arizona, Tucson.
Stone, Tammy
   1987   An Examination of Mogollon Corrugated Pottery.
          In "Mogollon Variability," edited by C. Benson
          and S. Upham, pp. 89–106. *University Museum
          Occasional Papers* 15. New Mexico State Univer-
          sity, Las Cruces.
   2003   Social Identity and Ethnic Interaction in the West-
          ern Pueblos of the American Southwest. *Journal
          of Archaeological Method and Theory* 10(1):
          31–67.
Stull, Brian P.
   1998   A Cultural Resource Survey of the Arizona Game
          and Fish Department's Cluff Ranch Water Pipe-
          line and Access Easement, Graham County,
          Arizona. Project No. 98–16. *Technical Report*
          120. Kinlani Archaeology, Ltd., Tucson.
Sullivan, Alan P., III, and Anthony S. Tolonen
   1998   Evaluating Assemblage Diversity Measures with
          Surface Archaeological Data. In *Surface Ar-
          chaeology*, edited by Alan P. Sullivan III, pp.
          143–155. University of New Mexico Press, Albu-
          querque.
Tatman, Oscar A.
   1931   Archaeological Notes from Ruins Located Three
          Miles east of Solomonsville, Arizona on land
          owned by Donald Curtis. MS on file, Henderson
          Museum, University of Colorado, Boulder.
Taylor, Peter, Mary Farrel, William Gillespie,
and Chris LeBlanc
   2002   Heritage Resource Report: Gillespie III Prescribed
          Burn, Safford Ranger District, Coronado National
          Forest. Cultural Resources Report 2002–04–025.
          MS on file, Coronado National Forest Office,
          Tucson.
Torres-Saillant, Silvio
   1997   Diaspora and National Identity: Dominican Migra-
          tion in the Postmodern Society. *Migration World
          Magazine* 25(3): 18–22.

Tuohy, Donald R.
   1960   *Archaeological Survey and Excavation in the Gila
          River Channel between Earven Dam Site and
          Buttes Reservoir Site, Arizona.* MS on file, Arizo-
          na State Museum, University of Arizona, Tucson.
Turner, Raymond M., and David E. Brown
   1994   Sonoran Desertscrub. In *Biotic Communities:
          Southwestern United States and Northwestern
          Mexico*, edited by David E. Brown, pp. 181–221.
          University of Utah Press, Salt Lake City.
Tyberg, Joel J.
   2000   Influences, Occupation, and Salado Development
          at the Solomonsville Site. Master's thesis, Depart-
          ment of Anthropology, University of Colorado,
          Boulder.
Van Dyke, Ruth M.
   1999   Space Syntax Analysis at the Chacoan Outlier of
          Guadalupe. *American Antiquity* 64(3): 461–473.
Van Keuren, Scott
   1999   Ceramic Design Structure and the Organization of
          Cibola White Ware Production in the Grasshopper
          Region, Arizona. *Arizona State Museum Archaeo-
          logical Series* 191. University of Arizona, Tuc-
          son.
Van West, Carla R., and Jeffrey S. Dean
   2000   Environmental Characteristics of the A.D. 900–
          1300 Period in the Central Mesa Verde Region.
          Kiva 66(1): 19–44.
Vertovec, Steven
   2001   Transnationalism and identity. *Journal of Ethnic
          and Migration Studies* 27(4): 573–582.
Vint, James M.
   2000   Ceramic Dating of Sites and other Temporal
          Issues. In "Tonto Creek Archaeological Project:
          Artifact and Environmental Analyses, Volume I:
          A Tonto Basin Perspective on Ceramic Econ-
          omy," edited by James M. Vint and James M.
          Heidke, pp. 23–94. *Anthropological Papers* 23.
          Center for Desert Archaeology, Tucson.
Wallace, Henry D.
   2001   Time Seriation and Typological Refinement of the
          Middle Gila Buffware Sequence: Snaketown
          Through Soho Phase. In "The Grewe Archaeolog-
          ical Research Project, Volume 2: Material Cul-
          ture, Part I: Ceramic Studies," edited by David R.
          Abbott, pp. 177–261. *Anthropological Papers*
          99–1. Northland Research, Inc., Flagstaff.
Wasley, William W.
   1962   A Ceremonial Cave on Bonita Creek, Arizona.
          American Antiquity 27(3): 380–394.
Waters, Michael R., and John C. Ravesloot
   2001   Landscape Change and the Cultural Evolution of
          the Hohokam Along the Middle Gila River and
          Other River Valleys in South-Central Arizona.
          American Antiquity 66(2): 285–299.

Wauchope, Robert, Editor
  1956   Seminars in Archaeology: 1955. *American Antiquity* 22(2): Part 2.

Welch, John R.
  1995   Preservation, Research, and Public Interpretation at Pueblo Devol, an Arizona Cliff Dwelling. *Kiva* 61(2): 121–143.

Wiessner, Polly
  1983   Style and Social Information in Kalahari San Projectile Points. *American Antiquity* 48: 253–276.

Wilcox, David R., and Charles Sternberg
  1983   Hohokam Ballcourts and their Interpretation. *Arizona State Museum Archaeological Series* 160. University of Arizona, Tucson.

Wilson, Eldred D., and Richard T. Moore
  1958   Geologic Map of Graham and Greenlee Counties, Arizona. Arizona Bureau of Mines, University of Arizona, Tucson.

Woodson, M. Kyle
  1994   The Goat Hill Site: A Kayenta Anasazi Pueblo in the Safford Valley of Southeastern Arizona. Paper presented at the 67th Annual Pecos Conference, Mesa Verde, Colorado.

  1995   The Goat Hill Site: A Western Anasazi Pueblo in the Safford Valley of Southeastern Arizona. Master's thesis, Department of Anthropology, University of Texas, Austin.

  1999   Migrations in Late Anasazi Prehistory: The Evidence from the Goat Hill Site. *Kiva* 65(1): 63–84.

Yelvington, Kevin A.
  1991   Ethnicity as Practice? A Comment on Bentley. *Comparative Studies in Society and History* 33(1): 158–168.

Zedeño, María Nieves
  1994   Sourcing Prehistoric Ceramics at Chodistaas Pueblo, Arizona: The Circulation of People and Pots in the Grasshopper Region. *Anthropological Papers of the University of Arizona* 58. University of Arizona Press, Tucson.

Index

Abandonment, of northern
    Southwest, vii, 7
Adobe (cobble-reinforced)
    at Fischer Site, 19
    in Safford Valley, 14, 41–45,
        86, 89, 91, 95
Agave production, 22
Aggregation, of population, 97–98
Agriculture
    in the Aravaipa Valley, 98
    in the Safford Valley, 94, 98
    See also Canals; Rock-bordered
        grids
Amerind Foundation, ix
Archaeological Consulting
    Services, Inc., 22
Archaeological Research Services,
    23
Archaic period, 23
Architectural comparisons, pre and
    post migration, 39–45
Architectural construction
    techniques, 41–45
Architecture
    as expression of identity, 3–6, 8,
        32–45, 98
    space syntax analyses of, 4,
        56–64, 67–68, 94, 95
    See also Adobe (cobble-
        reinforced); Ballcourts; Com-
        pounds; D-shaped kiva;
        Entrybox complexes;
        Masonry (coursed); Pit
        houses; Room blocks
Arizona State Museum, ix, 77
Axes, at 76 Ranch Ruin, 24
Atlan Archaeology, Inc., 23
Archaeological sites. See by site
    name and by site number (AZ)
Aravaipa Valley
    agricultural potential of, 98

archaeological research in,
    23–27
architecture in 32–45, 94
ceramic manufacture and
    exchange in, 79–85
ceramics in, 54
chronological sequences for,
    20–21, 24–27
corrugated ceramics in, 29–32
Kayenta and Tusayan migration
    into, 10, 25–27, 94
limited research in, 10
room blocks in, 22–24, 32, 41
AZ BB:3:22 (ASM)
    architecture at, 43
    ceramics at, 83
    migrant and indigenous
        coresidence at, 91
AZ CC:1:3 (ASM), ceramics at, 50,
    51, 52
AZ CC:1:55 (ASM), ceramics at,
    74
AZ CC:2:23 (BLM)
    architecture at, 62, 87–88, 94
    as migrant enclave, 87–88, 94,
        98
    ceramics at, 50–54, 87, 94
    dating of, 87
    defensible location of, 87, 94
    integration score at, 61
    location of, 65, 87
AZ CC:2:33 (BLM)
    architecture at, 91
    ceramics at, 54, 91
    location of, 65
AZ CC:2:69 (ASM), ceramics at,
    32, 55–56
AZ CC:2:185 (ASM)
    architecture at, 34–35
    ceramics at, 31–32, 49–50
    space syntax analyses at, 59–64

AZ CC:289 (ASM), archaeological
    research at, 23
AZ CC:2:290 (ASM),
    archaeological research at, 23
AZ CC:2:291 (ASM),
    archaeological research at, 23
AZ V:16:8 (ASM)
    chronology at, 24
    excavations at 18, 24
AZ V:16:10 (ASM)
    chronology at, 24
    excavations at, 18, 24

Ballcourts, in Safford Valley, 14,
    18
Blue River, as obsidian source, 69
Bonita Creek Cache, 18
Bordieu, Pierre, 2
Brillouin statistics, of decorated
    ceramics, 48–54
Brown, Jeffrey, 18–19
Buena Vista Ruin
    archaeological research at, 18,
        19, 23
    ceramics at, 30–32, 49–52, 66,
        78, 89, 93
    migrant indicators at, 89–91, 93,
        97
    room count at, 64
Bureau of Land Management, viii,
    ix, 17, 22
Bylas phase
    architecture during, 36, 39, 43,
        44
    dating of, 18, 19, 22, 24–25
Bylas phase sites, space syntax
    analyses of, 59–64

Canals, prehistoric, 18, 22, 23, 94,
    98
Center for Desert Archaeology, viii

Ceramic compositional analyses, 73–85
Ceramics
   as expression of identity, 3–6, 28–32, 46–56, 98
   assemblages (decorated) of, 47–56, 91–92, 94
   corrugated, 14, 19, 28–32, 85, 91
   diversity measures of, 48–54, 95, 96
   glaze-decorated ware, 75
   perforated plates, 14, 32, 39, 40–41, 44–45, 51–52, 54, 56, 66, 72, 77, 78, 83–84, 85, 87, 89, 91, 93
   plain ware, 19
   Cibicue Painted Corrugated, 28, 30
   Cibola White Ware, 14, 25, 75, 76
   Cliff Polychrome, 82
   Gila Polychrome, 19
   Maverick Mountain series, 13–14, 23, 54–56, 67, 73–76, 78, 82–85, 87, 88–91, 93, 94, 99
   McDonald Corrugated, 28, 30
   Middle Gila Buff Ware, 82, 83, 85, 86, 93
   Mimbres Black-on-white, 75, 76, 82–83, 85, 89
   Mogollon Brown Ware, 51
   Pinto Polychrome, 82
   Roosevelt Red Ware, 19, 51, 54, 56, 75, 76, 78, 79, 82, 85, 86, 89, 93, 95
   Safford Variety Middle Gila Buff Ware, 14, 77, 83, 85, 86, 89–91, 94
   Salado Red, 30
   San Carlos Red-on-brown, 14, 24, 55–56, 67, 75, 76, 82, 83, 85, 86, 89–91, 93, 94
   San Simon series, 73–76
   Snowflake Black-on-white, 24
   Tsegi Orange Ware, 14
   Tularosa Black-on-white, 24
   Tularosa Fillet Rim 28, 30
   White Mountain Red Ware, 14, 25, 75, 76, 89
Chichilticale, ruins of, 19, 24

Cliff dwellings, evidence of migrants in, 99
Cluff Ranch Site
   ceramics at, 32, 49–50
   space syntax analyses at, 59–64
Cobble-reinforced adobe. *See* Adobe
Communities of practice, 3, 29
Compound layouts, 14, 22, 23, 33, 94
Convex articulation, as measure of space syntax, 58–64, 94
Convex space, definition of, 57
Coronado National Forest, ix, 17, 77
Cotton, cultivation of, 22
Courtyard spatial organization, 33
Cow Canyon, as obsidian source, 69–72
Crary Site
   archaeological research at, 23
   ceramics at, 50, 74
   source of obsidian at, 72
   space syntax analyses at, 59–64
Cremation areas, 19
Crescent Ruin
   architecture at, 35
   ceramics at, 31–32, 54, 79–81, 95
   location of, 66
   petrofacies of, 79
   plan of, 36

Daley Site, archaeological research at, 23
Dating
   of AZ CC:2:23 (BLM), 87
   of AZ CC:2:185 (ASM), 35
   of Bylas phase, 18, 19, 24–25
   of canals, 23
   of Classic period, vii
   of Eden phase, 22, 24
   of Goat Hill or Middle Classic phase, 32, 33
   of Goat Hill Site, 14, 35, 87, 88
   of Rattlesnake Mesa Site, 32
   of Safford or Fort Grant phase, 19, 32
   of Two Dog phase, 19
   of Yuma Wash Site, 35
Davis Ranch Ruin
   architecture at, 89

   migration to, 99
Defensible location
   of AZ CC:2:23 (BLM), 65, 94
   of Goat Hill Site, 13, 65, 87, 94
   of Haby Pueblo, 23
Depopulation. *See* Abandonment
Desert Archaeology, Inc., 23, 76, 77
Design styles, as expression of identity, 2
Dewester Site
   archaeological research at, 23
   ceramics at, 74, 78, 95
   room count at, 64, 95
Duality of structure, 2–3, 9, 46, 98
Duffen, William, 23–24
Duwe, Sam, 77

Eagle Pass Site
   archaeological research at, 19
   architecture at, 34–35
   ceramics at, 50–52, 54, 95
   convex space in, 58
   evidence of migrants at, 99
Earven Flat Site
   archaeological research at, 18
   architecture at, 35
   ceramics at, 50
   source of obsidian at, 72
Eastern Arizona College, ix, 19
Eastern Arizona College Minutemen, 19
Eden phase
   architecture during, 36, 39, 44
   ceramics during, 51, 94
   dating of, 22, 24
   migration during, 85
Eden and Bylas phase transition, Hohokam influence during, 72
Enculturation, passive indicators of, 2, 4
Entrybox complexes, at Goat Hill Site, 13, 87
Environmental conditions, as reasons for migration, vii, 6–7
Epley's Ruin, excavations at, 18, 23
Ethnicity, definition of, 9–10
Exchange
   of ceramics, 76–86, 87, 89, 91, 93, 95
   of obsidian, 69–73, 85, 87

Fewkes, Jesse Walter, 18
Fischer Site
  archaeological research at, 19
  ceramics at, 19, 31, 55–56, 78
Fitting, James E., 19
Fort Grant phase, 54, 82
Fort Grant Pueblo
  archaeological research at, 23
  ceramics at, 30, 49–50, 82,
    89–91
  migrant indicators at, 89–91
  source of obsidian at, 72
Fort Grant Silo Site
  ceramics at, 55–56
  migrant and indigenous
    coresidence at, 91

Giddens, Anthony, 2–3
Goat Hill or Middle Classic phase
  architecture during, 33–36, 39,
    43, 44, 94
  ceramic variability during, 94
  ceramics during, 51, 54
  definition of, 25
  room area during, 36–41
  settlement location during,
    64–67, 87
Goat Hill or Middle Classic phase
  sites
    obsidian prevalence at, 70–71
    space syntax analyses of, 59–64
Goat Hill Site
  archaeological research at,
    10–14, 18, 19, 22–23
  architecture at, 10–14, 34–35,
    41, 87, 94
  as migrant enclave, 10–14, 87,
    94, 97–99
  ceramics at, 10, 84, 87
  dating of, 14, 35, 87, 88
  defensible location of, 13, 65,
    87, 94
  integration score at, 61
  space syntax analyses of, 59–64
  suprahousehold migrant group
    at, 97–98
Graham County Historical Society,
  ix
Grasshopper region, 5
Grid convexity, as measure of
  space syntax, 58–64, 94

Habitus, 2, 3, 8
Haby Pueblo
  archaeological research in, 23
  ceramics at, 30, 54, 83
  location of, 66
Hartmann, William, 24
Homelands, return to, 8, 15
Hearths, slab-lined, 88
Hooker Ranch Site, archaeological
  research at, 23

Identity
  as expressed through space
    syntax analyses, 57–64,
    67–68
  definition of, 8–10, 32–33
  expressions of, 9, 87
  material correlates of, 1–6,
    28–45, 46–47
  renegotiation of, 8, 15, 54, 56,
    61, 62, 67–68, 94, 96–100
Inequalities, between migrants and
  locals, 7–8, 14, 64–67, 95, 96
Integration, of Kayenta and
  Tusayan migrants, 95–96, 100
Integration score, as measure of
  space syntax, 58–64
Irrigation. *See* Canals

Jernigan, Wesley, 22

Kayenta and Tusayan area,
  migration from, 7, 14, 25,
  87–100. *See also* Abandonment
Kivas
  at AZ CC:2:23 (BLM), 87–88
  at Krider Kiva Site, 22
  at 76 Ranch Ruin, 24
  D-shaped, 10–14, 87
Krider Kiva Site
  archaeological research at, 19,
    22
  architecture at, 34–35, 61,
    89–91
  ceramics at, 54, 55, 56, 74,
    89–91
  migrant indicators at, 89–91
  space syntax analyses at, 59–64

Lavayen, Carlos, 77
Layton Site, archaeological
  research at, 19

Lee, Betty Graham, ix, 19, 24
Lippencott South Site
  ceramics at, 32, 49–50
  space syntax analyses at, 59–64
Lippincott North Site
  architecture at, 35, 61
  ceramics at, 50, 52
  integration score at, 61
  room count at, 64

Marijilda Site
  archaeological research at, 18
  architecture at, 12, 41, 88, 94
  as migrant enclave, 88, 94, 98
  ceramics at, 88, 94
  integration score at, 61
  location of, 64–65
Masonry, coursed, at Goat Hill
  Site, 10–14, 41, 87
McEuen Cave, archaeological
  research at, 23
Mealing bins, 24
Mesa Site, archaeological research
  at, 19
Mesa Verde region, abandonment
  of, 6–7
Methodist Church Site, archaeological research at, 18, 19, 23
Migrant enclaves, integration of,
  64, 87–100. *See also* AZ
  CC:2:23 (BLM); Goat Hill Site;
  Marijilda Site
Migration model, refined, 97
Miksa, Elizabeth, 77
Migration
  archaeological identification of,
    vii–viii, 1–2, 4, 88–92,
    99–100
  as process vs. event, 15, 100
  community level of, 5–6, 96, 97
  definition of, 5
  household level of, vii, 5–6, 15,
    28–32, 45, 88, 91, 92, 96–98,
    100. *See also* AZ CC:2:23
    (BLM)
  identity affected by, viii, 3,
    8–10, 14–15, 87–100
  individual level of, 4, 5
  into occupied territory, 7, 14
  into unoccupied territory, 7
  of ancestral Puebloans, vii,
    10–14

Migration (*continued*)
  reasons for, vii, 6–7, 8
  risks of, 6
  routes of, 99
  scales of, 5–6, 14, 47, 87–100
  social consequences of, vii,
    7–10, 14–15, 46–47, 91–100
  suprahousehold level of, vii,
    5–6, 15, 32, 87, 88, 91, 92,
    97, 98, 100. *See also* Goat
    Hill Site; Marijilda Site
Mills, Jack and Vera, 19
Mimbres migration, 76, 85
Mimbres region, 5
Museum of Northern Arizona, ix
Mule Creek, as obsidian source,
  69–72
Murphy Site (AZ CC:1:52 ASM)
  archaeological research at, 23
  ceramics at, 74
Murphy Site (AZ CC:2:103 ASM)
  archaeological research at, 18
  ceramics at, 32, 54

National Science Foundation, vii

Obsidian, sourcing of, 69–73, 85
Owens, Rex, ix, 19
Owens-Colvin Site
  archaeological research at, 19
  ceramics at, 31–32, 79
Oxidation analyses, of ceramics,
  73–76

P Ranch Canyon Site, ceramics at,
  30
Pentagon Site
  archaeological research at, 23
  ceramics at, 54, 83
  location of, 66
  space syntax analyses of, 57,
    59–64
  total site area comparisons, 57
Petrofacies, in Safford and
  Aravaipa valleys, 77–85, 93
Petrographic analyses, of ceramics,
  75–85, 86, 89, 93
Picketpost Mountain, as source of
  obsidian, 72
Pit houses, in Safford Valley, 22,
  23, 33, 89

Plazas
  at Marijilda Site, 88
  in Safford Valley, 33, 88, 95
Point of Pines Site
  D-shaped kiva at, 13
  Maverick Mountain phase at, 19
  migration into, 5, 10, 19, 99
Population increase, as indicator of
  migration, 5–6. *See also*
  Aggregation
Pothunting, vandalism, viii, 16, 24,
  88, 89
Practice theory, 3

Rattlesnake Mesa Site
  ceramics at, 31, 32, 54
  dating of, 32
  location of, 66
Reeve Ruin
  ceramic similarities with, 19
  migration to, 99
Resource procurement activities, 22
Richardson Orchard Site, ceramics
  at, 49–50
Richness statistics, of decorated
  ceramics, 48–54
Rincon Canyon Site, 18
Rock-bordered grids, 18, 22, 32
Room blocks
  at AZ CC:2:33 (BLM), 91
  at Fischer Site, 19
  at Goat Hill Site, 10–14, 87
  at Haby Pueblo, 23
  at Marijilda Site, 88
  at 76 Ranch Ruin, 23–24
  in Safford Valley, 23, 33–45,
    85, 91, 94–95
Room Contiguity Index, 33–36, 45
Rule, Pamela, 19–22

Safford or Fort Grant phase
  architecture during, 35–36, 39,
    44–45, 94–95
  ceramics during, 19, 32, 51
  dating of, 19
  integrated settlements during,
    67, 68
  room area during, 36–41
  settlement location during,
    64–67
Safford or Fort Grant phase sites

  obsidian prevalence at, 70–71
  space syntax analyses of, 59–64
Safford Valley
  archaeological research in,
    16–27
  architecture in, 14, 18, 33–45
  chronological sequences for,
    20–21, 24–27
  corrugated ceramics in, 29–32
  CRM projects in, 16–19, 22, 23
  environment of, 16
  kivas in, 10–14, 22, 24, 32
  migration into, 10–14, 18, 19,
    22–23, 25–27, 36, 69, 92–
    100. *See also by site name
    and by site number (AZ)*
  Pueblo Viejo district of, 16, 18,
    25
  room blocks in, 10–14, 18, 19,
    22–24, 32, 41
  San Carlos district of, 16
San Francisco River, as obsidian
  source, 69
San Pedro River Valley region,
  migration into, 5, 10, 89, 99
San Pedro River Valley sands,
  ceramic temper of, 83
Sauceda Mountains, as obsidian
  source, 72
76 Ranch Ruin
  archaeological research at, 23
  ceramics at, 82
Sharon Site, ceramics at, 31–32
Silver Creek region, migration into,
  5, 8
Social integration, 56–64, 67–68
Social marginalization, 64–67, 93
Space syntax analyses, 56–64,
  67–68, 94, 95
Spatial integration, 60–61, 67
Spatial marginalization, of
  migrants, 64–67
Spear Ranch Site
  archaeological research at, 18,
    19
  ceramics at, 74, 89–91
  location of, 64–65
  migrant indicators at, 89–91
Structuration, 2–3
Subsistence activities, 23
Sunset School Site, archaeological
  research at, 23

SWCA Environmental Consultants, Inc., 22, 23

Tatman, Oscar, 18
Technological styles
    as expression of identity, 2–5, 69
    intrusive and indigenous, 89–92
    of architecture, 32–45, 69, 87
    of corrugated pottery, 29–32, 87, 91
Temper, ceramic. *See* Petrographic analyses
Tierra Right of Way Services, Inc., 23
Tonto Basin
    architecture in, 33, 36, 41
    marginal resources in, 98
    migration into, 5, 8
Tucson Basin region, migration into, 5

Two Dog phase
    dating of, 19, 89
    migration during, 85
Two Dog Site, archaeological research at, 19

University of Arizona, 18
University of California at Berkeley, 22
University of Colorado, 18
University of New Mexico, 22
University of Texas at Austin, 22
Upper Gila Valley region, migration into, 5
U.S. Forest Service, 22

Wall niches, at 76 Ranch Ruin, 24
Water control features, 22, 98. *See also* Canals; Rock-bordered grids

Wes Jernigan Site
    ceramics at, 31–32
    migrant and indigenous coresidence at, 91, 94
Whitmer Site, archaeological research at, 18
Woodson, M. Kyle, 10–11
Wooten-Claridge Terrace Site
    archaeological research at, 23
    ceramics at, 50, 95
    rooms at, 95

Yuma Wash Site
    archaeological research at, 18, 23
    architecture at, 34–35, 43
    ceramics at, 31–32, 49–50, 52, 55–56
    location of, 64–65
    migrant and indigenous coresidence at, 94

Abstract

Abundant archaeological evidence indicates that at least one group of migrants from the Kayenta and Tusayan areas of northeastern Arizona arrived in the Safford Valley in the last decades of the thirteenth century. This research examines population movement from northeastern Arizona to the Safford and Aravaipa valleys of southeastern Arizona in ways specific to understanding the scale at which these migrations occurred and the effect these migrations had on the expressions of identity of both migrant and indigenous groups. Data from the Goat Hill Site and 34 additional sites in the Safford and Aravaipa valleys provides a region-wide perspective on population movement in these areas during the Classic Period (A.D. 1200–1450).

This study involved a two-stage approach to identifying migration and its consequences in the archaeological record. First, an analysis of the technological style of low visibility utilitarian ceramics and domestic architecture provided an opportunity to distinguish between household and suprahousehold level groups in the archaeological record. Once these groups were identified, high visibility decorated ceramics and the space syntax of domestic architecture were used to determine how the people in these two groups expressed their identity and if those expressions of identity changed following migration into the Safford and Aravaipa valleys. The identification of provenances of a sample of decorated ceramics and of obsidian, obtained through petrographic and X-ray fluorescence analyses, clarified the degree of interaction between groups living in the Safford and Aravaipa valleys and those outside this region, helping to determine if the patterns observed could be explained by social mechanisms other than migration.

This study revealed that several groups of puebloan migrants arrived in both suprahousehold level and household level groups during the thirteenth and fourteenth centuries, first settling independently of local populations, and then intermingling with local populations at mixed settlements. Initially, as migrant and indigenous populations remained segregated from each other, they continued their premigration identities and each group remained distinct. However, as these populations began to live together at mixed settlements, they

Resumen

Abundante evidencia arqueológica indica que por lo menos un grupo de inmigrantes originarios de las áreas de Kayenta y Tusayán en Arizona septentrional arribó al valle de Safford en las últimas décadas del siglo XIII. Esta investigación examina el movimiento de población del noreste de Arizona a los valles de Safford y Aravaipa en el sureste de Arizona especificamente para comprender la escala de las migraciones y el efecto que éstas tuvieron en las expresiones de identidad, tanto de los inmigrantes como de los grupos indígenas. Datos obtenidos del sitio Goat Hill y de 34 sitios adicionales en los valles de Safford y Aravaipa proveen una perspectiva regional sobre el movimiento de la población durante el período clásico (1200–1400 D.C.).

Este estudio consistió de dos etapas para investigar la migración y sus consecuencias en el registro arqueológico. Para empezar, un análisis del estilo tecnológico de cerámica utilitaria de baja visibilidad y arquitectura doméstica proveyeron la oportunidad de distinguir entre familias individuales y grupos de familias en el registro arqueológico. Una vez que estos grupos fueron identificados, la cerámica decorada de alta visibilidad y la sintaxis de la arquitectura doméstica se utilizaron para determinar la manera en que estos dos grupos expresaron su identidad, y si esas expresiones de identidad cambiaron después de la inmigración a los valles de Safford y Aravaipa. La identificación de proveniencia de una muestra de cerámica decorada y de obsidiana, obtenidas a través de análisis petrográfico y químico (XRF), clarificaron el grado de interacción entre los grupos que vivieron en estos valles y aquéllos de fuera de esta región, ayudando así a determinar si los patrones observados se debieron a mecanismos sociales distintos de la inmigración.

Este estudio reveló que algunos grupos de inmigrantes Pueblo arribaron en familias o en grupos de familias durante los siglos XIII y XIV, primero asentándose independientemente y luego mezclándose con la población local en asentamientos heterogéneos. Inicialmente, cuando los inmigrantes estuvieron separados de la población local, ellos continuaron con sus identidades de pre-inmigración y cada grupo se mantuvo distinto. Sin embargo, cuando estas poblaciones empezaron a vivir en el mismo asentamiento, ellos rencgo-

renegotiated their identities in order to deal with the day-to-day realities of living with people with whom they had little or no previous experience. Through this process, migrant and indigenous groups formed a new identity that incorporated elements of the premigration identities of both groups. With these results, the author created and refined a model of the effects of migration on identity to present a better understanding of the social consequences of ancient migrations.

ciaron sus identidades para asi poder vivir la realidad diaria de compartir el espacio con gente desconocida. A través de este proceso, los inmigrantes y los grupos indígenas formaron una nueva identidad que incorporó elementos de ambas identidades. Con estos resultados, el autor creó y refinó un modelo de los efectos de la migración sobre la identidad que sirve para explicar las consecuencias sociales de las migraciones antiguas.

ANTHROPOLOGICAL PAPERS OF THE UNIVERSITY OF ARIZONA

1. **Excavations at Nantack Village, Point of Pines, Arizona.** David A. Breternitz. 1959. (O.P.)
2. **Yaqui Myths and Legends.** Ruth W. Giddings. 1959. *Now in book form.*
3. **Marobavi: A Study of an Assimilated Group in Northern Sonora.** Roger C. Owen. 1959. (O.P.)
4. **A Survey of Indian Assimilation in Eastern Sonora.** Thomas B. Hinton. 1959. (O.P.)
5. **The Phonology of Arizona Yaqui with Texts.** Lynn S. Crumrine. 1961. (O.P., D)
6. **The Maricopas: An Identification from Documentary Sources.** Paul H. Ezell. 1963. (O.P.)
7. **The San Carlos Indian Cattle Industry.** Harry T. Getty. 1964. (O.P.)
8. **The House Cross of the Mayo Indians of Sonora, Mexico.** N. Ross Crumrine. 1964. (O.P.)
9. **Salvage Archaeology in Painted Rocks Reservoir, Western Arizona.** William W. Wasley and Alfred E. Johnson. 1965. (O.P.)
10. **An Appraisal of Tree-Ring Dated Pottery in the Southwest.** David A. Breternitz. 1966. (O.P.)
11. **The Albuquerque Navajos.** William H. Hodge. 1969. (O.P.)
12. **Papago Indians at Work.** Jack O. Waddell. 1969.
13. **Culture Change and Shifting Populations in Central Northern Mexico.** William B. Griffen. 1969. (O.P.)
14. **Ceremonial Exchange as a Mechanism in Tribal Integration Among the Mayos of Northwest Mexico.** Lynn S. Crumrine. 1969. (O.P.)
15. **Western Apache Witchcraft.** Keith H. Basso. 1969.
16. **Lithic Analysis and Cultural Inference: A Paleo-Indian Case.** Edwin N. Wilmsen. 1970. (O.P.)
17. **Archaeology as Anthropology: A Case Study.** William A. Longacre. 1970.
18. **Broken K Pueblo: Prehistoric Social Organization in the American Southwest.** James N. Hill. 1970. (O.P., D)
19. **White Mountain Redware: A Pottery Tradition of East-Central Arizona and Western New Mexico.** Roy L. Carlson. 1970.
20. **Mexican Macaws: Comparative Osteology.** Lyndon L. Hargrave. 1970. (O.P.)
21. **Apachean Culture History and Ethnology.** Keith H. Basso and Morris E. Opler, eds. 1971.
22. **Social Functions of Language in a Mexican-American Community.** George C. Barker. 1972. (O.P.)
23. **The Indians of Point of Pines, Arizona: A Comparative Study of Their Physical Characteristics.** Kenneth A. Bennett. 1973. (O.P.)
24. **Population, Contact, and Climate in the New Mexico Pueblos.** Ezra B. W. Zubrow. 1974. (O.P.)
25. **Irrigation's Impact on Society.** Theodore E. Downing and McGuire Gibson, eds. 1974. (O.P.)
26. **Excavations at Punta de Agua in the Santa Cruz River Basin, Southeastern Arizona.** J. Cameron Greenleaf. 1975. (O.P.)
27. **Seri Prehistory: The Archaeology of the Central Coast of Sonora, Mexico.** Thomas Bowen. 1976. (O.P.)
28. **Carib-Speaking Indians: Culture, Society, and Language.** Ellen B. Basso, ed. 1977. (O.P.)
29. **Cocopa Ethnography.** William H. Kelly. 1977. (O.P., D)
30. **The Hodges Ruin: A Hohokam Community in the Tucson Basin.** Isabel Kelly, James E. Officer, and Emil W. Haury, collaborators; Gayle H. Hartmann, ed. 1978. (O.P.)
31. **Fort Bowie Material Culture.** Robert M. Herskovitz. 1978. (O.P.)
32. **Artifacts from Chaco Canyon, New Mexico: The Chetro Ketl Collection.** R. Gwinn Vivian, Dulce N. Dodgen, and Gayle H. Hartmann. 1978. (O.P.)
33. **Indian Assimilation in the Franciscan Area of Nueva Vizcaya.** William B. Griffen. 1979. (O.P.)
34. **The Durango South Project: Archaeological Salvage of Two Late Basketmaker III Sites in the Durango District.** John D. Gooding. 1980. (O.P.)
35. **Basketmaker Caves in the Prayer Rock District, Northeastern Arizona.** Elizabeth Ann Morris. 1980. (O.P.)
36. **Archaeological Explorations in Caves of the Point of Pines Region, Arizona.** James C. Gifford. 1980. (O.P.)
37. **Ceramic Sequences in Colima: Capacha, an Early Phase.** Isabel Kelly. 1980. (O.P.)
38. **Themes of Indigenous Acculturation in Northwest Mexico.** Thomas B. Hinton and Phil C. Weigand, eds. 1981. (O.P.)
39. **Sixteenth Century Maiolica Pottery in the Valley of Mexico.** Florence C. Lister and Robert H. Lister. 1982. (O.P.)
40. **Multidisciplinary Research at Grasshopper Pueblo, Arizona.** William A. Longacre, Sally J. Holbrook, and Michael W. Graves, eds. 1982. (O.P.)
41. **The Asturian of Cantabria: Early Holocene Hunter-Gatherers in Northern Spain.** Geoffrey A. Clark. 1983. (O.P.)
42. **The Cochise Cultural Sequence in Southeastern Arizona.** E. B. Sayles. 1983. (O.P.)
43. **Cultural and Environmental History of Cienega Valley, Southeastern Arizona.** Frank W. Eddy and Maurice E. Cooley. 1983. (O.P.)

44. Settlement, Subsistence, and Society in Late Zuni Prehistory.   Keith W. Kintigh. 1985. (O.P., D)

45. The Geoarchaeology of Whitewater Draw, Arizona.   Michael R. Waters. 1986. (O.P.)

46. Ejidos and Regions of Refuge in Northwestern Mexico.   N. Ross Crumrine and Phil C. Weigand, eds. 1987. (O.P.)

47. Preclassic Maya Pottery at Cuello, Belize.   Laura J. Kosakowsky. 1987. (O.P.)

48. Pre-Hispanic Occupance in the Valley of Sonora, Mexico.   William E. Doolittle. 1988. (O.P.)

49. Mortuary Practices and Social Differentiation at Casas Grandes, Chihuahua, Mexico.   John C. Ravesloot. 1988. (O.P.)

50. Point of Pines, Arizona: A History of the University of Arizona Archaeological Field School.   Emil W. Haury. 1989.

51. Patarata Pottery: Classic Period Ceramics of the South-central Gulf Coast, Veracruz, Mexico.   Barbara L. Stark. 1989.

52. The Chinese of Early Tucson: Historic Archaeology from the Tucson Urban Renewal Project.   Florence C. Lister and Robert H. Lister. 1989. (O.P.)

53. Mimbres Archaeology of the Upper Gila, New Mexico.   Stephen H. Lekson. 1990. (O.P.)

54. Prehistoric Households at Turkey Creek Pueblo, Arizona.   Julie C. Lowell. 1991. (O.P.)

55. Homol'ovi II: Archaeology of an Ancestral Hopi Village, Arizona.   E. Charles Adams and Kelley Ann Hays, eds. 1991. (O.P., D)

56. The Marana Community in the Hohokam World.   Suzanne K. Fish, Paul R. Fish, and John H. Madsen, eds. 1992.

57. Between Desert and River: Hohokam Settlement and Land Use in the Los Robles Community.   Christian E. Downum. 1993. (O.P., D)

58. Sourcing Prehistoric Ceramics at Chodistaas Pueblo, Arizona: The Circulation of People and Pots in the Grasshopper Region.   María Nieves Zedeño. 1994.

59. Of Marshes and Maize: Preceramic Agricultural Settlements in the Cienega Valley, Southeastern Arizona.   Bruce B. Huckell. 1995.

60. Historic Zuni Architecture and Society: An Archaeological Application of Space Syntax.   T. J. Ferguson. 1996.

61. Ceramic Commodities and Common Containers: Production and Distribution of White Mountain Red Ware in the Grasshopper Region, Arizona.   Daniela Triadan. 1997.

62. Prehistoric Sandals from Northeastern Arizona: The Earl H. Morris and Ann Axtell Morris Research.   Kelley Ann Hays-Gilpin, Ann Cordy Deegan, and Elizabeth Ann Morris. 1998.

63. Expanding the View of Hohokam Platform Mounds: An Ethnographic Perspective.   Mark D. Elson. 1998.

64. Great House Communities Across the Chacoan Landscape.   John Kantner and Nancy M. Mahoney, eds. 2000.

65. Tracking Prehistoric Migrations: Pueblo Settlers among the Tonto Basin Hohokam.   Jeffery J. Clark. 2001.

66. Beyond Chaco: Great Kiva Communities on the Mogollon Rim Frontier.   Sarah A. Herr. 2001.

67. Salado Archaeology of the Upper Gila, New Mexico.   Stephen H. Lekson. 2002.

68. Ancestral Hopi Migrations.   Patrick D. Lyons. 2003.

69. Ancient Maya Life in the Far West Bajo: Social and Environmental Change in the Wetlands of Belize.   Julie L. Kunen. 2004.

70. The Safford Valley Grids: Prehistoric Cultivation in the Southern Arizona Desert.   William E. Doolittle and James A. Neely, eds. 2004.

71. Murray Springs: A Clovis Site with Multiple Activity Areas in the San Pedro Valley, Arizona.   C. Vance Haynes, Jr., and Bruce B. Huckell, eds. 2007.

72. Ancestral Zuni Glaze-Decorated Pottery: Viewing Pueblo IV Regional Organization through Ceramic Production and Exchange.   Deborah L. Huntley. 2008.

73. In the Aftermath of Migration: Renegotiating Ancient Identity in Southeastern Arizona.   Anna A. Neuzil. 2008.

Anthropological Papers listed as O.P., D are available as Docutech reproductions (high quality xerox) printed on demand. They are tape or spiral bound and nonreturnable.